The Return of Grand Theory
in the Human Sciences

Canto is a new imprint offering a range of
titles, classic and more recent, across a
broad spectrum of subject areas and
interests. History, literature, biography,
archaeology, politics, religion,
psychology, philosophy and science are
all represented in Canto's specially
selected list of titles, which now offers
some of the best and most accessible of
Cambridge publishing to a wider
readership.

The Return of Grand Theory in the Human Sciences

edited by

Quentin Skinner

Professor of Political Science
University of Cambridge

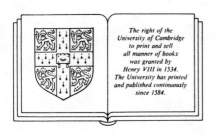

The right of the
University of Cambridge
to print and sell
all manner of books
was granted by
Henry VIII in 1534.
The University has printed
and published continuously
since 1584.

Cambridge University Press

Cambridge
New York   Port Chester   Melbourne   Sydney

Published by the Press Syndicate of the University of Cambridge
The Pitt Building, Trumpington Street, Cambridge CB2 1RP
40 West 20th Street, New York, NY 10011, USA
10 Stamford Road, Oakleigh, Melbourne 3166, Australia

First published 1985
Reprinted 1986 (twice), 1987, 1988
Canto edition 1990

Printed in Great Britain by
Billing & Sons Ltd, Worcester

Library of Congress catalogue card number: 84–28566

British Library Cataloguing in Publication Data

The return of Grand Theory in the human sciences.
1. Social sciences
I. Skinner, Quentin
300'.1 H61

ISBN 0 521 39833 9 paperback

RB

Contents

Contributors

Barry Barnes is Reader in the Science Research Unit at the University of Edinburgh

James Boon is Professor of Anthropology at Cornell University

Stuart Clark is Lecturer in History at the University College of Swansea, University of Wales

Anthony Giddens is Professor of Sociology at the University of Cambridge and a Fellow of King's College

David Hoy is Professor of Philosophy at the University of California at Santa Cruz

Susan James is Lecturer in the Faculty of Philosophy at the University of Cambridge and a Fellow of Girton College

William Outhwaite is Lecturer in Sociology at the University of Sussex

Mark Philp is Lecturer in Politics at the University of Oxford and a Fellow of Oriel College

Alan Ryan is Professor in the Department of Politics, Princeton University

Quentin Skinner is Professor of Political Science at the University of Cambridge and a Fellow of Christ's College

Preface

My principal debt as editor of this book is owed to Michael Mason of the Talks department at BBC Radio 3. It was with Mr Mason that I originally discussed the idea of commissioning a group of essays about recent theoretical developments in the human sciences. As a result, eight of the following chapters first took shape as contributions to a series of talks on that general theme which Mr Mason produced for Radio 3 in the spring of 1984. The talks were broadcast under the title *The Return of Grand Theory* and were subsequently printed in *The Listener*. I am deeply grateful to Mr Mason for persuading the BBC to run the series, for prompting me to approach the contributors, and for providing all of us who took part in the broadcasts with the benefit of his expert advice on the range of topics to be covered and the best means of presenting our arguments.

I am also very grateful to Jeremy Mynott of the Cambridge University Press, as a result of whose guidance and encouragement the broadcasts have now been turned into a book. At his suggestion, the original scripts were all revised and greatly expanded; the bibliography and guides to further reading were added; and two further chapters were commissioned, the one by David Hoy on Derrida and the one by James Boon on Lévi-Strauss. Jonathan Sinclair-Wilson served as editor of the volume as it went through the Press, and did so with his habitual calm and efficiency. Penny Souster acted as our sub-editor, and carefully sorted out a number of last minute difficulties.

I should also like to express my appreciation to all those who have contributed to this book. They have helped me at every stage, providing me with many valuable suggestions about coverage as well as meeting their own deadlines with cheerfulness and complete absence of fuss. Finally, in writing and revising my Introduction I have incurred a number of debts: to various readers who wrote to

The Listener about the original broadcasts, whose criticisms I hope I have managed to accommodate; and above all to Anthony Giddens and Susan James, both of whom commented on successive drafts of the Introduction with meticulous care, as well as offering me a great deal of indispensable support and advice throughout the production of the book.

I have taken the opportunity of an early reprint to correct some small errors. For pointing them out I am indebted to the original contributors and, above all, to Keith Thomas for his exceptional vigilance.

Quentin Skinner

1 Introduction:
the return of Grand Theory

by Quentin Skinner

Writing almost exactly twenty-five years ago about the state of the human sciences in the English-speaking world, the American sociologist C. Wright Mills isolated and castigated two major theoretical traditions which he saw as inimical to the effective development of what he described, in the title of his book, as *The Sociological Imagination*.[1] The first was the tendency – one that he associated in particular with the philosophies of Comte and Marx, Spencer and Weber – to manipulate the evidence of history in such a way as to manufacture 'a trans-historical strait-jacket' (Wright Mills 1959: 22). But the other and even larger impediment to the progress of the human sciences he labelled Grand Theory, by which he meant the belief that the primary goal of the social disciplines should be that of seeking to construct 'a systematic theory of "the nature of man and society"' (ibid.: 23).

Wright Mills was unusual among sociologists of his generation in attacking the pretensions of Grand Theory in the name of imagination rather than science.[2] But his hostility towards the construction of abstract and normative theories of human nature and conduct was an attitude he shared with most of the leading practitioners not merely of sociology but of all the human sciences in the English-speaking world at that time. Many of the same suspicions were echoed, for example, by students of history. It is symptomatic that, at the time of which I am speaking, the leading English historian was widely held to be Sir Lewis Namier. For Namier was not merely at his happiest when chronicling the detailed manoeuvres of individual political actors at the centres of political power; he was also a sarcastic critic of the belief that any general social theories (or flapdoodle, as he preferred to call them) could possibly be relevant to the explanation of political behaviour or the processes of social change (Namier 1930: 147; Namier 1955: 3–4).

We even encounter a similar scepticism among moral and political theorists of the same generation, a scepticism expressed in the form of two related claims that enjoyed widespread support. One was that, to cite a notorious title of Daniel Bell's, the 'end of

---

[1] Wright Mills 1959. As well as attacking these theoretical orientations, Wright Mills singled out a third tendency he deplored, the tendency of sociological investigations to degenerate into the study of 'a series of rather unrelated and often insignificant facts' (ibid.: 23).

[2] This had the valuable effect of putting him at odds with the 'end-of-ideology' theorists, of whom he was one of the earliest critics.

ideology' had been reached (Bell 1960). The attempt to formulate general social or political philosophies thus came to be treated as little better than a confused and old-fashioned failure to keep up with the scientific times. Connected with this was the positive injunction to abandon the study of the grand philosophical systems of the past, with their unsatisfactory mixture of descriptive and evaluative elements, in order to get on with the truly scientific and purportedly value-neutral task of constructing what came to be called 'empirical theories' of social behaviour and development.[3] The effect of all this was to make it appear that two millennia of philosophising about the social world had suddenly come to an end.[4]

This drive towards a science of politics and society was in turn encouraged by the view then prevailing as to the proper relationship between philosophy and the other cultural disciplines. A philosopher was taken to be someone whose basic concern is to explicate general concepts by way of analysing the meanings of the terms used to express them. One implication of this commitment was that it must simply be a mistake to suppose that the true business of moral, social and political philosophy can ever be to provide us with reasoned defences of particular ideals or practices. To cite two other characteristic works of the fifties, the aim was held to be that of studying not morality itself but merely (in R. M. Hare's title) the 'language of morals'; not politics itself but merely (in T. D. Weldon's title) the 'vocabulary of politics' (Hare 1952; Weldon 1953). With the philosophers themselves proclaiming that there was nothing systematic for them to tell us about the substantive moral and political issues of the day, the burgeoning of a purely empirical science of society seemed assured.

Further support for such scientific aspirations came from some of the leading philosophical doctrines, even dogmas, of the same period. Within the philosophy of science, a positivist account of what constitutes an explanation largely held sway. To explain a puzzling set of facts was taken to be a matter of showing that their occurrence can be deduced and hence predicted from a known natural or at least statistical law.[5] The prestige of this analysis not only served to direct social scientists to look for regularities as the

[3] For a classic instance of this approach, especially as applied to the politics of democratic states, see Lipset 1960. For a classic critique, see Taylor 1967: 25–57.

[4] See Laslett 1956: vii: 'For the moment, anyway, political philosophy is dead.'

[5] For one of the most influential statements see Hempel 1965: 245–95 and for the claim that this model applies equally to historical explanations cf. ibid.: 231–43.

only acceptable basis for explaining social phenomena. It also required them to believe that there was no reason in principle why human actions should not be viewed and explained in just the same way as natural events.[6] The result was that 'man as a subject for science' – to cite the title of a well-known essay by A. J. Ayer – came to seem not just a possible but the only respectable goal for the social disciplines (Ayer 1967: 6–24).

Finally, the idea of a science of society gained specific direction as well as general encouragement from the widespread endorsement of what Barry Barnes describes (in Chapter 5 of this book) as 'rationalist' assumptions about the practice of science itself. Among philosophers of science who adopted a generally 'rationalist' stance, Karl Popper and his numerous disciples probably exercised the most powerful influence upon the conduct of the social disciplines. Popper's most important contribution was to put into currency a particular view of what can properly be said to count as a scientifically respectable belief. A belief is rationally grounded, Popper maintained, and hence scientifically respectable, if and only if it has been submitted to a 'crucial experiment' designed to falsify it, and has succeeded in passing that test. If a statement – or a body of statements in a theory – fails the test of falsifiability, or proves incapable of submitting to it, we have a clear indication that nonsense is being talked (Popper 1959: 78–92). With this suggestion, the social disciplines found themselves provided with a ready and easy way of separating purportedly factual from merely normative or metaphysical assertions, and thereby placing themselves on the straight and narrow path towards becoming genuine sciences. Popper himself urged these distinctions with passionate conviction throughout his polemic on the 'open society and its enemies': piecemeal empirical research in the human sciences was alone commended, while Marxism, psychoanalysis, and all forms of Utopian social philosophy were together consigned to the dustbin of history (Popper 1945: II, 212–80).

Times have certainly changed. During the past generation, Utopian social philosophies have once again been practised as well as preached; Marxism has revived and flourished in an almost bewildering variety of forms; psychoanalysis has gained a new theoretical orientation with the work of Lacan and his followers; Habermas and other members of the Frankfurt School have continued to reflect on the parallels between the theories of Marx and

[6] For a typical statement of this view see Brodbeck 1968: 58–78.

Freud; the Women's Movement has added a whole range of previously neglected insights and arguments; and amidst all this
turmoil the empiricist and positivist citadels of English-speaking
social philosophy have been threatened and undermined by successive waves of hermeneuticists, structuralists, post-empiricists, deconstructionists and other invading hordes.

By now, with the dust of battle subsiding, it seems possible to take
stock, and this is what we have tried to do in this book. We have
focused on a number of individual thinkers who have played, we
believe, a role of exceptional importance in helping to bring about
these changes of theoretical allegiance. But at the same time we have
tried to place them in a wider intellectual context, our aim being to
illuminate the more general character of the upheavals and transformations that have served to restructure the human sciences over
the past quarter of a century.[7]

II

Among these general transformations, perhaps the most significant
has been the widespread reaction against the assumption that the
natural sciences offer an adequate or even a relevant model for the
practice of the social disciplines. The clearest reflection of this
growing doubt has been the revival of the suggestion that the explanation of human behaviour and the explanation of natural events
are logically distinct undertakings, and thus that the positivist contention that all successful explanations must conform to the same
deductive model must be fundamentally misconceived. From many
different directions the cry has instead gone up for the development
of a hermeneutic approach to the human sciences, an approach that
will do justice to the claim that the explanation of human action
must always include – and perhaps even take the form of – an
attempt to recover and interpret the meanings of social actions from
the point of view of the agents performing them.

Some recent social theorists have sought to reconcile these two
traditions – very much in the spirit of Max Weber – by arguing that
a satisfactory theory of social explanation must take account of
both the meanings and the causes of social phenomena.[8] But others

---

[7] For the idea of the 'restructuring' of social and political theory, see Bernstein 1976.
[8] Habermas upholds this position against Gadamer on the one hand and the positiv-
ists on the other in Habermas 1971a: 301–17. Among English social theorists,
Runciman has commended Weber for adopting this position in Runciman 1972
and explored its implications himself in Runciman 1983.

have rejected the possibility of such an accommodation, reverting instead to the far more radical suggestion – the suggestion of such earlier writers as Dilthey and Collingwood – that we should view the task of the historian and the sociologist in purely interpretative terms.[9] One important influence on these developments has been exercised by Wittgenstein's later philosophy, with its anti-positivist insistence that the meaning of an utterance is a matter of its use, and thus that the understanding of any meaningful episode – whether an action or an utterance – always involves us in placing it within its appropriate 'form of life'.[10] Of even more direct relevance, however, to the practice of the human sciences has been the adoption of a similar viewpoint by Hans-Georg Gadamer, the subject of the second chapter in this book. Drawing in part on Dilthey, but above all on Heidegger, Gadamer has argued in his major treatise, *Truth and Method*, that the one appropriate model to invoke in seeking to understand a social action is that of interpreting a text: a model in which we are not in the least concerned with the search for causes or the framing of laws, but entirely with the circular process of seeking to understand a whole in terms of its parts, and its parts in terms of the contribution they make to the meaning of the whole (Gadamer 1975a).

At the same time, however, Gadamer has injected a new element of scepticism into this long-standing debate. By emphasising the limitations of our own horizons, the prejudices and preconceptions we inevitably bring to bear upon the task of understanding another form of life, Gadamer has cast doubt on whether we can ever hope to reach the traditional goal of interpretation, that of grasping an alien action, utterance or text 'objectively' in its own terms. The most we can ever hope for, he concludes, is a 'fusion of horizons', a partial rapprochement between our present world, from which we can never hope to detach ourselves, and the different world we are seeking to appraise (Gadamer 1975a: 267–74).

From such doubts it has proved a short step to the anarchistic conclusion that we ought not to think of interpretation as a method of attaining truths at all, but ought rather – in the words of Paul Feyerabend's title – to be 'against method' (Feyerabend 1975).

[9] For the renewal of interest in these writers, see for example Gadamer 1975a: 153–234 (on Dilthey): Skinner 1969 and Dunn 1980: 2–4 (on Collingwood). For an important restatement of a similar case see Taylor 1971.

[10] Wittgenstein 1958: esp. 8–12. For the centrality of this concept in Wittgenstein's later philosophy see Cavell 1976: 44–72. For its application to the social sciences see Winch 1958.

Feyerabend has mainly applied this insight to scientific theories, arguing that we ought to remain as unconstrained and imaginative as possible in dreaming up alternatives to existing bodies of alleged knowledge.[11] Even more unsettling, however, has been the growing refusal, even in the case of literary interpretation, to treat the recovery of an intended meaning as any part of the interpreter's task. Here the leading iconoclast has been Jacques Derrida, the subject of the third chapter in this book. Derrida is fond of pointing to examples in which, due to the presence of some semantic ambiguity, together with the absence of any context that tells us how to 'take' what has been said, the result is an utterance we cannot hope to interpret with any certainty at all. He then generalises this insight to entire texts and oeuvres, insisting that we never have enough authority to privilege any one interpretation over another. The hermeneutic enterprise, he concludes, is actually a mistake: what is needed instead is what he calls (in the title of one of his most recent books) 'dissemination', the activity of illustrating with more and more examples the ultimate illegibility of texts (Derrida 1981a).

III

Along with these proliferating philosophical doubts about the possibility of modelling the social disciplines on a traditional image of the natural sciences, a series of moral objections have been raised of recent years against the positivist ambition to construct a science of society. One of the first victims of this development proved to be the 'end-of-ideology' argument. MacIntyre and others quickly pointed out that the thesis itself amounted to little more than an ideological reading of consensus politics, one in which silence was (recklessly, as it turned out) taken for agreement (MacIntyre 1971: 3–11). Habermas subsequently went on to emphasise a deeper level of moral bankruptcy encouraged by this vision of political life. As he argued in *Legitimation Crisis*, to claim that politics is a purely technological affair, and thus that ideology must have come to an end, has the effect of grounding the stability and even the legitimacy of the state on its capacity to maintain a high level of technological success, above all by delivering a sustained rate of economic growth.

---

[11] 'There is only *one* principle that can be defended under *all* circumstances and in *all* stages of human development. It is the principle: *anything goes*' (Feyerabend 1975: 28). Cf. also Feyerabend 1981 for the use of historical case-studies to exemplify the merits of an anarchistic approach.

The danger is obvious: in times of economic recession, such states will be unable to call on any wider or more traditional loyalties on the part of their citizens, with the result that economic difficulties will readily and dangerously mutate into crises of legitimacy (Habermas 1975: 33–94). It is a striking fact that, although Habermas presents this diagnosis from a Marxist perspective, a number of political writers from the so-called New Right have lately developed a remarkably similar attack on the moral limitations of *laissez-faire* capitalism, defending a form of conservatism founded not on free markets and the minimalist state, but rather on an almost Hegelian sense that the values of community, loyalty and deference must be prized and cultivated above all.[12]

Even more vociferous doubts about the normative presuppositions of positivism have been voiced of recent years by the psychologists. To perceive all human behaviour in lawlike, causal terms – as R. D. Laing and his associates have especially protested – presupposes that the question to ask about abnormal behaviour must always be what malfunction is prompting it. But this is to overlook the possibility that the behaviour in question may be strategic, a way of trying to cope with the world. And this oversight, Laing has argued, has the effect of reducing the agents involved to objects of manipulation when they deserve to be treated as subjects of consciousness.[13]

Behind this move towards an existential psychology can be discerned the authority of Sartre, to whom Laing and his followers owe an evident intellectual debt. Among more recent theorists, however, undoubtedly the most influential of those who have come to think in these terms has been Michel Foucault, the subject of the fourth chapter in this book. For the past two decades – before his tragically early death in 1984 – Foucault devoted himself to compiling historical case-studies about the treatment of such issues as madness, sexuality and criminality in our society, his aim being to demonstrate that claims to understand such phenomena have increasingly become associated with techniques of social control. As a philosopher, Foucault's central concern came to be that of forging a link between such claims to knowledge and the exercise of coercive power. As a moralist, his aim became that of urging us to break out of the prison we have increasingly built around ourselves in the

---

[12] For a representative statement of this commitment by an English commentator, see Scruton 1980. For an American example, see Will 1984.

[13] See Laing 1960; for Laing on Sartre see ibid.: 94n, 95–6.

name of scientific expertise. His was an almost romantic protest – one with a long pedigree among critics of industrial capitalism – against the routines and disciplines of our society, a protest which he combined with a call to resist and destroy the so-called human sciences in the name of our own humanity.

These various lines of attack on the very idea of a social science have in part derived, and have drawn great strength, from increasing doubts as to whether the sciences themselves are truly capable of living up to their own image as paradigms of the rational pursuit of knowledge. Here the most influential scepticism has been expressed by Thomas Kuhn, whose work is discussed in Chapter 5 of this book. Citing extensive evidence from the history of science, Kuhn has argued in his classic study, *The Structure of Scientific Revolutions*, that scientific communities rarely if ever espouse a Popperian ideal of seeking counter-examples to existing hypotheses and accepting as knowledge only such propositions as survive such tests. Normal science, as Kuhn calls it, instead proceeds by seeking confirmation of existing theories, theories whose authority is generally invoked to dispose of awkward counter-examples rather than being abandoned in the light of them. Whereas Popper had sought to question a Humean analysis of rational belief, Kuhn's analysis reinstates it.[14] To this account Kuhn adds that, if we wish to explain the acceptance or rejection of particular scientific hypotheses, what we need to invoke are the established customs of science as a profession, not merely the purportedly rational methods of disinterested scientists. In a fascinating parallel with Foucault's thought, the practice of science is thus depicted as a means of controlling what is permitted to count as knowledge.

Kuhn's most basic contention is that the reason why the sciences do not and cannot emulate a Popperian account of their practice is that our access to the facts in the light of which we test our beliefs is always filtered by what Kuhn has called our existing 'paradigms' or frameworks of understanding (Kuhn 1970: 43–51). To put the point more starkly, there *are* no facts independent of our theories about them, and in consequence no one way of viewing, classifying and explaining the world that all rational persons are obliged to accept. Rival theories can of course be compared, but not against an objective scale: in the end they are simply incommensurable, with the result that their exponents may be said (in Kuhn's Idealist-

---

[14] This contrast between Popper and Kuhn is well brought out in Mortimore and Maund 1976: 11–33.

sounding metaphor) to be living and working in different worlds (Kuhn 1970: 134–5).

Kuhn's attack on standard notions of scientific rationality bears some resemblance to Quine's celebrated onslaught on what he calls the empiricist dogma of supposing there to be a categorical distinction between concepts and facts (Quine 1953: 20–46). It is also somewhat reminiscent of Wittgenstein's insistence that all our attempts to understand what we call the facts will always be relative to the framework of a particular form of life. Where all these influences have flowed together, as they have for example in Richard Rorty's remarkable book, *Philosophy and the Mirror of Nature*, the outcome has been nothing less than a disposition to question the place of philosophy as well as the sciences within our culture. If our access to reality is inevitably conditioned by local beliefs about what is to count as knowledge, then the traditional claim of the sciences to be finding out more and more about the world as it really is begins to look questionable, or at least unduly simplified. Moreover, if there is no canonical grid of concepts in terms of which the world is best divided up and classified, then the traditional role of philosophy as the discipline that analyses such concepts is also thrown into doubt.[15] Epistemology, conceived in Kantian terms as the study of what can be known with certainty, begins to seem an impossibility; instead we appear to be threatened with the spectre of epistemological relativism.[16]

Among those who have argued in this way, the study of history has increasingly proved to be a fertile source of inspiration and evidence. Foucault's writings constantly seek to confront our sense of how the world needs to be seen with the very different record of how it has in fact been seen at different times. Kuhn similarly presents himself as an historian, seeking to investigate the actual behaviour of scientific communities in such a way as to undermine, by reference to the historical record, some of the *a priori* commitments of contemporary philosophers of science. Partly in consequence of these developments, a number of historians as well as ethnographers have in turn become quite explicit in presenting their own studies as further ammunition in the fight against naive realism and associated normative views about human nature and rationality. Among his-

[15] Rorty 1979: esp. 315–56. For a discussion, see Skinner 1981.
[16] Some argue that this spectre has in fact materialised, and that we have no reason to be alarmed by it. See Rorty 1979 for a cautious statement; Barnes and Bloor 1982: 21–47 for a less cautious one.

torians of science, historians of moral and political philosophy, and above all among cultural anthropologists, the study of the alien and the exotic has increasingly been held to take its point from the capacity of other ages and other cultures to offer us counter-examples to some of our most cherished presuppositions and beliefs.[17]

IV

By this stage in my survey, however, it may begin to sound paradoxical to speak of all these sceptical strands of thought as contributions to a return of Grand Theory in the human sciences. If there is one feature common to all the thinkers I have singled out, it is a willingness to emphasise the importance of the local and the contingent, a desire to underline the extent to which our own concepts and attitudes have been shaped by particular historical circumstances, and a correspondingly strong dislike – amounting almost to hatred in the case of Wittgenstein – of all overarching theories and singular schemes of explanation. With some of the writers I have mentioned, moreover, this has led – implicitly with Foucault, quite explicitly with Feyerabend – to a form of conceptual relativism so strong as to seem almost self-defeating,[18] and to something like the project of seeking to demolish the claims of theory and method to organise the materials of experience. To describe such sceptics as grand theorists may well sound dangerously like missing the point.

To this apparent paradox, however, there are two responses to be made. One is that the joke, so to speak, is on the sceptics themselves. Although they have given reasons for repudiating the activity of theorising, they have of course been engaged in theorising at the same time. There is no denying that Foucault has articulated a

[17] Among historians of science, this commitment is especially marked among anarchists (see for example Feyerabend 1975: esp. 47–53) and among exponents of the so-called 'strong programme' in the sociology of knowledge. For a general statement of the latter approach see Barnes 1974 and for applications see Bloor 1976 and Barnes 1977. Among historians of moral and political philosophy, MacIntyre 1966 has proved to be an influential model. For more recent examples see Tuck 1979: esp. 1–4, Skinner 1984: 193–221 and Taylor 1984: 17–30. From the perspective of cultural anthropology Geertz has provided the best statement of an analogous case. See especially the concluding chapter of Geertz 1980 and the Introduction to Geertz 1983. For a much more sceptical view, however, of the utility of our traditions of thought, see Dunn 1979.

[18] For this charge, urged especially against Foucault, see Putnam 1981: 150–73. For the claim that a similar incoherence afflicts Kuhn's arguments see Davidson 1984: 183–98.

general view about the nature of knowledge, that Wittgenstein presents us with an abstract account of meaning and understanding, that Feyerabend has a preferred and almost Popperian method of judging scientific hypotheses, and even that Derrida presupposes the possibility of constructing interpretations when he tells us that our next task should be that of deconstructing them. There can be no doubt, moreover, that all these anti-theorists have had a decisive impact in redirecting the efforts of social philosophers in the present generation, if only by exposing the inadequacies of received beliefs. There is no paradox, in short, in giving pride of place to the icono-clasts: almost in spite of themselves, they have proved to be among the grandest theorists of current practice throughout a wide range of the social disciplines.

My second and main response is that, after surveying the contri-butions made by these 'all-purpose subversives',[19] my story is still only half-told. We next need to note that, during the past two decades, there has also been an unashamed return to the deliberate construction of precisely those grand theories of human nature and conduct which Wright Mills and his generation had hoped to outlaw from any central place in the human sciences.

This can be seen most obviously in the case of moral and political philosophy. Here, somewhat ironically, the destructive work of the sceptics has served to clear the ground on which the grandest theor-etical structures have since been raised. To understand how this has come about, we need only recall the strong emphasis placed by most of the writers we have so far been considering on the idea that concepts are not timeless entities with fixed meanings, but should rather be thought of as weapons (Heidegger's suggestion) or as tools (Wittgenstein's term), the understanding of which is always in part a matter of seeing who is wielding them and for what purposes. But if this is granted, then the orthodoxy I cited at the outset – that the task of moral or political philosophy is to analyse *the* language of morals, or *the* vocabulary of politics – is automatically discredited. To cite Foucault's way of putting the objection, there is simply no such changeless grid of concepts and meanings awaiting neutral analysis.[20]

The void thus created at the centre of analytical moral and politi-cal philosophy has now been filled by a reversion to the two most time-honoured objectives of these disciplines. One has been a

[19] The phrase is from Geertz 1983: 4, speaking in particular of Foucault and Kuhn.
[20] For reference to this objection and a valuable discussion, see Rorty 1979: 330.

renewed willingness directly to address the most pressing evaluative issues of the day.[21] As a result, such topics as the justice of war, the social causes of famine, the responsibility of man for nature, the welfare of animals, the limits of political obligation, the rights of the unborn, of future generations, and above all the risks of being 'defended to death', all these and many other kindred questions of obvious urgency have again become the staples of philosophical debate.[22] But the other and even more startling development has been a return to Grand Theory in the most traditional and architectonic style, the style employed by the great normative system-builders of earlier centuries. Moral and political philosophers have ceased to be in the least shy of telling us that their task is that of helping us to understand how best to live our lives.[23] Throwing off their purely linguistic preoccupations, they have gone on to revive a heady and recognisably Platonic view of their discipline as essentially concerned with elucidating the character of the good life and the boundaries of a free and just society. So much high seriousness has this generated, indeed, that there are even some signs that the charge of triviality regularly levelled at the subject in its meta-ethical days may be replaced by a no less justified accusation of undue sententiousness and self-importance.[24]

It is of course true that such lofty aspirations had never been completely repudiated, at least in German – and hence to some extent in American – social philosophy. The names of Herbert Marcuse and Hannah Arendt immediately spring to mind.[25] A comparable commitment, however, now informs the work of many writers trained in the more rarified atmosphere of analytical philosophy. The effect has been to initiate an energetic and profound debate between two rival theories of social and political life, each of which has now

[21] The title of Thomas Nagel's collection of essays (Nagel 1979) neatly suggests the change of perspective: the concern is now with 'mortal questions'.

[22] By now there is a large body of literature on most of these themes. For distinguished contributions (many of which contain helpful bibliographies) to the discussions of each of the topics mentioned in the text, see respectively Walzer 1977; Sen 1981; Passmore 1974; Regan and Singer 1976; Dunn 1980; Sumner 1981; Parfit 1984; Prins 1983.

[23] This aspiration, resting as it does on objectivist ideas about justice and 'human flourishing', exists in strong tension with the sceptical and almost relativist tendencies prevalent in so much contemporary social science, and has begun to elicit protests as a result. See for example Geertz 1984.

[24] The dangers of excessive pretension are candidly acknowledged in Scheffler 1982: vi.

[25] See especially Arendt 1958 and Marcuse 1964 – Arendt's title in particular suggesting nothing less than a global set of concerns.

become highly systematic in structure as well as ambitious in scale.

Of these two schools of thought, the one that has enjoyed more prominence in recent years has been based on emphasising, in Kantian vein, the absolute separateness of persons and the alleged sanctity of their individual rights. Among legal theorists, Ronald Dworkin in particular has invoked these principles to question the assumptions of legal positivism in *Taking Rights Seriously* (Dworkin 1978a). Even more influentially, a number of political theorists have employed a similar approach to challenge the tenets of utilitarianism, thereby seeking to restore the idea of distributive justice to the centre of our political thought. One such writer has been Robert Nozick, whose *Anarchy, State and Utopia* deduces a minimalist account of the powers of the State from a recognisably Lockean vision of individual citizens as the bearers of inalienable rights (Nozick 1974). But the most systematic of these recent attempts to found a general theory of justice on the basis of our civil and economic liberties has been made by John Rawls, whose writings are discussed, along with those of his followers, in Chapter 6 of this book. Perhaps the most remarkable feature of Rawls's major treatise, *A Theory of Justice*, is that he presents it as an extension and generalisation of a number of insights originally owed to the social-contractarian thinkers of the seventeenth and eighteenth centuries (Rawls 1971: vii–viii). He presents it, that is, as a continuation of precisely that style of abstract theorising about the nature of man and society which we find in Locke, Rousseau and Kant, but which was supposed to have been finally superseded (so the end-of-ideology theorists assured us) by the coming of a purely empirical science of politics.

For all the prominence of these philosophies of right, however, the terms of debate in recent legal and political theory have still been largely set by the defenders of utilitarianism, the other style of Grand Theory prevalent among contemporary exponents of the moral sciences. Even among those who have aspired to demolish the entire structure of utilitarian thought, it has still proved necessary to pose the central issue in the form of asking whether one is For or Against utilitarianism.[26] Moreover, a number of the most original and ambitious theorists continue to be for rather than against. Among legal philosophers, the peerless contributions of H. L. A. Hart have ensured that the case for a generally utilitarian perspec-

[26] See for example Smart and Williams 1973. Utilitarianism remains a major reference-point for most of the contributors to Sen and Williams 1982.

tive has never lacked for eloquent defence.[27] And in moral philosophy, the range and depth of Derek Parfit's new treatise, *Reasons and Persons*, reminds us, should any reminder be needed, how powerful are the resources available to those who emphasise the autonomy of individuals less than the welfare of societies as a whole (Parfit 1984). The debate continues, in short; and it does so in an idiom that Hume and Kant – the respective tutelary deities of the rival creeds – would have recognised without much difficulty.

V

If we turn to the wider fields of sociology and social philosophy, we find similar signs of a return to Grand Theory even more in evidence. Here one of the major preoccupations has become that of trying to furnish a satisfactory response to the sceptics, the irrationalists, the protagonists of the 'strong programme' in the sociology of knowledge and the numerous other exponents of apparently relativistic threats to the foundations of the human sciences.[28] The study of rationality has thus come to be a major focus of research, together with the study of its limits, including the investigation of such familiar but philosophically intractable phenomena as self-deception, the wider notion David Pears has described as motivated irrationality and the further subversions of reason Jon Elster has discussed under the heading of 'sour grapes'.[29]

Of those who have taken the concept of rationality as their central theme, perhaps the most ambitious and tenacious has been Jürgen Habermas, whose voluminous writings form the subject of the seventh chapter in this book. Habermas is of course one of the most prolific and wide-ranging of all contemporary social philosophers, and his interests are so diverse as to defy any easy paraphrase. But he has certainly made it one of his abiding concerns to analyse what he takes to be the constituent elements of purely rational communication. His method has been to construct a counterfactual model of what he calls 'the ideal speech situation', his aim being to elucidate the nature of the circumstances in which we might be capable of reaching a fully rational appraisal of our own social predicament,

[27] See especially Hart 1961 and Hart 1968.
[28] For an outline of these movements and a response to them, see Hollis and Lukes 1982: 1–20. See also Hollis 1977, Hollis 1982: 67–86, Lukes 1982: 261–305 and the general survey in Bernstein 1983.
[29] See Pears 1984, Elster 1983, and for connected arguments see also Elster 1978 and 1979.

undisturbed by external constraints or ideological preferences. This ideal of 'undistorted' communication is already present in Habermas's earliest writings, most notably in his Inaugural Lecture of 1965, 'Knowledge and Human Interests', and it remains one of his central preoccupations, surfacing once again to play a vital role in his recent two-volume study, *A Theory of Communicative Action*.[30]

As well as making a distinctive contribution to debates about human rationality, Habermas has played a major part in helping to revive two traditions of Grand Theory that had both fallen into considerable disrepute under the hegemony of positivism. He has devoted a great deal of respectful attention, especially in his most recent writings, to the highly abstract theories of social structure developed by Talcott Parsons – thereby resurrecting the grand theorist whom Wright Mills had above all hoped to bury with ridicule.[31] But of far greater importance has been Habermas's role in helping to bring about the immense resurgence of interest in Marxism over the past two decades. It is true that he criticises Marx, whose aspiration to uncover laws of social development leaves insufficient space, according to Habermas, for the role of 'reflexivity' and thus of conscious agency in the processes of social change. But as Anthony Giddens points out in Chapter 7 below, there can be little doubt that, in presenting his own ideas as a 'reconstruction of historical materialism', Habermas is in effect offering himself as a Marx for our times.

Habermas's doubts about the more mechanistic aspects of Marxism, together with his insistence that we need to develop a 'critical theory' of our own society, are commitments that place him squarely within the mainstream of 'humanist' approaches to Marx's thought. Humanist Marxism has been an influential movement in recent times, widely propagated not only by the followers of the Frankfurt School in Germany, but also by such writers as E. P. Thompson in England and above all by the admirers of Sartre, Merleau-Ponty and other founders of existential Marxism in France.[32] Since the late 1960s, however, a fierce attack on this way

---

[30] See Habermas 1971a: 311–15 and cf. Habermas 1984.

[31] See the discussion in Habermas 1984 and cf. the satirical account in Wright Mills 1959: 25–49.

[32] On the humanist Marxism of the Frankfurt School see Connerton 1980, and for a more critical appraisal see Geuss 1981. For E. P. Thompson's humanistic assumptions see Thompson 1978 and for an extended critique see Anderson 1980; for an analysis of the issues at stake see James 1984. On the French movement of existential Marxism see Poster 1975.

of reading Marx has gathered momentum, above all in France and especially in the writings of Louis Althusser and his disciples, whose theories are discussed in Chapter 8 of this book. Concentrating on the strongly determinist features of Marx's later works, to the deliberate exclusion of the more humanistic elements familiar from the so-called Paris Manuscripts of the 1840s, Althusser has systematically argued the case for treating Marx as the one genuine scientist of society, scientific in the strict sense of offering a fully causal analysis of the mechanisms of social change.

The most salient and challenging feature of Althusser's philosophy has been his uncompromising determinism, his willingness to work out with complete consistency the implications of Engels's celebrated observation to the effect that the course of European history would have been no different if Napoleon had never lived. Althusser has perhaps gone furthest in this attempt to outlaw our ordinary notions of agency and responsibility from social explanation, but a similar tendency to lay all the emphasis on the determining effects of social and linguistic structures has been a prominent feature of many other grand theories in contemporary social science, especially in France. The two most obvious and influential examples are discussed in the final two chapters of this book. One is Claude Lévi-Strauss's attempt to develop and practise a structuralist anthropology, one in which the apparent diversity of different cultures will be related to, and subsumed under, an account of the general laws that govern our mental operations and in consequence determine both our systems of signs and the fabric of our beliefs. Finally, the other group of practising structuralists we consider are the historians of the so-called *Annales* School, whose whole approach to the past has been conditioned by the desire, as Fernand Braudel expresses it, 'to transcend the individual and the particular event' (Braudel 1980: 6–11).

This form of Grand Theory has in turn been taken up by a number of social philosophers both in England and in the United States. The question of the relative weight to be assigned to agents and structures has indeed become a central preoccupation with the younger generation of social theorists in both countries, and a brisk debate has ensued. Perhaps unsurprisingly, most of those who have taken part have continued to insist that both categories remain indispensable.[33] More recently, however, the general case in favour of a more

---

[33] See for example Giddens 1979: 49–95 and Dunn 1982.

structuralist approach has also been defended, while at the same time a number of writers – notably Perry Anderson and Theda Skocpol – have succeeded in deploying the evidence of historical case-studies in such a way as to press the argument for a more deterministic stance.[34]

Meanwhile the discipline of history, normally the least reflective of the social sciences, has been comprehensively reorientated – especially in the United States – through the impact of the *Annales* historians. The study of individual political actors, together with the whole Namierite tradition of focusing primarily on political history, have both been widely repudiated.[35] Instead, historians have increasingly paid homage to the very different credo embodied in that Bible of *Annales* historiography, Fernand Braudel's history of the Mediterranean in the early-modern period. Braudel insists that the beliefs and the behaviour of even the most significant historical agents are determined by the economies and institutions of the societies within which they operate, while these are in turn determined largely by the exigencies of climate and geography. It follows, as he puts it, that mountains, not rulers, come first, and that historians need to adopt a far more sociological as well as deterministic perspective in order to come to grips with the implications of that fundamental fact.

VI

The return of Grand Theory has brought with it many clashes of titans: Gadamer has debated with Heidegger, Lévi-Strauss with Sartre, Kuhn with Feyerabend, Dworkin with Hart, Nozick with Rawls, Foucault with Derrida and Habermas with almost everyone. I have not tried in the above outline to smooth out these differences in the name of producing a neat account; all I have tried to do is to furnish something in the nature of a map, seeking to situate a number of leading figures roughly in their appropriate places in the current intellectual landscape. It is obvious, however, that what I have produced is the merest sketch, and that what is needed if we wish to familiarise ourselves with the somewhat rugged terrain I

---

[34] For a general defence, drawing on the work of both Althusser and the *Annales* School, see James 1984; for case-histories see Anderson 1974 and Skocpol 1979.
[35] But there are signs of revolt, as Stone 1979 notes, even in the United States, while in England the study of 'high politics' has remained widespread and has even become increasingly fashionable.

have been surveying is a series of more detailed and more expert guides. And this, of course, is the purpose which will I hope be served by the individual chapters of this book.

2

Hans-Georg Gadamer

by William Outhwaite

The 'grand theorists' discussed in this book are all very different from one another, yet most of them agree in attaching enormous importance to the idea of frameworks which give meaning and significance to individual phenomena: Kuhn's paradigms or disciplinary matrices, Althusser's *problématiques*, Foucault's discourses, *epistemes*, and 'regimes'.

All these frameworks are guides to understanding, but at the same time guides to action. The disciplinary matrix of particle physics makes it possible both to understand what the practitioners are up to, and to join in with them. Althusser's reconstruction of Marx's scientific problematic is intended to clarify the import of Marx's work (of which Marx was not fully aware) and to make possible the further development of more specialised 'regional' theories within Marxism. Foucault's frameworks seem at first sight to be more a matter of external historical description, yet even here we are brought to realise our inevitable complicity in the modern European regime of truth/power.

These two ideas – understanding seen firstly as a holistic process mediated by a complex framework and secondly as an active process of encounter and response – are also central to the work of the German hermeneutic philosopher Hans-Georg Gadamer. The framework notion of understanding is something he shares with the rest of the hermeneutic tradition; the stress on understanding as a matter of commitment is a theme he has taken from Heidegger, but made very much his own.

Hans-Georg Gadamer was born in 1900, studied under Heidegger and worked mainly at the universities of Marburg and Heidelberg. He retired officially in 1968 but remains extremely active. His main work, *Truth and Method*, was published in 1960, though not translated into English until 1975. Gadamer endorses the traditional conception of understanding an unfamiliar text or way of life as a holistic process, operating within a hermeneutic circle in which we move back and forth between specific parts of the 'text' and our conception of it as a totality. Understanding, in other words, is not a matter of simple addition of discrete elements. If, for example, I want to learn Serbo-Croat, one of the worst ways of doing so is to take an English–Serbo-Croat dictionary and work slowly through it. A more promising strategy is to build up a basis of simple sentences which are meaningful in themselves.

The traditional hermeneutic conception of understanding, as it developed in the Romantic period, is that it is something which is not automatic; it requires a certain openness of mind, an ability to put oneself into the place of the author of the book or the participants in the way of life. This notion of projection tends to be misunderstood in the Anglo-Saxon world as a mysterious kind of empathy, but what Dilthey and others really had in mind was a much more cerebral process based on a common sphere of experience:

Every single human expression represents something which is common to many and therefore part of the realm of objective mind. Every word or sentence, every gesture or form of politeness, every work of art and every historical deed are only understandable because the person expressing himself and the person who understands him are connected by something they have in common; the individual always experiences, thinks, acts, and also understands, in this common sphere. (Dilthey 1958: 146f)

Gadamer would I think be happy with this formulation. Where he diverges from the nineteenth-century tradition is in rejecting its stress on *method* (hence the title of his book). In a sense, the basis of this disagreement can be pinned down to two different interpretations of the traditional principle of understanding that 'meaning is to be read out of, not into the text: *sensus non est inferendus, sed eferendus*' (Wach 1929: 9). The first interpretation of this principle points towards the construction of precise methods to capture the meaning as it is in itself, stripping away any 'modern' assumptions or prejudices, just as a natural scientific experiment tries to exclude extraneous effects. As Gadamer puts it, '...the methodology of the modern historical sciences ... makes what has grown historically and has been transmitted historically an object to be established like an experimental finding – as if tradition were as alien and, from the human point of view, as unintelligible, as an object of physics' (Gadamer 1975a: xxi).

But how *can* we conceive a text as it is in itself, independently of the complex process by which we get access to it? It is here that Gadamer's alternative conception becomes relevant. For him, understanding is not a matter of trained, methodical, unprejudiced technique, but an encounter in the existentialist sense, a confrontation with something radically different from ourselves. Understanding involves *engagement* in Jean-Paul Sartre's sense. Gadamer's book could almost have been called *Against Method* or *Beyond Method*: he is concerned with a 'pre-understanding' which makes possible, but at the same time sets limits to, any interpretative technique.

Traditional hermeneutic theory postulates a subject who aims to understand an object (a text, a social practice, or whatever) as it is in itself. This means that the subject must be as open-minded and unprejudiced as possible, approaching the object without preconceptions. For Gadamer, by contrast, preconceptions or prejudices are what make understanding possible in the first place. They are bound up with our awareness of the historical influence or effectivity of the text; and without this awareness we would not understand it. It is impossible to understand the Bible or the Communist Manifesto without a knowledge of the role they have played in our history.

Our understanding of a text arises out of our position in a historical tradition, and this is in fact our link with the historical influence or effectivity of the text itself (Gadamer 1975a: xxi). Understanding is not a matter of forgetting our own horizon of meanings and putting ourselves within that of the alien texts or the alien society; it means merging or fusing our own horizons with theirs. In Gadamer's view, hermeneutic theory has paid too much attention to the detached way in which we tend to interpret literary texts, and not enough to the more practical concerns of legal or theological interpretations, where the outcome is not just a better understanding of a text but its actual incorporation into our own lives.

As Gadamer puts it in his Foreword to the second edition of *Truth and Method* (1975a: xix),

... the purpose of my investigation is not to offer a general theory of interpretation and a differential account of its methods (which E. Betti has done so well) but to discover what is common to all modes of understanding and to show that understanding is never subjective behaviour towards a given 'object', but towards its effective history – the history of its influence; in other words, understanding belongs to the being of that which is understood.

One way of clarifying Gadamer's opposition to nineteenth-century hermeneutics is to unpack the concept of subjective behaviour in this passage. For the traditional conception of hermeneutics, 'subjective' means an approach which is individual, idiosyncratic and arbitrary; this is contrasted with an objective approach which is trained, disciplined and methodical. Gadamer however wishes to transcend the subject–object division, or at least to relativise it to an objective context, that of the effective history of a text which is part of a tradition.

Here, he draws on Heidegger's account of understanding in *Being and Time*. 'Heidegger's temporal analytics of human existence (*Dasein*) has, I think, shown convincingly that understanding is not just one of the various possible behaviours of the subject, but the mode of being of [*Dasein*] itself' (1975a: xviii). In Heidegger's terms, interpretation is 'grounded existentially in understanding' (Heidegger 1962: 188):

In interpreting, we do not, so to speak, throw a 'signification' over some naked thing which is present-at-hand, we do not stick a value on it; but when something within-the-world is encountered as such, the thing in question already has an involvement which is disclosed in our understanding of the world, and this involvement is one which gets laid out by the interpretation. (Ibid.: 190-1)

Gadamer's conflict with traditional hermeneutics can also be elucidated in terms of his two central principles: the *universality* and the *historicity* of hermeneutics. The tradition which found its most systematic expression in Dilthey was universalistic in the sense that it aimed at a general methodology of the human sciences, grounded in the nature of human consciousness or *Geist* and in the concept of lived experience (*Erlebnis*). For Gadamer, as we have seen, the universality of hermeneutics means more than this; it is a fundamental dimension of all human consciousness as it is expressed in language; it encompasses human knowledge of nature as well as of human artefacts. For Gadamer, as for Heidegger, 'Being that can be understood is language.'

Historicity, too, was a fundamental theme of Romantic hermeneutics, but there it was understood in terms of historicism (*Historismus*); the historical diversity of human civilisations means that we must think ourselves into their categories in order to understand them. Here, historical distance is a methodological problem: for Gadamer, it is an ontological one since it affects the very nature of that which we try to understand. Our 'prejudices' are not an obstacle to knowledge so much as a condition of knowledge, since they make up the fundamental structure of our relationship with our historical tradition.

The example of art which makes up the first part of *Truth and Method* illustrates these differences. The Romantic conception of understanding a work of art in its own (reconstructed) context is not only impossible but pointless, given the fact of historical change and in particular our modern (and impoverished) conception of the aesthetic.

What is reconstructed, a life brought back from the lost past, is not the original. In its continuance in an estranged state it acquires only a secondary, cultural, existence... Even the painting taken from the museum and replaced in the church, or the building restored to its original condition are not what they once were – they become simply tourist attractions. Similarly, a hermeneutics that regarded understanding as the reconstruction of the original would be no more than the recovery of a dead meaning. (1975a: 149)

Hegel was right; these are 'beautiful fruits torn from the tree' (Hegel 1977: 455). Gadamer offers us a modified and sceptical Hegelian position: 'the essential nature of the historical spirit does not consist in the restoration of the past, but in thoughtful mediation with contemporary life' (1975a: 150).

As stated earlier, Gadamer's basic metaphor for this process of mediation is that of the fusion of horizons, in which we approach what we wish to understand, not in a state of factitious (because impossible) virginity, but with the prejudices which 'constitute the historical reality of [our] being' (1975a: 245).

What is at stake between these two conceptions of interpretation? Gadamer's lengthy polemics with Emilio Betti have helped to clarify the issues. Betti, committed to a methodological hermeneutics based on canons of interpretation, reproaches Gadamer with abandoning the ideal of the objectivity of interpretation. Gadamer's positive evaluation of prejudices and his exaggeration of the dimension of application within hermeneutics, amount to a conception in which 'the object of historical understanding does not consist of events but of their significance (which is related to the present), i.e. their significance for today'. This is 'a presumptuous self-assertion of subjectivity that would demote the process of historical interpretation to a mere mediation of past and present' (Betti 1962, quoted in Bleicher 1980: 81, 82).

In sum, Gadamer ducks the epistemological question posed to hermeneutics, which

is not a *quaestio facti* but a *quaestio juris*: it is concerned with the problem of justification which does not aim at ascertaining what actually happens in the activity of thought apparent in interpretation but which aims at finding out what one should do – i.e. what one should aim for in the task of interpretation, what methods to use and what guidelines to follow in the correct execution of this task. (Bleicher 1980: 84)

Betti's charge, then, is that Gadamer is not offering a theory of interpretation, but a mere descriptive phenomenology. Gadamer retorts that it is Betti who is deficient in offering nothing more than a methodology of hermeneutics. 'By being able to conceive the problem of hermeneutics only as a problem of method, he shows that he is profoundly involved in the subjectivism which we are endeavouring to overcome' (1975a: 466).

The easy way to resolve this dispute is to say that, whatever their different conceptions of the proper role of philosophy, Betti and Gadamer are simply talking about different aspects of the hermeneutic enterprise. One might say that Gadamer's philosophical hermeneutics aims to describe the basic starting-point of hermeneutics, which Betti is more inclined to take for granted in constructing his canons of interpretation. It is, in the end, not clear whether Gadamer's conception is in contradiction with the standard view, here represented by Betti, or complementary to it. What is clear is that the dispute bears on endemic controversies in the human sciences about the ways in which the meaning of texts is produced and reproduced. In American literary theory, for example, E. D. Hirsch (1967) upholds a standard conception based on determinate meanings of texts, whereas Stanley Fish (1980) stresses the production of meaning by 'interpretative communities'.

In the rest of this essay I shall confine myself to the implications of Gadamer's conception for social theory, as reflected notably in the work of Jürgen Habermas and Anthony Giddens. Gadamer is important on two fronts: first, in reinforcing the long-standing opposition to positivistic accounts of the unity of the natural and the social sciences, and, secondly, in showing that the traditional hermeneutic critique of positivism remains tied to a conception of method whose implications are themselves positivistic.

The concept of 'understanding' most forcefully advanced by Dilthey in the nineteenth century has formed the basis for a view of the social sciences which stresses their difference from the sciences of nature (Outhwaite 1975). Understanding or, in German, *Verstehen*, has come to be understood as a method alternative to the study of casual connections between phenomena. The German sociologist Max Weber argued in the first two decades of this century that explanations in the social or cultural sciences must be both causally and meaningfully adequate (Weber 1968: 9ff). It is not enough, for example, to register the fact that Protestant merchants appeared to be more innovative than Catholics in early-modern Europe. The explanation of this correlation must be sought in the internal structure of Protestant and especially Calvinist religiosity: what it was *like* to be a Calvinist (Weber 1976). To give another example: Gresham's law that bad money drives out good is both empirically verifiable and rationally intelligible: people want to offload their dud currency as soon as possible and they hold on to the higher value coins. And we can understand why it makes sense for them to do so (Weber 1968: 18).

This traditional conception of understanding needs to be qualified in two ways, both of which are implicit in Gadamer's work. First, it is not enough to see understanding or *verstehen* as a method, for it is more than this: it is the way in which we get access to social reality in the first place. The natural sciences, too, interpret the phenomena they have to deal with, but the phenomena studied by the social scientist are crucially bound up with (though not identical with) the interpretations of them given by the members of the society being studied. And there is even something odd about speaking, as I have just done, of getting *access* to social reality since, as hermeneutic theorists have always stressed, we are already in it as (social) human beings.

Secondly, Gadamer's notion of engagement helps us to understand the consequences of the fact that we are rooted in the social world. The fact that we are ourselves human beings makes it possible for us to understand what it is like to be another human being, what it is (probably) like to hold the beliefs which other human beings hold, and so on. But this also means that we cannot simply record, in an objective and value-free way, the practices and beliefs of other human beings. The social scientist does not go out into the field as a *tabula rasa* and return with an account of what it is like to be a European car-worker or an African peasant; it is precisely the encounter between the social scientist's own beliefs and practices and those of the people he or she is studying which makes up whatever understanding we can have of another social reality.

Let me now examine these issues in a rather more detailed way. First, it is essential to bear in mind Gadamer's principle of the universality of hermeneutics. Understanding is *not* a special feature of the human sciences, but the fundamental way in which human beings exist in the world. 'Understanding ... shows the universality of human language-use (*Sprachlichkeit*) as a limitless medium that carries everything, not only the culture that has been handed down through language, but absolutely everything, because everything is incorporated into the realm of understandability in which we interact' (Gadamer 1976: 25). The problem about the sciences, for Gadamer as for Husserl (1970) and Heidegger (1962), is how they link up with this realm of human understanding: ... the central question of the modern age ... is ... how our natural view of the world – the experience of the world that we have as we simply live out our lives – is related to the unassailable and anonymous authority that confronts us in the pronouncements of science' (Gadamer 1976: 25). Hermeneutic reflection, like Husserl's transcendental phenomenology, is supposed to mediate between science and the life-world, and in particular between their respective languages. It was 'the specific merit and the specific weakness' of Greek science that it 'originated in the linguistic experience of the world. In order to overcome this weakness, its naive anthropocentrism, modern science has also renounced its merit, namely its place in the natural attitude of man to the world' (Gadamer 1975a: 412). Hermeneutical reflection, then, forms a bridge between the special sciences and the life-world, making explicit the presuppositions of the sciences, their forms of abstraction, and, most of all, their guiding conception of *method*. Gadamer puts it in Wittgensteinian terms: 'The language games of science remain related to the metalanguage presented in the mother tongue' (1976: 39).

All this must I think be accepted. Despite the vagueness of Gadamer's concept of the natural attitude to the world, it marks out an important area of enquiry: that of world-pictures, ideas of natural order, and so forth (cf., e.g., Dijksterhuis 1961). But what about the social and human sciences? It is interesting to note that Gadamer does not assimilate the social sciences to the human sciences or *Geisteswissenschaften*: philology, literary criticism, aesthetics, cultural history, etc. Instead, he draws a fairly conventional distinction between the natural sciences and the *Geisteswissenschaften* (Gadamer 1975a: 5ff) and then locates the social sciences somewhere in the middle. The essay (Gadamer 1976) cited above continues with the argument that the separation or alienation of science from our natural experience of the world is

without importance for the natural sciences as such. The true natural scientist knows how very particular is the realm of knowledge of his science in relation to the whole of reality... The so-called humanities (Humaniora) still relate easily to the common consciousness, so far as they reach it at all, since their objects belong immediately to the cultural tradition and the traditional educational system. But the modern social sciences stand in a peculiarly tense relationship to their object, a relationship which especially requires hermeneutical reflection. For the methodical alienation to which the social sciences owe their progress is related here to the human-societal world. (Gadamer 1976: 40)

Gadamer's view of the social sciences, so far as it can be disentangled from his more specific disagreements with Habermas,[1] is that they should indeed be conscious of the 'hermeneutic conditions' which apply to the 'verstehende Geisteswissenschaften' and their implications for the practice of social science. He notes that (some of the time?) the social sciences do not aim at understanding but rather 'incorporate linguistically sedimented truisms in their attempt to capture the real structure of society'. And even if they do aim at understanding, they are committed, *qua* sciences, to a methodically alienated form of understanding, which therefore requires further hermeneutic reflection.[2]

What then are the hermeneutic conditions which govern the *Geisteswissenschaften* and, whether or not they heed them, the social sciences as well? Gadamer's hermeneutic philosophy is concerned with the sort of understanding which is at work in our encounter with and participation in a cultural tradition – something which is prior to any systematic hermeneutic investigation. As noted above, this process of coming-to-understand is not a matter of unprejudiced appropriation of an object such as a text, but a 'fusion' of one's own 'horizon' of meanings and expectations ('prejudices') with that of the text, the other person, the alien culture.

Gadamer is therefore not offering a different methodology of understanding; nor is he 'against method' in Feyerabend's sense. Rather, he is concerned with processes which precede and underlie interpretative methods: 'The hermeneutics developed here is not, therefore, a methodology of the human sciences, but an attempt to understand what the human sciences truly are, beyond their method-

[1] The essay (Gadamer 1976) from which I have been quoting is a response to Habermas's 1967 critique *Zur Logik der Sozialwissenschaften* (Habermas 1971b). Habermas continued the exchange in his contribution to Gadamer's Festschrift, *Hermeneutik und Dialektik I* 1970. This essay, entitled 'The hermeneutic claim to universality', is translated in Bleicher 1980. See also Gadamer's reply in *Hermeneutik und Ideologiekritik* 1971.

[2] *Hermeneutik und Ideologiekritik* 1971: 66–7; Gadamer 1976: 27. This is an extremely obscure passage, and the translation, which Gadamer is said to have corrected (p.vii), diverges a good deal from the original.

ological self-consciousness, and what connects them with the totality of our experience of the world' (Gadamer 1975a: xiii).

Does this mean that Gadamer's hermeneutic philosophy leaves the human sciences as they are? Gadamer distinguishes between those sciences or research topics which are concerned with the meticulous investigation of a given area of reality, and those which are more a matter of reinterpreting a partially known reality in terms of current concerns. The latter description might fit, say, environmental science as well as the social sciences, parts of which seem to correspond more closely to Gadamer's conception of natural science. In the end, though, Gadamer is right that, if hermeneutics is universal, it impinges more strongly on the social sciences.

Why should this be so? One answer might be in terms of the nature of our interest in social phenomena. This is the dominant theme in the passage quoted above; it is developed further in Habermas's differentiation of three cognitive interests: control, communication and emancipation (Habermas 1971b). But any such conception must itself be grounded in the different nature of the domains of the sciences: in Gadamer's case the emphasis is generally on cultural *traditions* as the locus of understanding (*Verständigung*), whereas Habermas tends to refer directly to notions of communication and communicative action.

This is the point at which Gadamer's general thesis spills over into a set of special theses about the place of hermeneutics in the social sciences. These have been developed less by Gadamer himself than by social theorists, notably Habermas and Giddens, as well as by philosophers like Paul Ricoeur and Charles Taylor.

At the same time, however, Habermas has drawn heavily on Gadamer from the time of his early work on the logic of the social sciences (1971), through his critique of Dilthey's 'objectivism' to his recent 'Theory of communicative action' (1984). Giddens, too, has made significant use of Gadamer in his conception of the 'double hermeneutic' at the basis of the social sciences; as Giddens puts it (1976: 55): 'Dilthey's views, in modified form, are not without defenders today; but the main thrust of hermeneutic thinking, following the appearance of Gadamer's *Wahrheit und Methode* (1960), has been in a different direction.'

Earlier traditions of hermeneutic thinking in the social sciences centred on the concept of meaning as a *datum*. In Max Weber's classic formulation, 'the course of human action and human expressions of every sort are open to an interpretation in terms of meaning [*sinnvolle Deutung*] which in the case of other objects would have an analogy only on the level of metaphysics' (1975: 217–18). Weber attempted to incorporate this concept of interpretation into his account of social-scientific explanation, and thus to bridge the chasm which Dilthey and others had dug between 'explanation' and 'understanding'. That story does not need to be re-told here. What matters in the present context is that, in terms of a broader hermeneutic such as Gadamer's, this conception of understanding retains a dichotomy between subject and object and an objectivistic conception of interpretative method. It therefore neglects the element of existential encounter in communication which is prior to any systematic social theory. As Giddens put it in *New Rules of Sociological Method*, '*verstehen* must be regarded, not as a special method of entry to the social world peculiar to the social sciences, but as the ontological condition of human society as it is produced and reproduced by its members'.[3] This Heideggerian insight converges with some major traditions in social theory: first and most generally, the symbolic interactionist approach, with its stress on actors' definitions of the situation; secondly, Alfred Schutz's insistence, *contra* Weber, that typification is a process carried out by actors within the 'life-world' as well as by social scientists, and that the social scientist's data 'are the already constituted meanings of active participants in the social world' (Schutz 172: 10); thirdly, Wittgenstein's notion, developed by Peter Winch, of language games embedded in forms of life.

These variants of *verstehende* sociology are often loosely described as 'hermeneutics', and they certainly seem at first sight to correspond to the requirements of a hermeneutically oriented approach to the social world. They are however vulnerable to broadly based hermeneutic critique which argues, in essence, that their conception of meaning is too restricted and that they do not do justice to the hermeneutic basis of social theory. They confine themselves largely to the study of the 'subjective meanings' actually or supposedly present in the actors' heads, at the expense of the more general underlying structures of meaning which the hermeneutic tradition considers equally important (Bleicher 1982).

Symbolic interactionism, for example, focuses as its name implies on interaction; structural aspects of social life are reduced in a social-psychological manner to socialisation, role-taking and

---

[3] Giddens 1976: 151. This passage is quoted with approval in Habermas's most recent book, *Theorie des kommunikativen Handelns* (1984: I, 162).

related phenomena. Conversely, in the phenomenological tradition, the focus is on cognitive phenomena, the relation between different typifications, such that the whole enterprise comes to resemble a sociology of knowledge and, in Berger and Luckmann's *Social Construction of Reality* (1967), is explicitly presented as such. The related approach recommended by Wittgenstein and Winch brings out more sharply one of the problems which arise here: a language-game and its associated view of the world is not a cab which one can get in and out of at will. The hermeneutic process, to repeat Gadamer's metaphor, is not the replacement of the interpreter's 'horizon' by that of the object of study, but a dialogical process in which the two horizons are fused together.

Winch's *Idea of a Social Science* (1958) has had a deservedly powerful impact on discussion of these issues within the English-speaking world. His Wittgensteinian conception of discrete forms of life suffers however from both theoretical problems of relativism (which Winch does not consider a problem – see his introductory quotation from Lessing) and the practical problem that there are relatively few (and increasingly few) societies whose world-views are hermetic to the degree which he presupposes (cf. Gellner 1974). Habermas's Gadamerian critique of Winch is helpful here: 'Winch seems to have in mind a linguistic version of Dilthey. From his free-floating position the language analyst can slip into and reproduce the grammar of any language-game, without himself being tied to the dogmatism of his own language-game, which would govern the language analysis as such' (Habermas 1971b: 243–4).

This upshot of the hermeneutic critique of *verstehende* sociology is that it must broaden its concept of meaning and recognise the interactive or dialogical dimension to the clashes between alternative frameworks of meaning. In other words, hermeneutic theorists object to the restriction to subjective meaning and to an exclusively subject–object conception of science. As Giddens puts it at the end of *New Rules of Sociological Method*

The mediation of paradigms or widely discrepant theoretical schemes in science is a hermeneutic matter like that involved in the contacts between other types of meaning-frames. But sociology, unlike natural science, deals with a pre-interpreted world, where the creation and reproduction of meaning-frames is a very condition of that which it seeks to analyse, namely human social conduct: this is why there is a double hermeneutic in the social sciences ... the observing social scientist has to be able first to grasp those by concepts, i.e. penetrate hermeneutically the form of life whose features he wishes to analyse or explain. (1976: 158–9)

This need not of course involve a dialogue in the literal sense; the point is that there is a virtual dialogue in which insiders' and observers' conceptions interact. Even when the interpreter feels constrained to reject the actors' view as totally *illusory*, it remains relevant that the actors have that view and that the interpreter be able to describe it accurately. Much of the time, of course, social science (like any other science) appears as a critique of common-sense conceptions, but it is important to recognise the way in which common sense is also constitutive of the social reality which the members of society produce and reproduce. This is the basis of Giddens's distinction between 'practical consciousness, as tacit stocks of knowledge which actors draw upon in the constitution of social activity, and ... "discursive consciousness", involving knowledge which actors are able to express on the level of discourse' (1979: 5).

Here Giddens takes on board, but also modifies, the ethnomethodological principle that members of society should not be treated as 'cultural dopes' but as knowledgeable and skilled performers who 'bring off' society as a practical accomplishment. However, where ethnomethodology conflates practical and discursive consciousness and all too often treats them as invulnerable to sociological critique, Giddens insists on the distinction:

The logical status of the knowledge applied by social actors in the production and reproduction of social systems ... has to be considered on two levels. On the methodological level, what I label 'mutual knowledge' is a non-corrigible resource which the social analyst necessarily depends upon, as the medium of generating 'valid' descriptions of social life. As Wittgenstein shows, to know a form of life is to be able in principle to participate in it. But the validity of description or characterisations of social activity is a distinct issue from the validity of 'knowledge' as belief-claims constituted in the discourse of social actors. (1979: 5–6)

So far, I have argued for the acceptance of the hermeneutic approach to social theory and the associated critique of various forms of *verstehende* sociology. In the rest of this essay I shall indicate some limitations of the hermeneutic programme, as it has been reformulated by Gadamer.

The natural starting-point for this discussion is again the concept of critique. I shall suggest that, while it is wrong to reject hermeneutics as uncritical *per se*, it does have problems in handling what

Habermas calls systematically distorted communication. This points us beyond hermeneutics to more structuralist and materialist conceptions of social theory – themselves of course hermeneutically grounded.

It is easy to see how the impression has arisen that hermeneutic theory is uncritical. In its association with theological apologetics and with aesthetics it has traditionally been concerned to find meaning, truth and beauty even in the most unpromising locations. As Paul Ricoeur put it at the beginning of *Freud and Philosophy*, hermeneutics is polarized beween two projects: the 'recollection of meaning' and the 'exercise of suspicion': 'According to the one pole, hermeneutics is understood as the manifestation and restoration of a meaning addressed to me in the manner of a message, a proclamation, or as is sometimes said, a kerygma; according to the other pole, it is understood as a demystification, as a reduction of illusion.'[4]

Gadamer's conception of hermeneutics is well towards the former pole; this emerges most starkly in his opposition to Habermas's stress on emancipation: 'the purpose of sociological method as emancipating one from tradition places it at the outset very far from the traditional 'purpose and starting point of the hermeneutical problematic with all its bridge building and recovery of the best in the past' (Gadamer 1976: 26).

Gadamer goes on to reject the critique of authority which Habermas takes over from the Enlightenment (ibid.: 33); he concludes severely:

The unavoidable consequence to which all these observations lead is that the basically emancipatory consciousness must have in mind the dissolution of all authority, all obedience. This means that unconsciously the ultimate guiding image of emancipatory reflection in the social sciences must be an anarchistic utopia. Such an image, however, seems to me to select a hermeneutically false consciousness... (ibid.: 42)

Passages like these, however, say more about Gadamer's personal conservatism than about the intrinsic nature of his hermeneutic philosophy. The real problem is that, as Habermas puts it, 'Hermeneutic consciousness remains incomplete as long as it does not include a reflection upon the limits of hermeneutic understanding' (1980: 190). In other words, the problem for hermeneutic theory is not just

---

[4] Ricoeur 1970: 26. The latter approach, Ricoeur argues, is dominated by Marx, Nietzsche, and Freud.

that communication may be systematically distorted by extraneous causal influences (Bleicher 1982: Conclusion), but that linguistic communication is in any case part of more general social processes, which should not be reduced to communication alone. The thesis of hermeneutic universality commits, once again, the epistemic fallacy: from the fact that interpretative processes are a significant part of what goes on in the social world, and that our access to the social world is necessarily via our understanding of these interpretative processes (Giddens's double hermeneutic), it does not follow that this is all that exists, or can be known to exist. The production and reproduction of social structures is partly a matter of the interpretations given to them by actors, but also of what Durkheim called 'deeper causes which are opaque to consciousness' (see Lukes 1971: 231).

Despite these problems in adopting Gadamer's hermeneutics wholesale, it is clear that his radicalisation of the hermeneutic approach has had and is having a powerful influence in Anglo-Saxon social theory. It has become increasingly clear that social scientists can no longer pass over the hermeneutic foundations of their practice, nor consign them to the domain of an optional *verstehende* sociology. This is no less true of those like Roy Bhaskar and myself who are arguing for the relevance, even to the social sciences, of a realist philosophy of science and whose main interests are in structural macrosociology (Bhaskar 1979; Outhwaite 1983).

Habermas has summarised, with exemplary clarity, four aspects in which a philosophical hermeneutic is relevant to the sciences and the interpretation of their results.

(1) Hermeneutic consciousness destroys the objectivist self-understanding of the traditional *Geisteswissenschaften*. It follows from the hermeneutic situatedness of the interpreting scientist that objectivity in understanding cannot be secured by an abstraction from preconceived ideas, but only by reflecting upon the context of effective-history which connects perceiving subjects and their object. (2) Hermeneutic consciousness furthermore reminds the social sciences of problems which arise from the symbolic pre-structuring of their object. If the access to data is no longer mediated through controlled observation but through communication in everyday language, then theoretical concepts can no longer be operationalised within the framework of the pre-scientifically developed language-game of physical measuring... (3) Hermeneutic consciousness also affects the scientistic self-understanding of the natural sciences... The legitimation of decisions which direct the choice of research strategies, the construction of

theories and the methods for testing them, and which thereby determine the 'progress of science', is dependent on discussions within the community of scientists... A philosophical hermeneutic can show the reason why it is possible to arrive at a rationally motivated but not at a peremptory consensus on this theoretic level. (4) Hermeneutic consciousness is, finally, called upon in ... the translation of important scientific information into the language of the social life-world. (Bleicher 1980: 186–7)

Perhaps the most important consequence of all this is the recognition that the results of the social sciences are even more open-ended and open to question than those of the natural sciences, even when the latter are understood in a post-Kuhnian manner (cf. Bhaskar 1979: 62). All science is implicitly committed to a distinction between its concepts, theories and descriptions and the facts of the matter. To give a realist interpretation of scientific theories does not require us, indeed it forbids us, to assume that we have attained some ultimately valid description of the world. As Bhaskar puts it (1978: 250): 'Things exist and act independently of our descriptions, but we can only know them under particular descriptions. Descriptions belong to the world of society and of men; objects belong to the world of nature. We express [our understanding of] nature in thought.' In the case of the social sciences, however, there is a peculiarly intimate connection between scientific theorising and other human projects and practices. Social theory is both value-impregnated and value-generating. Gadamer's notion of dialogue has a peculiar poignancy here.

Gadamer's influence on Anglo-Saxon social theory has been slow to develop, for reasons of language and disciplinary specialisation, and it remains largely indirect. And yet it has, in a lasting way, reshaped our thinking about the nature of social theory.

FURTHER READING

There is a certain irony in proposing a 'method' for understanding Gadamer, but the following suggestions may be helpful. A gentle way into Gadamer's own writings is via his essays in Gadamer 1981 and Gadamer 1976. *Truth and Method* (1975a) itself, though long, is not as fearsome as it appears. Another way to approach Gadamer's work would be through a more general discussion of the hermeneutic tradition such as Palmer 1969 or Bleicher 1980. The latter work is more difficult, but also more rewarding; it contains a quite helpful glossary and texts by Betti, Gadamer, Habermas and Ricoeur.

Ricoeur's view of Gadamer can be found in Ricoeur 1981; see also Thompson 1981. Gadamer's exchanges with Habermas are only partly available in English; in Gadamer 1976, Dallmayr and McCarthy 1977 and Bleicher 1980; the last of these contains Habermas's important essay, 'The Hermeneutic Claim to Universality'. See also Gadamer 1975b. These and the other texts are in the German reader, *Hermeneutik und Ideologiekritik*. (Other useful German sources include Gadamer's Festschrift, *Hermeneutik und Dialektik* (1970), and the historical anthology by Gadamer and Boehm (1976) which includes an introductory essay by Gadamer.) The Gadamer–Habermas debate has been an important reference point for discussions of the relationship between hermeneutics and modern social theory, such as Outhwaite 1975, Dallmayr and McCarthy 1977, Bauman 1978 and Bleicher 1982. Gadamer's hermeneutics is important for the work of Anthony Giddens; see, in particular, Giddens 1976 and the first essay in Giddens 1982. Another impressive attempt to deal with issues raised by Gadamer's work is Bernstein 1983, which contains an interesting letter from Gadamer to Bernstein. Wolff 1975 concentrates on the implications of philosophical hermeneutics for the sociology of art.

3

Jacques Derrida

by David Hoy

Jacques Derrida asked himself in a recent essay whether future philologists would be able to understand what past and present philosophers meant by the word 'representation' if our current natural languages died out. Whether the language were French or English would not make a difference, for his point is that 'representation' is only a term in a philosophical vocabulary that is itself like a dead language (Derrida 1982a: 298). To put his point differently, philosophers and other theorists should recognise that although the word is taken as the name for a supposedly eternal philosophical problem, its meaning has changed radically throughout the history of philosophy and we are mistaken if we think we are using it in the same ways, or even if we think it still has a genuine use. Worries about whether the mind and its ideas represent reality appropriately are displaced when people become unsure that they know what they mean by 'idea'. Shifting to the problem of how *language* represents reality avoids the problems of the mentalistic vocabulary and terms like 'idea', but construing representation as reference has not ended debate between realists and idealists.

Derrida's intervention implies that if there are inevitable problems accompanying the use of the notion of representation, it does not follow that these are *eternal* problems for philosophy and the human sciences. By constructing and using an alternative theoretical vocabulary in which the metaphor of representation did not occur, the problems would disappear. Of course, other problems would be sure to arise, so there is no guarantee that philosophy or the sciences would be better served by the new way of speaking and thinking. The normative notion of progress would have to be given up along with that of representation, for 'progress' is part and parcel of the image of representation construed as closer and closer approximation to reality. Whether we need to think that knowledge 'grows' or 'progresses' in any more than a purely quantitative sense is an idea Derrida and other French post-structuralists challenge.

Giving up the normative ideal of progress has a significant cost, however. Uncertainty is part of the price. If we are going to encounter further problems in the new way of thinking, ones we do not yet foresee, why should we not stick to our present vocabulary? At least we know what its problems are, and the problems with the new vocabulary might be equally unsolvable. Moreover, we might be buying something we do not need. After all, we do not know for certain that we cannot solve the 'eternal' problems, and we can assume we have made some progress to the extent that the failures of our predecessors teach us which approaches will not work. The bargain becomes especially disadvantageous considering the strangeness and self-alienation that would result from the change. Our educated familiarity with the difficulties of the traditional problems gives us a sense of continuity with the past and of kinship with earlier thinkers, including our own earlier selves.

That Derrida is willing to pay the price is evident from the strangeness of his style. More significant than his style, however, are his substantive readings of texts from the history of philosophy. He focuses not on the central ideas or arguments, but on marginal metaphors and other rhetorical devices that most interpreters gloss over. As opposed to interpreters who purport to enable us to read the text, Derrida would make us unable to read it. Instead of assuming the text succeeds in establishing its message, Derrida's strategy is to get us to see that it does not work. In short, he does not reconstruct the text's meaning, but instead deconstructs it. Deconstruction reveals not only how the text gives the impression of working, but insofar as the text can be found to have rhetorical devices deliberately perpetuating this illusion, how it really works against itself. A text would work (and would be a work) if it succeeded in being a unified, coherent whole, perhaps communicating a message, but in some more general way representing or recreating a reality external to it. Deconstruction shows the failure of a work's attempt at representation and, by implication, the possibility of comparable failure by any such work, or by any text whatsoever. For philosophical texts deconstruction can accomplish this by showing how the supposedly literal level is intensively metaphorical. For literary texts it can show an ambivalent attitude towards the inevitable movement of the metaphorical towards the literal.

If the bargain is such a bad one, however, what would motivate so many recent theorists, especially in literary studies, to accept it? 'Ennui' is one possible factor. The problems that would arise in the alternative vocabulary would at least be fresh ones. The challenge alone would also supply some motivation. To create a novel theoretical vocabulary and to put it into practice is a difficult and risky task, requiring ingenuity and luck. Also, writing and thinking in a new style when most others are still working in the old style generates a revivifying adversary situation. Splenetic reactions serve only to reinforce the identity of the emergent movement, and may even be a desired result.

The real motivation comes, however, from the situation in which philosophy finds itself when Derrida begins to develop his strategy of deconstruction. I will discuss two themes, the end of philosophy and the critique of humanism. There are other features, but emphasising the former allows me to show connections with a familiar theme in Anglo-American philosophy, and introducing the latter should give a sense of the uncommonness of the continental perspective. Unless we can see what seems so different about that perspective, we will not perceive how it could be a novel source of inspiration for anglophone theorists and critics, or at least one that guards against parochialism.

The death of the grand tradition of humanism

The first theme concerns how the contemporary philosophical scene stands in relation to the philosophical tradition. Like both Wittgenstein and Heidegger, Derrida and other French post-structuralists see the grand tradition of metaphysics as having ended. However, Derrida resists unduly easy talk about the death of philosophy or of man, and about overcoming metaphysics (Derrida 1981b: 6). His deconstructions show in contrast that, in the absence of a clear alternative to the grand tradition and its eternal problems, theories that supposedly avoid metaphysics tend to remain trapped in the old vocabulary and dilemmas.

Derrida is generally classified as a post-structuralist because of his criticism of structuralist linguistics (Saussure) and anthropology (Lévi-Strauss). Structuralism is itself an end-of-philosophy development, since it is the attempt to make philosophical speculation unnecessary. Just as the modern physical sciences replaced philosophical speculation about the nature of matter with more heuristic, empirical description, philosophical reflection about the nature of man was to be superseded by sciences like linguistics and anthropology. Derrida's major work, *Of Grammatology*, and one of the first essays by which he became translated and well-known among anglophone intellectuals, 'Structure, Sign, and Play in the Discourse of the Human Sciences', argue that Saussure and Lévi-Strauss still relied on problematic metaphysical assumptions in setting up their enterprises, and thus had not succeeded in freeing themselves from the philosophical difficulties they were attempting to avoid.

Derrida agrees with the structuralists that metaphysical assumptions can no longer be genuinely believed, so he is not trying to bring the grand tradition back to life. Instead, he deconstructs current attempts to get beyond metaphysics by showing latent metaphysical strains entailed by retaining as 'natural' such oppositions as those between speech and writing, mind and body, inside and outside, good and evil, accident and essence, identity and difference, presence and absence, space and time, the literal and the figurative, or even male and female. Although these distinctions are supposed to be obvious and value-neutral, their use in both the tradition and the more recent sciences suggests that in practice one pole in these oppositions is privileged over the other. Derrida's critical analysis of these distinctions shows how in their use the dualisms are at once negated and preserved (*aufgehoben*, in Hegel's sense). We seem to be forced into the impossible position of saying about these 'unde-cidable' oppositions, 'Neither/nor, that is, *simultaneously* either *or*' (Derrida 1981b: 43).

The second current running through continental theory is a reaction to the humanism of existentialism and of certain versions of Marxism. Derrida undermines the structuralist attempt to develop the sciences of man by challenging the conception of man. In an essay called 'The Ends of Man' he plays on different senses of end, including both that of man's coming to an end and that of the tra-ditional goals or ends of mankind (Derrida 1982b). Reflection on the second sense leads us to ask whether these ideals have been ful-filled, and doubts may even make us wonder whether they have been counterproductive, dooming us to eternal disappointment.

The French post-structuralists follow Nietzsche in thinking that one way to free ourselves from the despair produced by our failure to realise our ideals is to free ourselves from the conception of man they presuppose. We can bring 'man' to an end by showing that the conception is itself a historically relative one whose beginnings we can date and thus whose end we can imagine, and have perhaps already experienced. The invention of new terms and vocabularies, like Derrida's 'differance' or Foucault's 'power/knowledge', is supposed to waken us, if not from our dogmatic slumber as Hume did for Kant, at least from what Foucault calls our 'anthropological sleep' (Foucault 1970: 340). Kant is precisely the one who fell into this sleep with his Copernican Revolution in philosophy, which put man at the centre of things. Kant explicitly introduces the anthropo-logical question, 'what is man?', into philosophy, and thus condemns the post-Kantian tradition to an unfortunate anthropo-logism, or idealism, or *humanism*. The critique of humanism is thus often directed against Kant, and against the ideals of the Enlightenment that he built into our understanding of what philosophy is.

The French post-structuralists inherit the task of criticising humanism from Martin Heidegger. Heidegger's enterprise involves a critique of the humanism he finds rampant in the neo-Kantianism of his time. But humanism is hard to avoid, and the later Heidegger has to criticise the tendency of his own early works like *Being and Time* to sound like pieces of philosophical anthropology. Hence, in 1947 he writes the 'Letter on Humanism' to distance his work from the tendency of Sartre to read it as philosophical anthropology. Heidegger insists that Sartre is still doing philosophical anthropology and has therefore misread him. Heidegger was trying instead to create a new philosophical vocabulary precisely to avoid psychologistic terms like consciousness or subjectivity that still feature in Sartre.

This critique of Sartre by Heidegger is one reason French phenomenology is no longer so prominent in the current philosophical scene. Moreover, the tendency of the times is to move away from humanism, from a philosophy devoted to analysing consciousness, toward an emphasis on linguistic structures and social practices. There is also, of course, a political corollary to this critique of humanism. Sartre and Merleau-Ponty become outdated not only because they were still trying to do phenomenology, but also because as Marxists they were Marxist humanists.

At the risk of oversimplifying the critique of philosophical humanism, I will condense it into five main points, suggesting briefly in each case the reason for criticising it. First, Heidegger sees humanism as metaphysical because of the privilege it gives to man, its ascription to man of a 'universal essence'. Heidegger raises this point in his critique of Sartre, and Derrida agrees that Sartre's philosophy proves that, in Heidegger's words, 'every humanism remains metaphysical' (Derrida 1982b: 116). Sartre misinterprets Heidegger's claim that *Dasein*'s essence lies in its existence, and takes this as privileging 'human-reality's' subjectivity. Sartre has not freed himself from the tradition of taking consciousness as the paradigm of philosophy, and his metaphysical bias is shown in his conception of man as the being who desires to be like God. Heidegger, in contrast, does not want to talk about man only, but about man only insofar as there is something more than man. This rejection of humanism, of the privilege given to man, Heidegger thinks, does not entail that his thinking is anti-humanistic or inhumane. On the contrary, Heidegger is trying to avoid the subjectivism and idealism he thinks make traditional humanism itself inhumane, and and to lay the basis for a higher humanism, one that does not worship man as the centre and telos of all being.

The second feature of humanism that Heidegger, Derrida and Foucault call into question is the concept of autonomy. In this respect they follow an aspect of Hegel's criticism of the Kantian notion of the autonomy, and Hegel's insistence that human beings are social and historical beings, not transcendent, noumenal ones. Husserl and the earlier Sartre of *Being and Nothingness* do not adequately recognise the social and historical conditions of the formation of beliefs and practices.

What Kant says about the autonomy of the moral personality is closely connected with his views about how the mind is instrumental in constructing the world we experience. The third feature of philosophical humanism that its critics challenge is thus the postulation of a constituting consciousness. Of course, Sartre had long before attacked Husserl's Kantian notion of the transcendental ego. But the post-structuralists who want to go beyond humanism and metaphysics see Sartre's denial of the transcendental ego as not much better than an affirmation of it. They project instead a total philosophical revolution, or at least a change in vocabulary, where either affirming or denying subjectivity would no longer have a point.

This idea of a philosophical revolution is the fourth difference from traditional humanism, which is generally Whiggish about history. A Whig in philosophical parlance assumes that our superiority over the past is proof of the truth of our theories and the falsity of those of our predecessors. Kant is famously Whiggish for his claim that he understood Plato better than Plato understood himself because Kant could now express exactly the theses for which Plato was merely groping to find the right words (*Critique of Pure Reason* A314/B370). Whiggishness is the belief that science progresses, that knowledge grows in a cumulative fashion and, in short, that we know better than our predecessors did, even to the point of understanding them better than they understood themselves. Whereas Kant sees his Copernican Revolution as being of a piece with the cumulative growth of knowledge, the new historicists see philosophical revolutions as producing not necessarily better forms of knowledge, only different ones. Or if this sounds too baldly relativistic, their point could be rephrased. They could believe that their revolutionary change of vocabularies is justified by the historical fact that the old vocabularies are perceived as degenerative dead ends. This degeneration could be seen either implicitly from within the old vocabulary, or explicitly when the old vocabulary is deconstructed by those who no longer believe in it.

Not only do Foucault and Derrida give up humanism's belief in *epistemological* progress, they also give up its belief in *social-historical* progress, which is the fifth and last, but probably most important feature of the critique of humanism. The main targets are Enlightenment thinkers, and especially Kant. Not only does Kant think of knowledge as cumulative and progressive, he maintains we have to believe that history is as well. Man's nature for Kant is such that despite man's inextirpable propensity to evil, history will see man progressing inevitably toward a 'perfect constitution', a maximally free civil society. Hegel and his twentieth-century interpreter Alexander Kojève continue to point dialectically towards such progress. The French post-structuralists abandon dialectics and see themselves as at the end of history in a different sense. Whereas Hegel sees himself as being near its culmination and fulfilment, Foucault, Derrida, and other modern Nietzscheans see history, like God, as 'ending' in the sense of 'dying'. Nietzsche's parables suggest that God died long ago in that man gave up believing in God (probably sometime during the Enlightenment) and man put himself in God's place (for instance, by way of Kant's Copernican Revolution in philosophy). Similarly, the post-structuralists think faith in the progressive character of history was lost (probably during the nineteenth century), and we are only now, long after the death, coming to realise the consequences of these changes of belief.

Sometimes Foucault and Derrida, like Nietzsche or even Heidegger, look wistfully for a 'beyond', but generally their point is that there really is no such thing as 'history'. The progressive story of man told by speculative philosophers of history is understood to be simply a fiction, now bankrupt, a dead metaphor from a defunct rhetoric. 'Philosophy' conceived as the account of the nature of man is itself part of this fiction, and is even its hero, since the progress of freedom was equated with the progress of man's reason.

The French attitude toward the grand tradition of philosophy is not even like Wittgenstein's. The later Wittgenstein wanted to bring philosophy to an end, and thereby implied he thought it was still alive. The French post-structuralists think the Kantian and Husserlian conception of philosophy as 'rigorous science' is today in rigor mortis. The thought that just as physics should give fundamental explanations of matter, philosophy should generate absolute and uncontestable explanations of mind, reason, experience or truth is one that we cannot conceive giving up. As Derrida himself concedes, who could not invoke truth? But this rigid conception of philosophy has long been not only unproductive, but worse, counterproductive and parochial. It tends to preclude exploring other possible things 'philosophy' could be, such as hermeneutics.

Grammatology as radical hermeneutics

Of course, even the end-of-philosophy diagnosis is itself a philosophical position of sorts, and there are specific criticisms and theses at stake. Since I see Derrida's position growing out of Heidegger's, I think it is best understood as a variant of a branch of continental philosophy called hermeneutics. Derrida's position is more radical than those of other hermeneutic philosophers such as Paul Ricoeur or Hans-Georg Gadamer, and he is often explicitly critical of hermeneutics. Moreover, he is critical of Heidegger for falling back into the metaphors of the metaphysical tradition in the later Heidegger's talk about Being. Since the basis of the criticism is that Heidegger and hermeneutics do not go far enough, I think Derrida is best understood not as doing something completely different from hermeneutical philosophy, but as pushing the latter to its limits. Perhaps Derrida even pushes it beyond the limits of reason, but situating him within a broader type of theory makes it possible to test his uncommon suggestions against objections that are consistent with his starting point.

Hermeneutics is the philosophical concern with the theory of understanding and interpretation. For philosophers the primary interest in hermeneutics depends on whether it can bring out features that are not justly treated by the traditional theory of knowledge. To make the essential points in a schematic way, I shall use Richard Rorty's tactic of contrasting hermeneutics with epistemology, adding the suggestion that the relation between the two need not be one of inevitable conflict (Rorty 1979: Part III; see Hoy 1980, 1981a, 1982a). Whereas epistemology describes how knowledge is possible, hermeneutics describes how understanding is possible, with the reservation that understanding is not reducible to knowledge, as some epistemologists hold, but on the contrary that knowledge is best seen as a subdivision of understanding. Earlier in this century hermeneutics found itself polemically opposed to positivist and empiricist theories aiming at a reduction of all human and social understanding to a model of explanation drawn from the natural sciences. With the retreat of positivist and empiricist assumptions, however, theorists of the methodology of the social and human sciences could get on with detailed exploration of the methods of those disciplines.

To highlight the contrasts between epistemology and hermeneutics, I will sketch in the major tenets of each. Since Kant epistemology has been a foundationalist enterprise, one attempting to separate knowledge from other forms of belief with the intention of ascertaining what is objectively certain. In contrast, hermeneutics rejects the idea that the primary task of philosophy is to supply foundations and guarantee certainty. It sees knowledge as pragmatically relative to contexts of understanding. The paradigm of understanding becomes not the seeing of medium-sized physical objects, as for epistemology, but the interpretation of texts. Hermeneutics is opposed to a representational model of the mind, but it argues that the rejection of representation does not entail relativism. Although it holds that there is no physicalistic 'fact of the matter' to be properly represented by interpretations, nevertheless there are constraints on what gets taken as proper or improper interpretation.

In contrast to the foundationalist urges of epistemology, hermeneutics maintains that understanding is always already interpretative. This difference has at least four consequences. First, whereas epistemology searches for a privileged standpoint as the guarantee of certainty, hermeneutics maintains there is no uniquely privileged standpoint for understanding. For Derrida and other theorists such as Gadamer this result has the practical consequence of removing any special authority from the speaker or the author for determining the meaning of what is said or written. The major focus of Derrida's early work is on the tendency of theorists since Plato to take speaking as the primary place for determining linguistic meaning, and to consider writing a derived phenomenon. Derrida does not want to invert this usual ordering so much as to suggest that linguistic meaning is derived not from the psychological intentions of speakers but from the structure of language itself. Despite his criticisms of some features of Saussure's linguistics, Derrida's own conception of grammatology incorporates Peirce's notion that we think only in signs, and Saussure's view of the arbitrariness of the relation of the sign and what it signifies. Derrida adds an anti-Platonic note in his scepticism about the possibility of determining a single referent (the 'transcendental signified') for language as a whole. There is no extra-linguistic way to determine whether the world has a stable or consistent nature that language could mirror. Thus, the practitioners of deconstruction often go beyond the modest hermeneutic claim that there is no writing or reading that is not already itself an interpretation to the more radical assertion that any apparently coherent system of thought can be shown to have underlying, unresolvable antinomies, such that there are multiple and conflicting readings that must be held simultaneously.

Second, whereas epistemology is usually based on visual perception as the paradigm case for instances of knowledge, hermeneutics takes reading rather than seeing as the paradigm of understanding. To emphasise this shift Derrida criticises logocentrism and the metaphysics of presence for assuming unmediated access to the givens of sensory and mental experience. His term 'differance' is an antidote to the stress on presence. It means both different and deferred. For instance, any feature of experience requires other, not actually present features of experience to make sense and to count as a genuine experience. So Derrida, like most other recent academic philosophers, challenges traditional philosophical belief in immediate, indubitable features of mental life like ideas or sense data, intentions or perceptions. Although Derrida does not deny that there are psychological intentions, he does not give them any special privilege since they are never fully transparent to the agent or author (Derrida 1982b: 326; Derrida 1977: 213; see Hoy 1981a: 99ff). Much as 'intention' is an unverifiable hypothesis constructed by the interpreter, 'perception' is not a given, but a theory-laden notion, one that is constructed to fit the needs of particular epistemological theories from Plato to the empiricists. Hermeneutical philosophers have found it at best unhelpful, and at worse, misleadingly sterile.

As a result of the concern with the historical methods of the humanities, hermeneutics has developed the theory of reading. Reading a text is different from seeing a physical object in many respects, but one important difference is that there seem to be no special problems about whether the object exists independently of perception. Reading is not the same as seeing black marks on a page. Unlike the proverbial tree in the forest, a text and its meanings come to be only in acts of reading. Even in cases where what is being understood is not a written document (for instance, in understanding an action or a society), hermeneutic theorists may treat what is being understood as a text-analogue and the process of understanding it as like reading. So when social scientists or anthropologists interpret a society they may have to explore or use literary devices such as narrative and metaphor in much the same ways that novelists or literary critics do. Where deconstruction goes further, however, is in answering the questions whether there are limits on how a text can be read, and whether it succeeds in referring beyond itself to say something true or false about an independent reality. Giving up the referential ideal of a transcendental signified leads deconstructionists to say that if a text seems to refer beyond itself, that reference can finally be only to another text. Just as signs refer only to other signs, texts can refer only to other texts, generating an intersecting and indefinitely expandable web called intertextuality.

A third contrast follows when theorists abandon the ideal of representing the object as it really is independent of our representational apparatus. Lacking self-evident axioms that are forever beyond question, interpretations can be called into question at any moment and possibly supplanted. Thus, in contrast to the epistemological insistence on the atemporal truth of instances of knowledge, hermeneutics must take into account that understanding changes, and thus that interpretations require continual re-examination. This difference is one of emphasis. Epistemology is surely correct in its insistence, but hermeneutic theory must recognise and do justice to the fact that interpretations have their historical lives and limits. Interpretations are judged not only on the truth of their various assertions, but also on such changing factors as their usefulness, richness and range. Deconstruction simply accelerates the rate of change by deliberately seeking out the undecidable oppositions built into interpretations, and by playing on the text's polysemy to proliferate the possible interpretations.

A crucial reason why interpretations must be re-examined and altered is that they always depend, however implicitly, on the self-understanding of the interpreter, the discipline and the time. The fourth contrast is thus between the epistemological denial that reflection can disrupt self-evident tenets and the hermeneutic thesis that any interpretative understanding is laden with self-understanding, so that changes in self-understanding eventuate in changes in the understanding of the subject matter. Within hermeneutics itself there is a further question, however. Is this change in self-understanding a continuous development, one in which we get a truer and more complete picture of ourselves? Or do we change along with changing our interpretations? Change in the latter sense is akin to the kind of example where we say something we think is obvious, and then retract or modify it when we see it can be taken differently. (In Wittgenstein's example, 'Teach the children a game' is not a licence to teach them to gamble, but the statement does not explicitly preclude gambling either.) Derrida's position is more like the latter insofar as there is no 'self' that exists prior to or independently of the interpretations. Change of interpretation and thus of self-interpretation is not necessarily a story of inevitable progress toward rational maturity, but of chance. No single interpretation can claim to be the final one, and the practice of deconstruction leads to the proliferation of interpretations.

Undecidability and dissemination

Derridean deconstruction can thus be understood as agreeing with the hermeneutical critique of the metaphilosophical self-understanding of traditional epistemology, but also as taking that critique to its extreme limits and applying it against traditional hermeneutics as well. Derrida called his own early approach 'grammatology', and his method is referred to as 'deconstruction'. In his later writings, however, he stresses how much more radical than hermeneutics his position and method are. His approach is one of giving critical readings of texts to bring out unperceived contradictions or duplicitous tensions that undermine the coherence and cogency of the texts. Traditional hermeneutics implies that such deconstruction must always be preceded and should always be followed by a reconstruction recapturing the unity and truth of the original text. To emphasise his break with the tradition Derrida calls what he does in a recently translated book of the same title, 'dissemination'. Dissemination is not simply deconstruction without reconstruction. It is not only a method of reading, but a feature of all texts and all thinking, a feature supposedly covered over by the hermeneutical attempt to recover the unity of the text in a coherent account. The hermeneutical effort to decide among all the possible interpretations inevitably fails, says Derrida, because of the essential 'undecidability' of textual meaning.

Undecidability is a central theme in the literary theory that evolved from a group of people associated with the journal *Tel Quel*, particularly Julia Kristeva in her 1969 book, *Semiotikè*. Unlike Kristeva, who adapted her arguments from Goedel's famous proof of the undecidability of propositions in formalised axiomatic systems, Derrida sets up his examples more after the fashion of Freud. In an essay on primal words Freud is interested in examples from ancient languages of single words with antithetical meanings. So Derrida's paradigms are usually not propositions, but single words with opposed meanings where the context does not un-equivocally eliminate one or the other of the meanings. Derrida thus locates undecidability at the syntactical rather than the semantic level when he says that these words 'have a double, contradictory, undecidable value that always derives from their syntax' (Derrida 1981a: 221).

There is a further difference between Kristeva's Goedelian unde-cidability and Derrida's more Freudian conception. For Kristeva un-decidability results from the fact that texts refer only to other texts, and the network of intertextuality forms a universe that is said to be infinite. This theoretical notion of infinity fails, however, to make sense of the actual practice of interpretation. As Jonathan Culler remarks about Kristeva's notion of the intertextual universe, 'it is difficult to make that universe as such the object of attention' (Culler 1976: 1384). He notices that Kristeva herself pays attention to which editions an author could have known when that would make an interpretative difference. So in Kristeva's own practice the intertextual domain gets narrowed down to specific texts, and often even to *one* other text. For Derrida, in contrast, the inability to decide in a given case is the result of neither the vague indeterminacy of an infinity of associated meanings, nor the interpreter's indecisive-ness (or lack of knowledge). Both of the contradictory meanings must be seen in the single word at once. Infinity comes in later than it does for Kristeva, and for a more simple reason, namely, that from a contradiction anything and everything follows. So dissemination is the interpretative practice (or play) of exploring the supposedly infinite interplay of syntactic connections without any necessity, whether moral or methodological, of worrying about the semantic dimension of reference and truth-value.

Derrida's practice is not always strictly analogous to the model derived from Freud. For one thing, dissemination does not seek a final interpretation. The proliferation of contexts allowing for further associative possibilities can apparently go on indefinitely. So if Derrida's model does not start with infinity, it ends up with it. For another, Derrida does sometimes pick out larger units than single words as examples of undecidability. For instance, in an essay on Nietzsche entitled 'Spurs' he gives as an example an isolated fragment found among Nietzsche's notes, a single sentence in quotation marks saying 'I have forgotten my umbrella' (Derrida 1979: 122ff.; see Blondel 1974, and Hoy 1981b, 1982b). For Derrida this is a paradigm case of undecidability because the words are translatable and unambiguous, but nevertheless interpreting them seems impossible. Since this scrap of paper is now completely separated from its original context, whatever that was, traditional philological methods fail.

Derrida then extends the problem by suggesting that Nietzsche's entire corpus also stands in quotation marks, such that a univocal, systematic account of his philosophy cannot be recreated. By spinning out, or disseminating, the intimations introduced by Nietzsche's frequent use of quotation marks around key terms, Derrida's reading challenges the hermeneutic attempt to understand the texts, that is, to decide what is to count as possible and impossible meanings of the writings, or as proper and improper readings. This particular sentence may simply echo the possibility that there is no 'totality' to Nietzsche's writing, and 'no measure to its undecipherability' (Derrida 1979: 135). Hermeneutics may not think of itself as a version of metaphysics, but the hermeneutic desire to decipher the univocal meaning of the text may mirror the desire of metaphysics for a complete and comprehensive account of the meaning of everything, for the truth of the whole and the unity of the world. Derrida's implied charge is that hermeneutics is still confined to the metaphysical epoch, and refuses to see how Nietzsche's undecipherability is part of the 'difficult thought' that Nietzsche has somehow transcended those confines. The issue is thus not simply the trivial one of how to interpret the umbrella passage. The case not only defeats, but exposes the unquestioned and all-too-metaphysical assumptions of the serious hermeneutic reader who thinks that a text cannot be understood unless the surrounding context or the underlying reference can be discovered. A text with no decidable meaning would show the poverty of hermeneutics and the richness of dissemination, since when hermeneutics reaches its limits, dissemination is only beginning. A further insinuation is that the practice of dissemination may free us from an unduly restricted conception not only of philology, but also of philosophy. All philosophical writings may eventually be found to be similarly undecipherable.

Derrida is at least consistent in accepting that what holds for Nietzsche's text applies to Derrida's as well. He raises the question whether 'Spurs' itself has any decidable meaning. To tell the truth, he says, it does not. This information will not help a reader in the interpretative search for the presence or absence of such meaning, however, since the best way to lie and dissimulate is precisely to say that one is telling the truth (Derrida 1979: 137). At this point two misunderstandings of Derrida should be avoided. The first is that, like Nietzsche, Derrida is sometimes taken to be denying the possibility of truth, but I think he is more plausibly interpreted as trying to avoid assertions about the nature of truth, or at least anything stronger than that truth is trivial, and not the main issue for his concerns. He says instead that there are too many statements that are true, and the practical difficulty of interpretation is in selecting from the plethora of truths a useful subset: 'there is no such thing either as the truth of Nietzsche, or of Nietzsche's text... Indeed there is no such thing as a truth in itself. But only a surfeit of it. Even if it should be for me, about me, truth is plural' (Derrida 1979: 103).

The second misunderstanding concerns the extent to which quotation marks block reference and truth. Since the entire sentence 'I have forgotten my umbrella', as it stands in the original, is already in quotation marks, the identification of the context and referents of the terms is prevented. But there is nothing mysterious here, and Derrida is himself treating the sentence not as an utterance in use in a discourse, but simply as the name of a sentence in a natural language. Not to recognise that he considers the sentence to be mentioned but not used is to fall into the trap of confusing use and mention. Both Nietzsche and Derrida dance close to the line between mention and use, but the more charitable interpretation of their claims is to say not that they are themselves confused about the distinction, but that they are setting a trap for the unwary. If they are deliberately misleading, they are probably themselves fully aware that it would be a mistake to say that the use of quotation marks within a text makes it impossible in principle to decipher the significance of those quotation marks or the implied meanings of the words.

The rhetorical consequence of treating Nietzsche's entire work as if it were in quotation marks, and thus as if it had an undecidable truth-value, is that philosophy becomes like fiction. Derrida's view thus appears to be yet another variant on the theory of fictional statements as being neither true nor false because they do not even attempt to refer to reality. They are simply uttered in tacit quotation marks and thereby not asserted to be true. What Sir Philip Sidney says of the poets, that they do not affirm anything and therefore never lie, Derrida would seem to say of the philosopher as well. The twist is that philosophers traditionally believe themselves to be stating truths, and write accordingly. Derrida's novelty here thus consists less in what he says about literature than in the implied claim that philosophy is simply another fictional genre. He thereby dramatises his opposition to Heidegger's conception of philosophy and poetry as ways of getting in touch with an underlying level of meaning with which the history of metaphysics has lost contact. For Derrida, Heidegger fails to understand that Nietzsche is the very thinker who destroys philosophy through his initiation of what Derrida calls 'the epochal regime of quotation marks' (Derrida 1979: 107). In this epoch it becomes characteristic of textuality as such to be in quotation marks. Methods of interpretation, like deconstruction itself, must desist from the search for either 'hidden meaning' or some causal relation to an aspect of external reality.

In the essay 'Plato's Pharmacy' Derrida carries this criticism of the separation of philosophy and poetry back to the point where the distinction was first instituted. He finds another important case of undecidability in Plato's attack on writing in the *Phaedrus* (Derrida 1981a; see Hoy 1982a). However marginal and trivial the example may seem, Derrida's reading implies that since the example occurs at the beginning of the history of philosophy, it is decisive for Western thought. Derrida draws our attention to Plato's frequent presentation of writing as a drug, a *pharmakon*. This single word can be translated in either of two ways, as 'cure' or as 'poison', and, like a drug, which way it is taken will make all the difference in the world. Philosophy is built on the ability of the philosopher to use such differences, but without making a real difference. Hemlock, for instance, is a drug that poisons Socrates, but Socrates uses both rhetoric and metaphysics to prove that by taking the hemlock he is really being cured. The narcotic effect of words leads us to take reality as a dream, or dreams as reality, and philosophy loses sight of the difference.

Foucault's critique

Derrida's reading of Plato's critique of writing is contestable, and one of his strongest critics is Michel Foucault. Foucault has criticised Derrida's entire metaphilosophy, not because it is metaphilosophy, but because Foucault finds its practical implications to be inadequate. Foucault is similarly an 'end-of-philosophy' metaphilosopher, but he does not write metaphilosophical deconstructions of the history of philosophy. Instead he writes concrete histories of practical attempts to gather social and psychological knowledge.

Foucault thinks Derrida's practice of bracketing questions about textual truth blinds him to the fact that Plato's critique of writing is really about truth and not about the difference between writing and speech:

If you read the *Phaedrus*, you will see that this passage is secondary with respect to another one which is fundamental and which is in line with the theme which runs throughout the end of the text. It does not matter whether a text is written or oral – the problem is whether or not the discourse in question gives access to the question of truth. (Foucault 1983: 245–6)

For Foucault some interpretations are more fundamental than others, and thus can be decided. On his reading of the *Phaedrus* the decisions about how to understand the relation of writing, speech and truth cannot be understood apart from a more enveloping concern with techniques for the art of living.

Foucault's philosophical claim depends on recognising that at the beginning of philosophy there is not a sharp separation between epistemology or theoretical philosophy on the one hand and moral and social, or practical philosophy on the other. Truth and goodness are considered distinct and unrelated matters only later, and the early modern period understands them differently. Foucault thinks that what is going on behind Plato's question about the relation of writing and memory is the emergence of a vogue for keeping notebooks for personal and administrative use. 'This new technology', he claims, 'was as disrupting as the introduction of the computer into private life today' (Foucault 1983: 245). Furthermore, this practice of writing down and keeping notes was used from the beginning as part of the process of training oneself. It became an important technique in the service of the new idea of virtue as governing oneself perfectly, of self-knowledge and self-mastery. The technique could be used in parallel at both the personal and the public levels: 'The ancients carried on this politics of themselves with these notebooks just as governments and those who manage enterprises administered by keeping registers' (Foucault 1983: 246).

Whether Foucault's interpretation is supported by the historical and textual evidence, this exchange serves to illustrate an important line of criticism of Derrida's attempt to restrict interpretation to a purely syntactic and textual level. Foucault wants to bring out the social practices that the text itself both reflects and employs. By linking the question of writing with 'the technical and material framework in which it arose' (Foucault 1983: 245), he is not claiming to be giving just a more accurate *historical* interpretation. His concern with the social and political dimensions of the text is not only scholarly, for he also wants to make us aware of the extent to which similar or different practices today are political. That is, by becoming aware of practices that are so common we forget to think about them, and then by seeing that they perpetuate attitudes and self-understandings we ought to question, we may want to consider whether there is not too great a discrepancy between our ideals and our practices.

For Foucault, then, Derrida's own decision to avoid questions about the extent to which the text arises out of and reflects underlying social practices itself reflects a social practice. Derrida's practice thus appears to be methodologically deficient. By deliberately restricting itself to textual analysis, the question of evaluating textual analysis as a social and political practice, which it also is, cannot be raised. Since this practice serves to blind interpretation to the social and political dimension altogether, it is also politically deficient. That is, insofar as textual undecidability precludes raising questions about truth, and thus truth in normative, social and political matters, it perpetuates the status quo.

The politics of post-structuralism

Derrida's initial line of reply to Foucault's criticism could be to point out that Foucault's own reading of the *Phaedrus* depends on understanding the statements and figures in the text, and thus, if Derrida's own disseminative reading is right, Foucault's reading would depend on overlooking the undecidability that underlies the passages about writing. So Foucault would first have to rebut the details of Derrida's analysis of those passages. Instead of pursuing the intricacies of that debate, however, I will conclude by focusing instead on the larger, more political issues involved. From the greater distance of anglophone observers of the continental scene, the similarities between Derrida and Foucault, and their shared differences from other European philosophers, are likely to be more pertinent. Those observers may caution us to recall Bertrand Russell's point that there is no reason to think any particular politics follows from any particular epistemology. However, since hermeneutics is dealing with 'understanding' rather than 'knowledge' construed in some narrow sense, and since the context-dependence of understanding will invariably include social, historical and political horizons, a philosophy of interpretation cannot avoid the question whether its theory has political ramifications.

The debate is not restricted to German or French philosophers, but includes some mainstream anglophone philosophers as well. Hilary Putnam joins Jürgen Habermas, for instance, in a general condemnation of the relativism they see in both Foucault and Derrida. Putnam remarks that in trying to break completely with tradition, as Nietzsche did in trying to invent a new and better morality, what gets produced is a monstrosity (Putnam 1981: 216). Hegel made similar remarks about the desire to found all at once a new and better society. Foucault and Derrida realise these difficulties, and despite occasional slips usually avoid speaking of what things will be like after the genealogical deconstructions destroy the grand tradition once and for all. They refuse to explain what lies beyond our tradition (which is theirs as well, of course), yet at the same time they try their best to disrupt it by getting us to see it not as a harmonious, progressive whole, a cosy web of beliefs, but as a tissue of fabrications, a patchwork of remnants. They accept the idea that we have come to be what we are through our own historical tradition, but they wish to disturb its authority. They thus reject the hermeneutics of Heidegger and Gadamer as being still too metaphysical. Hermeneutics is old-fashioned and logocentric in that it assumes that texts or the 'call of Being' have an authoritative say to which we must listen respectfully. Derrida and Foucault seem to think the critique of humanism is not complete until the respect for the authority of meaning is seen through and perhaps abandoned.

The difference here thus goes beyond being an epistemological one, and takes on a political tone. Hermeneutics as practised by Heidegger and Gadamer is predicated on a respect for authority and tradition. To the left of this apparently conservative faith in authority and tradition stand not only Derrida and Foucault, but also Habermas. Habermas, however, does not recognise Foucault and Derrida as true leftists. On the contrary, he labels them both as neo-conservatives (Habermas 1981: 13). Nevertheless, Habermas's critique of Gadamer's hermeneutics is similarly directed against

Gadamer's respect for authority (see Hoy 1978: 117–28). Habermas's view is roughly that no authority is legitimate unless, counterfactually, it could be articulated and agreed to in an ideal speech situation where there were no social constraints, no power relations, to distort the exchange of information and the formation of a consensus. Notice that in the ideal speech situation the 'authority' is not really in force, since there is in principle nothing that is left unthought and undiscussed.

Gadamer's view is that this idealisation is too remote from practice. Practical understanding in real contexts is, he maintains, inevitably shot through with authority and prejudgements. Foucault's own reply to Habermas would probably be to agree with Gadamer on this point. However, since even this bit of agreement might confirm the charge of conservatism, Foucault would have to go further than Gadamer and claim that the appeal to an idealised speech situation could itself serve the purpose only of extending existent power relations and, therefore, only of perpetuating oppression. Derrida's belief that the truth-claims of philosophy are undecidable (presumably even under ideal speech conditions) would put him on Foucault's side against Habermas.

One can see, then, why Habermas labels these French attacks on all authority as conservative. Their claims appear so extreme that resisting authority in practice seems either futile or simply sporadic and without direction. The French philosophers must strike him as being reduced to a frustrated resentment of society and tradition, lacking any norms by which to sustain a legitimate programme of criticism.

How Foucault could respond to this charge, I shall leave aside except for the brief remark that Foucault is doing social criticism, but he is doing it by pointing to inconsistencies between *our* norms and *our* practices. This internal criticism does not require postulating *a priori*, counterfactual ideals. Similarly, Derrida's cases rest on textual analysis, not on *a priori* claims. The main question about Derrida remains the one Foucault raises, namely, whether Derrida's method of textual analysis is too restricted in scope, and too evasive about the questions of truth and social context. Hermeneutics presses this issue by cautioning against the deconstructionist reduction of both philosophy and literature to merely rhetorical or fictional genres.

Hermeneutical philosophers should not have to disagree with Putnam's insistence in his essay 'Literature, Science, and Reflection' that for now science is still on our culture's centre stage, as the best model of knowledge we have (Putnam 1978: 83–94). Asking about literature, then, he maintains, much as Heidegger and Gadamer do, that literature should not be understood as noncognitive since it does give us some understanding and even knowledge. His view is that it gives us conceptual but not empirical knowledge by thinking up, but not testing, new and illuminating hypotheses.

The disadvantage of this way of putting the point is that literature thus seems like 'guessing', like a second-rate way of saying things that could be stated more precisely, and tested, by science. A better approach is to think of literature as giving us something like increased understanding, perhaps of the sort that arises from seeing and dealing with new kinds of situations. I therefore prefer Putnam's further suggestion (following Baker and Grice on Kant) that literature is like practical, particularly moral, reasoning. Through literature we confront different ways of dealing with the moral question of 'how to live'. Both Gadamer and Foucault have advanced similar claims, and the vision all three share implies there is no longer any need to think of literature as false or lying discourse, or even as non-asserting or pretending discourse.

Once there is no longer any need to combat prejudices against literature or presumptions about the rigorous, scientific character of philosophy, there is also no need to project pure disseminative unde-cidability as the new ideal of all writing. If dissemination is at times a useful antidote, in excess it may also be a poison. Dissemination and hermeneutics should not be contrasted so extremely. Decon-struction and dissemination obviously presuppose a prior construc-tion of the text's sense, for otherwise there would be nothing to disrupt. Even if the disseminative reading then succeeds in unsettling the prior understanding of the text, that there are difficult interpre-tative decisions in practice does not entail undecidability or the im-possibility of understanding in principle. Only an unduly demanding conception of what it is to justify and give reasons for in-terpretations would force us to infer from the difficulty of justifying particular contexts to the conclusion that there are no appropriate contexts. Giving up the ideal of determining the one and only appro-priate context by appeal to a decisive criterion like the author's intention does not unleash an undecidable infinity of readings. We do not lose all grounds for rejecting inappropriate criteria and contexts, but instead find other useful and valid criteria becoming more available.

Any good reading aims at balancing the complexity of the text against its sense. Dissemination and deconstruction are practical interpretative strategies ensuring that the complexity is not under-estimated. The hermeneutic sense-making activity is also required, however, to keep the dissemination from spinning off infinitely. Dissemination may disdain the all-too-hermeneutical desire to bring complexity and sense into a reflective equilibrium. The distrust of hermeneutics may be premised on the belief that the reconstruction of the text's sense will invariably sell complexity short, and bring the reading to a premature halt. The premise is unwarranted, however, if, even for the best of readings, complexity and sense rarely remain in equipoise. Hermeneutic theory has no investment in the ideal of the *final* reading. If reflective equilibrium is only ever anticipated, then even if one reading appears to attain it, the next reading, perhaps by the same reader, will most likely lose it, and will have to re-establish it by other means. Where a reading would come to an abrupt halt, especially in philosophy, would be with the discovery of the text's final undecidability, and thus its unintelligibility.

FURTHER READING

Those who have not read any of Derrida's texts and would like to do so in translation could start with *Positions* (1981b), which contains helpful interviews on his theory. Then they could turn to the theoretical essays, par-ticularly 'Differance' (translated in both *Margins of Philosophy* (1982b) and *Speech and Phenomena* (1973)) as well as Part One of *Grammatology* (1976). The best examples of his philosophical deconstructions are in *Margins of Philosophy* (including 'The Ends of Man'). *Writing and Dif-ference* (1978) contains the important critique of structuralism from the article, 'Structure, Sign, and Play in the Discourse of the Human Sciences', as well as an essay on Foucault, 'Cogito and the History of Madness'.

4

Michel Foucault

by Mark Philp

At first sight it might seem paradoxical to include Michel Foucault in a collection devoted to the resurgence of Grand Theory. For all Foucault's novel philosophical and historical insights, his work is above all iconoclastic in intent. His major concern is neither to offer new solutions to hoary philosophical problems, nor to provide a more adequate historical account of our current difficulties. He does both, but only in passing. His primary objective is to provide a critique of the way modern societies control and discipline their populations by sanctioning the knowledge-claims and practices of the human sciences: medicine, psychiatry, psychology, criminology, sociology and so on. The sciences of man have, he argues, subverted the classical order of political rule based on sovereignty and rights, and have instituted a new regime of power exercised through disciplinary mechanisms and the stipulation of norms for human behaviour. In workplaces, schoolrooms, hospitals and welfare offices; in the family and the community; and in prisons, mental institutions, courtrooms and tribunals, the human sciences have established their standards of 'normality'. The normal child, the healthy body, the stable mind, the good citizen, the perfect wife and the proper man – such concepts haunt our ideas about ourselves, and are reproduced and legitimated through the practices of teachers, social workers, doctors, judges, policemen and administrators. The human sciences attempt to define normality; and by establishing this normality as a rule of life for us all, they simultaneously manufacture – for investigation, surveillance and treatment – the vast area of our deviation from this standard.

Foucault offers us histories of the different modes by which human beings in our culture have been made subjects; and we should note the ambiguity of the term 'subject'. The human sciences have made Man both a subject of study and a subject of the State and have thereby subjected us to a set of laws which they claim define our very being – laws of speech, economic rationality, biological functioning and social behaviour. Through the practices of these 'sciences' we have become divided selves, treating sanity, health and conformity to social mores as components of our 'real selves', and repudiating as foreign to us our diseases, irrationalities and delinquencies. Man, as a universal category, containing within it a law of being, is, for Foucault, an invention of the Enlightenment – and his much discussed prediction of the dissolution of Man is arguably best understood as nothing more or less than the claim that the attempt to establish a political order upon a scientific understanding of human nature is both profoundly mistaken and profoundly unstable (cf. Foucault 1970: 387).

We can see, then, why speaking of Foucault in terms of a return to Grand Theory is ambiguous. Although he offers us novel philosophical positions and an often intriguing analysis of power and its place in maintaining political and social order, his primary concern is to aid the destruction of Western metaphysics and the sciences of man. He would deny that he is offering a new theory of social and political order because, above all, his concern is with the destruction of such theories, and their normalising and subjecting attempts to define some single, cohesive human condition. If Foucault's comments on the future are at best evasive; if he undercuts his own works by modestly disclaiming them as fictions; and if he frequently spends more time making clear what he is not saying than with stating his own position, it is because his aim is to attack great systems, grand theories and vital truths, and to give free play to difference, to local and specific knowledge, and to rupture, contingency and discontinuity. For Foucault, to act as a grand theorist is to commit the undignified folly of speaking for others – of prescribing to them the law of their being. It is to offer a new orthodoxy, and thus a new tyranny.

This general theme dominated Foucault's work throughout his thirty years as a writer. In that time he produced books on the history of the management of mental illness, the birth of clinical medicine, the development of biology, philology and economics, the methodology of the history of ideas, the origins of the prison and the history of sexuality. By 1970 his work had earned him sufficient reputation for him to be awarded a personal chair at the Collège de France in the History of Systems of Thought. His subsequent work, on the prison and on sexuality, was marked by a new concern with the functioning of power within social life. Although strong threads of consistency can be recognised through his works, he repeatedly went back over his earlier works and reworked his ideas – much to the delight of his many followers, and to the confusion and irritation of his equally numerous critics. Although this means that his work is not easily summarised, I shall try in what follows to indicate some of its major themes. In particular I shall discuss the themes of discourse, the power/knowledge relation, the place of genealogical enquiry, and the absence of a subject to history.

Foucault's primary unit of analysis is the discourse. A discourse is

best understood as a system of possibility for knowledge. He rejects
the traditional units of analysis and interpretation – text, oeuvre and
genre – as well as the postulated unities in science – theories, paradigms and research programmes. Foucault's analysis is not meant to
offer a definitive interpretation of the elusive meaning of a text, nor
does he seek to reconstruct the rationality of scientific discovery.
Rather his approach is more sceptical and nominalist than this; his
attention is focused on statements and objects of analysis. His
method is to ask what rules permit certain statements to be made;
what rules order these statements; what rules permit us to identify
some statements as true and some as false; what rules allow the construction of a map, model or classificatory system; what rules allow
us to identify certain individuals as authors; and what rules are
revealed when an object of discourse is modified or transformed – as
when homicidal monomania becomes viewed as moral degeneration or paranoid schizophrenia. Whenever sets of rules of these
kinds can be identified, we are dealing with a discursive formation
or discourse. Thus, Foucault is not especially concerned with those
statements which are held as true in a given field of knowledge.
Rather, he is attempting to reveal the sets of discursive rules which
allow the formation of groups of statements which are what Ian
Hacking calls 'true or false': statements, that is, which can only be
seen as true or false because we have ways to reason about them
(Hacking 1982: 49). That is why a discourse can be seen as a system
of possibility: it is what allows us to produce statements which will
be either true or false – it makes possible a field of knowledge. But
the rules of a discourse are not rules which individuals consciously
follow; a discourse is not a method or a canon of enquiry. Rather,
these rules provide the necessary preconditions for the formation of
statements, and as such they operate 'behind the backs' of speakers
of a discourse. Indeed, the place, function and character of the
'knowers', authors and audiences of a discourse are also a function
of these discursive rules.

A simple way to see something of the nature and force of
Foucault's line of approach is to consider systems of classification.
At the beginning of *The Order of Things* he quotes a passage from
the Argentinian writer Jorge Luis Borges, purportedly taken from a
certain Chinese encyclopedia, which divides animals into the following categories: (a) belonging to the Emperor, (b) embalmed, (c)
tame, (d) sucking pigs, (e) sirens, (f) fabulous, (g) stray dogs, (h)
included in the present classification, (i) innumerable, (k) drawn

with a fine camelhair brush, (l) *et cetera*, (m) having just broken the water pitcher, (n) that from a long way off look like flies (Foucault 1970: xv). As Foucault points out, what this fictitious classification suggests, by the stark impossibility of thinking it, is the limitation of our own system of thought. Because we are locked in our own discourse we simply cannot see how the animal world could be mapped in this way. When we classify objects we operate within a system of possibility – and this system both enables us to do certain things, and limits us to this system and these things.

There have been numerous classificatory systems for animals throughout history, each rooted in a different conception of the natural order of the world. However, we tend to assume that previous classifications are contaminated by religious and primitive forms of thinking and that only ours is truly free from error. But it is precisely this move which Foucault will not allow. Truth for Foucault is simply an effect of the rules of a discourse – we cannot claim that our classificatory systems mirror certain enduring features of the natural world which previous classifications distorted. There can be no question of the over-all truth or falsity of a classification or of a discourse – the relationship between words and things is always partial and rooted in discursive rules and commitments which cannot themselves be rationally justified.

In his earlier work Foucault undermined the truth-claims of discourses by stressing the arbitrary nature of discursive changes. He emphasised rupture and discontinuity in the history of ideas because doing so highlighted the fact that logic and rationality played no part in providing the foundations for discourses. In this earlier work, discourses often seemed to be highly abstract structures of thought which were unaffected by non-discursive elements such as social and political events and institutions, or economic processes and practices. In his more recent work, however, he has increasingly emphasised the constitutive role which power plays in knowledge. Once again, part of his point is to show that the human sciences are rooted in non-rational, contingent and frequently unsavoury origins. However, we should note that Foucault's claim that truth is merely what counts as true within a discourse is not easy to accept. If what Foucault says is true, then truth is always relative to discourse; there cannot be any statements which are true in all discourses, nor can there be any statements which are true *for* all discourses – so that, on Foucault's own account, what he says cannot be true! This is a complex and far from trivial problem, and we can recognise moves in Foucault's more recent work to avoid it. In particular, he has engaged in some judicious equivocation over the question of whether he is saying that truth is always relative to discourse, or whether he is claiming that truth has a political as well as an epistemological status: for example, whether he is claiming that psychiatric knowledge has no basis in truth, or whether he is simply claiming that psychiatric knowledge has become a part of an oppressive system of political rule. However, as I shall suggest in my concluding remarks, it may be that this equivocation is itself an important part of Foucault's argument.

It will be useful at this point to consider more precisely how and why Foucault puts the truth-claims of psychiatry and the human sciences into doubt. Take, for example, his discussion of Henriette Cornier and Catherine Ziegler:

In Paris in 1827, Henriette Cornier, a servant, goes to the neighbour of her employers and insists that the neighbour leaves her daughter with her for a time. The neighbour hesitates, agrees, then, when she returns for the child, Henriette Cornier has just killed her and has cut off her head which she had thrown out the window.

In Vienna, Catherine Ziegler kills her illegitimate child. On the stand, she explains that her act was the result of an irresistible force. She is acquitted on grounds of insanity. She is released from prison. But she declares that it would be better if she were kept there, for she will do it again. Ten months later, she gives birth to a child which she kills immediately, and she declares at the trial that she became pregnant for the sole purpose of killing her child. She is condemned to death and executed. (Foucault 1978: 3)

Foucault draws our attention to the fact that in their discussions of these and similar cases at the beginning of the nineteenth century, psychiatrists broke with a number of conventions. They broke with the eighteenth-century practice of referring to madness only in cases of dementia or imbecility (which disqualified the subject from inheritance in civil law) and furor – all of which were easily recognised by the layman. These 'new' cases were ones in which the crimes committed were not preceded, accompanied or followed by any recognisable form of insanity. Yet psychiatrists refused to follow the earlier conventions which held that it was inappropriate to refer to insanity in more serious cases of crime. They presented these 'new' crimes as crimes against the laws of nature – as crimes which were too horrific to be regarded simply as straightforward instances of the infringement of conventional codes and rules. They emphasised that these crimes were committed without profit, passion, reason or motive, and they argued that this made the crimes unintelligible, or insane. Yet the only evidence that they had for this insanity was the crime itself. Given these facts, Foucault claims: 'Nineteenth century psychiatry invented an entirely fictitous entity, a crime which is insanity, a crime which is nothing but insanity, an insanity which is nothing but crime' (Foucault 1978: 5–6). They called their creation 'homicidal monomania' – a category rooted in the preposterous claim that there are some kinds of insanity which are manifested only in outrageous crimes.

Although homicidal monomania has been consigned to the history books of psychiatry, we should not assume that our interpretations of crime have escaped the conflation of natural, rational and legal orders which originally produced this bizarre category of insanity. Homicidal monomania, by appealing to a natural order, produced a category which predicated both a set of crimes and a form of madness. It thereby provided an opening in the judicial system for psychiatric expertise which resulted in a shift in the focus of judicial practice from the crime to the criminal – from a concern with the criminal code and its infringement to a concern with the rationality of the criminal act, and thus to a concern with the character of the criminal and with his or her treatment or reform. Once a class of criminal acts was interpreted as arising from a form of insanity, once the questions of rationality, motive and reasons for action were posed, other crimes were also gradually opened up to questions about the character and the state of the criminal's mind. It was then only a short step to the concept of 'the criminal mind'. Also, once we allow a form of insanity which manifests itself only in crime, we also create the threat of the 'dangerous individual' – the individual who may suddenly erupt in a transgression of the natural and legal orders. As psychiatry moves into the judicial system, the courtroom moves into the community in an attempt to detect this threatening pathology. As crime increasingly becomes interpreted as a function of personality, character and mental states, we increasingly concern ourselves with the potential for deviance among those who have not yet transgressed the legal order, but who may do so. There is, then, a shift from the application of the legal penalty to the investigation and treatment of personality, and an associated shift from the enforcement of legal rules to the treatment of the community and its sources of delinquency. With the replacement of the category of homicidal mono-mania by that of moral degeneracy, and subsequently the replacement of this category by the study of the social pathology of delinquency, we have gradually shifted from the rule of law to an obsession with the creation of a normal and healthy population.

This shift has also brought about other curious consequences. The identification of a category of madness manifested only in horrific crimes, and the associated lesson that some crimes are too horrible to be performed by fully rational, psychologically normal agents, gave rise to interpretations of cause, action and responsibility which still dominate judicial practice, despite the fact that they are funda-mentally flawed. We have adopted a conception of responsibility for action which not only presupposes the existence of an unclouded consciousness, but also fixes on the rational intelligibility of the act and makes reference to the conduct, character and antecedents of the individual. We have also accepted the axiom that only free acts can be punished – so, to be responsible for an act, that act must have been free. Yet, paradoxically, the more psychologically determined the act – that is, the more consistent it is with who and what the indi-vidual is – the more legally responsible the actor is held; while the more incomprehensible the act – the more out of character and the less determined by motive or reason it is – the more it is excused. Psychological determinism thus becomes the index both of legal freedom and of legal and moral responsibility – while to act out of character is to act unfreely. The law thus becomes fraught with recurrent problems of motives, reasons and causes. And at the heart of the judicial process lies the belief that if an act is to be punishable it must be free, yet if it is to be free it must be necessary! Out of this conceptual melange has grown the territory of the non-legal expert in the moral, social and psychological sciences who scrutinises character, consistency and personality, who regulates the appli-cation of punishment and who exercises the apparatus of social sur-veillance: the psychiatrist, the probation officer, the welfare worker.

Foucault's argument is that our contemporary classifications of delinquency, indeed our entire way of thinking about crime and criminality, arise from a discursive formation which involves us in a a morass of confused conceptual commitments. He has no special concern with the truth-values of individual statements to be found in psychiatry and its associated disciplines. What interests him is the way in which statements which are 'true or false' rest on a way of thinking about and reacting to criminality, and that this way of thinking, contrary to its claims to scientific standing, cannot be rationally justified. We also get a sense of why Foucault is concerned with the functioning of power in modern society. Psychiatry and the other non-legal disciplines which police normality within the social order form a disciplinary force which has increasingly come to superintend the mores and life of our communities. But to appreciate fully the thrust of Foucault's argument we need to look in more detail at his discussion of the power/knowledge relation.

Foucault's view of power has changed since he first introduced the concept into his analysis. Fortunately, his more recent statements have been much more clearly formulated than his early comments (compare Foucault 1971, 1979 and 1982). He now sees power as a relationship between individuals where one agent acts in a manner which affects another's actions. Power relationships are to be distinguished from relationships based on consent or on violence – 'which acts upon a body or upon things; it forces, it bends, it breaks on the wheel, it destroys, or it closes the door on all possibilities' (Foucault 1982: 220). So power describes those relationships in which one agent is able to get another to do what he or she would not otherwise have done: 'it is always a way of acting upon an acting subject or acting subjects by virtue of their being capable of action'. And power 'is exercised only over free subjects, and only in so far as they are free' (Foucault 1982: 220). Power operates to constrain or otherwise direct action in areas where there are a number of possible courses of action open to the agents in question.

While much of what Foucault now says about power seems to fit comfortably enough with much liberal and radical thought, he departs from these standard accounts in his discussions of the power/knowledge relation. Contrary to the liberal view that power is essentially a force which impedes the development of knowledge by repression and constraint, Foucault argues that power is an integral component in the production of truth: 'Truth isn't outside power, or lacking in power... Truth is a thing of this world: it is produced only by virtue of multiple forms of constraint. And it induces the regular effects of power' (Foucault 1980: 131). Thus, for example, the existence of the human sciences presupposes the simultaneous existence of sets of power relations which have enabled their practitioners to structure the fields of possibility within which criminals, madmen, the sick, the old, the delinquent and the putatively normal have had to act. Through their power to put others into action, these practitioners have been able to observe, order, classify, experiment with and practise on these agents so as both to put their knowledge into practice, and to derive further 'knowledge' from their practices. We might say that once psychiatry had gained control of that esoteric class of agents classified as homicidal monomaniacs, they were able, through experimentation and surveillance, to develop new concepts and categories which were then taken back into the judicial arena and used to claim further areas and subjects for practice. This is not to say that their demands were uncontroversial – indeed, in these controversies we find specialists relying on their claims to specialised knowledge. That is, their claims to knowledge were also claims to power – the two become inextricably bound together.

We must also recognise that power, for Foucault, is not something delegated to the human sciences from the body traditionally seen as the central repository of power – the State. On the contrary, power is an inherent feature of social relations (because it must exist whenever we can act in a manner which will affect the way that others act). Because of this, power relations are always potentially unstable and potentially reversible – I may limit your choice of actions, but your actions may equally limit mine. However, while claiming that power relations are of this volatile form, Foucault goes on to argue that in modern society the human sciences, through their claims to knowledge and expertise, have transformed these unstable relations into general patterns of domination. As he says, 'We are subjected to the production of truth through power, and we cannot exercise power except through the production of truth' (Foucault 1980: 93). The modern State is not simply the eighteenth-century State plus the practices of the human sciences, which it has seen fit to legitimate so as to extend its control over its population. On the contrary, the human sciences grew out of Enlightenment demands for a rational order of governance – an order founded on reason and norms of human functioning, rather than on State power and the rule of law – and it was through the gradual growth and consolidation of their knowledge and practices that they colonised, transformed, and greatly extended the areas of State activity; with the result that State power mutated into its current disciplinary and normalising form. It is from the human sciences that we have derived a conception of society as an organism which legitimately regulates its population and seeks out signs of disease, disturbance and deviation so that they can be treated and returned to normal functioning under the watchful eyes of one or other policing system. State power, for Foucault, is the end point of analysis; it is built up from innumerable individual exercises of power which are consolidated and co-ordinated by the institutions, practices and knowledge-claims of the 'disciplines'. Without these knowledge-claims the co-ordination of power relations into patterns of domination could only be temporary and unstable. Once we recognise this, we can more easily see what Foucault is trying to do in his accounts of these discourses.

Foucault describes his accounts as genealogies. Genealogy involves a painstaking rediscovery of struggles, an attack on the tyranny of what he calls 'totalising discourses', and a rediscovery of fragmented, subjugated, local and specific knowledge. It is directed against the great truths, great systems and great syntheses which mark the power/knowledge matrix of the modern order. It aims to unmask the operation of power in order to enable those who suffer from it to resist. In the modern encoding of power, in discourses which discipline their participating populations and impose norms upon them, what is suppressed is local, differential knowledge − knowledge which is incapable of unity because it expresses the specific experiences of individuals and communities. Foucault gives voice to the anarchic urge, rather than to the urge for a new system (which is why he distrusts Marxism). His support is lent to those who resist the subjugating effects of power: those who, like some feminists, refuse to surrender their bodies to the established practices of medicine; those who resist professionals' attempts to claim specialised knowledge (as in the anti-psychiatry movement); those who demand the right to have a say in the manner of their death; those who resist ethnic, social, religious, sexual or economic domination or exploitation; and those who resist the identities imposed upon them by others − as women have begun to resist their subjection to men, children to parents, the sick to doctors, and as sections of the population have resisted interferences in their lives and environment by central and local authorities. These struggles are immediate responses to local and specific situations. Above all, they spring from the sheer recalcitrance of individuals; and Foucault's works are intended as a stimulant to this recalcitrance − they attempt to offer new spaces for the emergence of subjugated knowledge and for the organisation of resistance.

But does this mean that Foucault wishes to liberate, for example, the twentieth-century equivalents of Henriette Cornier and Catherine Ziegler? That he helped establish and run prison groups in the early 1970s might suggest that this is so; but his purpose is not quite so direct. His critique of the prison is meant to open up its doors and allow the prisoner the right to be heard. The prison has not worked as intended – no prison even approximates Bentham's vision of, and hopes for, the panopticon – and Foucault's view is that it merely serves as a void into which to cast the delinquent. The prison shuts the prisoner up (in both senses), and the resulting silence allows the professionals to make what claims they like as to the curative process being enacted. Foucault's criticism is directed against these professional claims. His aim is not a plan of reform but the liberation of the prisoners' voices through the practice of genealogical criticism:

If prisons and punitive mechanisms are transformed, it won't be because a plan of reform has found its way into the heads of the social workers; it will be when those who have to do with that penal reality, all those people, have come into collision with each other and with themselves, run into dead-ends, problems and impossibilities, been through conflicts and confrontations; when critique has been played out in the real, not when reformers have realised their ideals...

Critique does not have to be the premise of a deduction which concludes: this then is what needs to be done. It should be an instrument for those who fight, those who refuse and resist what is. Its use should be in processes of conflict and confrontation, essays in refusal. (Foucault 1981: 13)

On the one hand then, genealogy aims to stimulate the criticism and struggles which are suppressed by our current penal discourse, where the prisoner's only right is to obey the order of discipline. But there is also another purpose at work. In many ways Foucault's point in focusing our attention on Ziegler or Cornier, or on the many comparable cases which appear in his works, is not to denounce us for what we have done to them, but to show us what we have done to ourselves by doing these things to them. To show, that is, that we have made ourselves mad, sick and delinquent by seeking to treat the madness, sickness and delinquencies of others. By directing our surveillance beneath the surface of events to the hearts, minds and souls of the individuals before the bench, we have simultaneously opened ourselves to that gaze and accepted our subjection to it. And genealogy above all involves the repudiation of the truth-claims and the pretence of omniscience of the disciplines which now watch over us.

At the heart of Foucault's work lies the conviction that there is no constant human subject to history – that there is no valid philosophical anthropology – and thus no basis for claiming that we can identify a coherent and constant human 'condition' or 'nature'. Certainly, history does not reveal any such condition or nature. Nor is there any rational course to history: there is no gradual triumph of human rationality over nature – our own or otherwise – nor is there any over-arching purpose or goal to history (as Marx supposed). So the study of history can offer us no constants, no comfort and no consolation: history is both uncontrolled and directionless. In describing Nietzsche's historical work Foucault effectively describes his own:

Effective history differs from traditional history in being *without constants*. Nothing in man – not even his body – is sufficiently stable to serve as the basis for this self-recognition or for understanding other men ... History becomes effective to the degree that it introduces discontinuity into our very being – as it divides our emotions, dramatises our instincts, multiplies our body and sets itself against itself. (Foucault 1977b: 153–4)

The 'course' of history, the narrative of human agency from past to present, is an illusion. Our past is always an invention of our present – and *our* present, it seems, must always see itself as a peak preceded by the lowly foothills of our imagined past. Foucault attacks this progressive view of history. Against order he sets haphazard conflicts – against consensus, incessant struggle. There is and can be no end to struggle; individuals remain caught in webs of contingency from which there is no escape because there is no constant human nature, no essential human 'being' that can stand outside this web and act to counterpoise this flux and impose a narrative order. Struggle is both demanded by and is a condition of this patternless process. It is necessary to avoid domination, and yet it cannot guarantee liberation since the exercise of power over others is built on the premise that the tables can always be turned, dissolved or reconstituted. History, knowledge and the human subject are fundamentally rooted in contingency, discontinuity and iniquitous origins. For Foucault, we are poor things, and rarely our own.

While I have tried to give some indication of what Foucault is trying to do and of how he has gone about his task, I have not said much in criticism of his position. I want to conclude by making one brief criticism and then to suggest why criticism may be difficult to pin on Foucault.

My criticism concerns Foucault's abandonment of the human subject and his attempt to stimulate resistance and struggle. The problem is to understand why people *should* struggle and what they should struggle for. On Foucault's account, the sheer recalcitrance of individuals, what he calls their 'agonism' or thirst for struggle, ensures that they *will* struggle; but he offers us no grounds for encouraging resistance, nor for distinguishing between different struggles. To move from a claim that explains resistance to a claim that justifies and encourages it in certain contexts requires that we make some commitment to a conception of the human good, and this usually rests on some view of human nature and human subjectivity. I cannot see how Foucault can avoid doing something similar if he wishes to retain a critical dimension to his analysis – but doing so clearly sits uncomfortably with his repudiation of the human subject and his denial of a constant human nature. It is easy to see why Foucault does not want to talk about human nature, but not doing so leaves him open to the charge that his perspective simply encourages us to struggle for power regardless of how we wish to use it.

This criticism, and my earlier comments on Foucault's account of truth, provide typical examples of the way in which philosophical considerations are taken as decisive in the evaluation of historical method or in social and political theory. Yet these criticisms do not stick easily to Foucault because it is precisely this view of philosophy which Foucault attacks (and it is not at all clear what considerations can be taken as decisive between conceptions of philosophy). Foucault's philosophy is rooted in story-telling and in action. His histories, he says, are fictions which seek to forge connections, establish relationships and transgress the established order and unity of discourse. His intention is to throw our assumptions and certainties into question; to allow variety and difference their rightful place – a place obliterated by the subjugating sciences of man which have grown up under the dogmatic and scientistic tutelage of Western metaphysics, and which have established themselves as the agents of power within the modern State. It is, then, difficult to criticise Foucault without associating oneself with the system which he attacks – we either stand with him, or we stand condemned of subjugation. Yet it is possibly the great strength of Foucault's work that it makes neither course attractive: much of what he says is sufficiently close to reality to be discomfiting, and yet his own view offers no attractive certainties. If this is so, then Foucault has achieved his chief end, which he describes as being:

> To give some assistance in wearing away certain self-evidentnesses and commonplaces about madness, normality, illness, crime and punishment; to bring it about, together with many others, that certain phrases can no longer be spoken so lightly, certain acts no longer, or at least no longer so unhesitatingly, performed, to contribute to changing certain things in people's ways of perceiving and doing things, to participate in this difficult displacement of forms of sensibility and thresholds of tolerance, – I hardly feel capable of attempting much more than that. (Foucault 1981: 11–12)

We might want to say that this makes Foucault's philosophy coercive, in that it is concerned with producing effects rather than with rational argument and persuasion. But this misses the fact that if we are disturbed by what he says it is because his fictions are recognised as familiar. It is as if they bring to awareness our inchoate experience of life in the modern State.

Given this understanding of Foucault, we can see that he differs from many of the other theorists included in this survey of the resurgence of Grand Theory in that, for all his archaeological metaphors, he is not so much excavating a new territory for theory as undermining old areas of certainty. With the loss of the certainties insisted on by the sciences of man we are left, once more, with a field for our differences, struggles and resistances. This may leave us no longer sure who and what we essentially are, but Foucault will have succeeded if he has left us believing that no one can know this with greater certainty than ourselves.

FURTHER READING

To see the way Foucault's ideas have developed, those with sufficient stamina might consider working through the corpus of texts in chronological order. But this is not really necessary. Alan Sheridan's book on Foucault provides a brief and generally reliable but uncritical guide through the major works which can then be used as a basis for more selective reading from the primary texts (Sheridan 1980). Alternatively, those who wish to go straight to Foucault's work are best advised to start with *Discipline and Punish* (1977a) and to supplement this with some of Foucault's essays, in particular: 'About the Concept of the "Dangerous Individual"' (1978) and 'Questions of Method' (1981). There is a useful collection of other essays, edited by Colin Gordon, which gives a good indication of the breadth of Foucault's interests (Foucault 1980), and although Bouchard's earlier collection now seems a little dated it does contain the seminal piece 'What is an Author?' which made Foucault's reputation among post-structuralist literary critics (Foucault 1977b). Foucault's most recent book, *The History of Sexuality* (1979), is not quite so accessible as *Discipline and Punish*, but it does provide a thoroughly provoking account of one of the great obsessions of our time.

Those readers interested in the power/knowledge relation are advised to start with the piece that first signalled Foucault's interest, 'The Orders of Discourse' (Foucault 1971), to go on to Chapters 6 and 7 of Gordon's collection (Foucault 1980), and to come up to date with the *History of Sexuality* and the recent essay 'The Subject and Power' (Foucault 1982).

Yet Foucault's earlier works, although not always easy reading, remain stimulating and provoking contributions to their respective fields. *Madness and Civilisation* (1967) has had a major impact on work in the history of psychiatry; *The Birth of the Clinic* (1973), Foucault's tribute to his early supervisor in the history of science, Georges Canguilheim, offers an account of emergence of medical conceptions of pathology; *The Order of Things* (1970), one of Foucault's most complex works, is an often stunning analysis of the origins of economics, sociology and philology; while *The Archaeology of Knowledge* (1972), Foucault's major methodological treatise, although pre-dating the integration of power into his work, remains an inspiring monument to his philosophical inventiveness.

Secondary works on Foucault are now legion. Gordon (Foucault 1980) and Sheridan 1980 both provide bibliographies. But subsequent to these publications five book-length treatments of Foucault have appeared: Dreyfus and Rabinow 1982, Lemert and Gillan 1982, Major-Moetzl 1983, Racerskis 1983, and Smart 1983. And still more are promised. However, much of the secondary literature makes few concessions to the uninitiated reader, who will find them a poor substitute for the original works.

5

Thomas Kuhn

by Barry Barnes

Thomas Kuhn is one of the few historians of science whose work is well known to outsiders. His book, *The Structure of Scientific Revolutions*, published in 1962, has become a classic, a routine point of reference for discussion and debate throughout our culture generally. Needless to say, the book is more than a historical narrative. It uses the findings of historical research as the basis for a startlingly original account of the general nature of scientific knowledge. This has given the book a profound philosophical significance, at least in the English-speaking world where science has always occupied a special position in our philosophical thinking.

We have never been able to accept the frankly speculative approach of the Continental philosophers, or their grand metaphysical theories. In Anglo-Saxon philosophy we have always kept our feet firmly upon the ground, and refused to accept any but the most securely established claims. Our model forms of discourse have been ordinary language with its immediate intelligibility, and natural science with its precision and stringent standards of justification. Within epistemology in particular, natural science has served as a paradigm of knowledge, which has meant that all important accounts of the development of science have acquired an epistemological as well as an historical relevance.

Simply by virtue of its subject, therefore, Kuhn's book was of considerable philosophical interest. But it was the treatment he gave to that subject which established his importance. Kuhn offered a unique combination of scholarship and iconoclasm. Although scarcely anyone initially accepted his radically unorthodox philosophical treatment of science, it commanded respect because of the acknowledged competence of the historical work upon which it was based. Kuhn was quickly recognised as a brilliant devil's advocate, a formidable critic of established philosophical wisdom.

If we are to understand the full significance of Kuhn's work we must look first to this established wisdom. It is no mere abstract philosophy which Kuhn calls into question. Rather, it is a connected pattern of ideas and evaluations which together constitute a key component of our generally accepted modern world-view. Although the pattern is a complex one, incorporating elements of rationalism, individualism and the liberal faith in gradual evolutionary progress, I shall simply call it the myth of rationalism.

Rationalist doctrines emphasise the power of the reasoning capabilities which all individuals possess. Rationalist accounts of science see its growth as the product of individual acts of reasoning. By logical inference on the basis of their experience, individual scientists contribute to scientific progress, to the cumulative development of scientific knowledge and its gradually increasing correspondence with the reality it describes.

Only if individuals cease to be rational is progress threatened. The danger here is society. Social pressures, political passions, economic interests may bias the judgement of the individual so that he irrationally refuses to modify a cherished belief, or to accept a disagreeable one. Over time, these biases may transform thought into political ideology or religious dogma: they must be eliminated or neutralised if the understanding of nature is to be advanced, or a contribution to science made.

This very rudimentary rationalist account is widely accepted not just in philosophy, but in society at large. Note here how nicely it blends with the central political values of our modern liberal democratic societies. It sets men before nature just as they stand before our law, as equals. Reason, the possession of every man, is all that is needed to derive knowledge from experience. Everyone alike can do it. Equally important, there is a strongly individualistic emphasis in the rationalist account: progress flows from unconstrained individual decisions, just as is claimed by the current theories of our Treasury economists; and social interference introduces undesirable distortions into the system. Finally, the rationalist account reflects the cherished liberal ideal of gradual evolutionary change: scientific progress stands in this respect as a gratifying analogue of social progress. This is why I spoke earlier of the myth of rationalism; not simply to imply that rationalism is false, but to imply that it is generally believed in the way that a myth is believed, because of its happy congruity with other patterns of thought and activity.

Needless to say, philosophers have not been content simply to assume and develop the rationalist viewpoint: they have also thoroughly analysed it, seeking out its weaknesses and deficiencies. Some of the most powerful anti-rationalist arguments have been developed by rationalist philosophers themselves.

The most significant of these arguments, the recognised Achilles' heel of rationalism, derives from the theoretical character of scientific knowledge. Scientists invariably describe and explain phenomena in terms of a specific theory which they have invented or constructed. But, formally speaking, an endless number of theories can be constructed to be consistent with a particular body of data, just as an endless number of curves can be constructed to pass through any finite number of points. Logically, the notion of a single correct, or best-supported theory is, to say the least, an extremely dubious one; but historically it is a notion which scientists routinely and effectively employ, which is indeed essential in scientific research.

The problem of the logical underdetermination of scientific theories is not denied by rationalist philosophers; but they do betray their prejudices in the way that they treat it. They assume that rationalism *must* be correct and that the problem it faces is therefore but a minor difficulty – something which will eventually be resolved, even if we cannot see how at present.

Kuhn's attitude to this same difficulty could not be more different. Like the rationalists he cannot see how scientists reason securely from the data to the correct theory. But this leads him to ask whether the theory might not be accepted on some other basis. And to check this he turns to examine the actual practice of scientists, largely as it is set out and recorded in historical materials.

Kuhn investigates what research is typically like, most of the time, in any well-established and productive scientific field. It is, he concludes, largely devoted to the elaboration and extension of some generally accepted concrete scientific achievement. Such an achievement is the worked-out solution to a particular scientific problem or puzzle. It embodies both theory and technique, and shows by example how they should be used. Think, for example, of Mendel's work with pea plants, or Bohr's on the spectrum of hydrogen. An accepted achievement of this kind may solve but a single scientific problem, and solve it crudely and incompletely at that. But it will have been selected not for its present condition but its future promise, and its many weaknesses will simply be treated as temporary aberrations, the removal of which is part of the task of future work. The attraction of the achievement is indeed that it can serve as the basis for further research. Scientists give it the status of an authoritative model – a scientific paradigm, as Kuhn says – and they develop their own research around it and in analogy with it. Kuhn calls this kind of research 'normal science'.

'normal science' means research firmly based upon one or more past scientific achievements, achievements that some particular scientific community acknowledges for a time as supplying the foundation for its further practice. (Kuhn 1970: 10)

The success of a paradigm ... is at the start largely a promise of success discoverable in selected and still incomplete examples. Normal science consists in the actualization of that promise, an actualization achieved by extending the knowledge of those facts that the paradigm displays as particularly revealing, by increasing the extent of the match between those facts and the paradigm's predictions, and by further articulation of the paradigm itself. (ibid.: 23–4)

Kuhn stresses that in normal science a paradigm is never accepted purely out of logical considerations. Always there is evidence which supports it and evidence which calls it into question, arguments for and arguments against. It is used in research by agreement, not because of compelling justifications. And the research in which it is used assumes it, and does not attempt its justification. In normal science a paradigm is not judged or tested: it itself is the basis for judgement. Successful use of a paradigm adds to our knowledge of nature. Unsuccessful use of a paradigm only indicates the incompetence of the scientist, or the inadequacies of his equipment, or the existence of some unknown source of disturbance of the conditions of observation or experiment. A paradigm serves as the *conventional* basis for the evaluation of research: normal science relies upon consensus not logical compulsion.

Indeed, as Kuhn is at pains to stress, the consensual character of normal science goes yet deeper than this. Although a paradigm serves as the basis for the evaluation of research, there is no fixed and predetermined way of using it for this task. A paradigm, remember, is a specific scientific *achievement*, not a set of watertight instructions for producing or evaluating further achievements. A paradigm is not an algorithm: it does not provide scientists with rules for solving specific problems, rules which scientists can follow like so many rational automata. All it provides is itself, an example of good practice, which must be used directly as a concrete model of competent work. And scientists must themselves determine how the model is to be used and what particular pieces of scientific work stand in proper analogy to it. Thus, scientists doing normal science do not merely have to agree upon what should serve as the basis of their work; they have also to agree upon how it should serve that purpose in every particular case. They are obliged to employ a paradigm much as a judge employs an accepted judicial decision, as a *precedent* for future actions and future judgements, and not as a *determinant* of those actions and judgements (Kuhn 1970: 23).

Whereas on a rationalist view routine scientific work is a matter of passive obedience to rules, on Kuhn's account it involves the active elaboration of existing custom and convention. Thus, on Kuhn's account there is no compelling reason why scientists should not disagree as to the correct interpretation of existing knowledge, just as judges sometimes disagree as to the correct interpretation of existing laws and precedents. That scientists generally disagree less than judges is not something which Kuhn attempts to explain: he simply notes it as a fact. It is this fact, that high levels of agreement in perception, practice and judgement can be sustained on the basis of shared paradigms and in the absence of shared rules, which makes normal science possible. 'The practice of normal science depends upon the ability, acquired from exemplars, to group objects and situations into similarity sets which are primitive in the sense that the grouping is done without an answer to the question, "Similar with respect to what?"' (Kuhn 1970: 200. For further discussion of this difficult but important point see Kuhn 1970: ch. 5 and Postscript, sect. 3; and Barnes 1982: ch. 2).

Needless to say, the account of normal science presented so far is fundamentally incomplete, and raises many further questions. In particular, we need to know how scientists become committed to their paradigms, and how that commitment is maintained. The key is to regard scientists as participants in a tradition of research, and research as the characteristic activity of the subculture carrying the tradition. Paradigms then appear as the inherited knowledge of scientists: they are accepted from the ancestors as the basis for research, developed and elaborated in the course of that research, and passed on in their developed and elaborated forms as the accepted knowledge of the next generation. On this account, paradigms, the core of the culture of science, are transmitted and sustained just as is culture generally: scientists accept them and become committed to them as the result of training and socialisation, and the commitment is maintained by a developed system of social control. The many long years involved in specialised scientific education are essentially a period of apprenticeship, when the formidable authority of teacher and text, backed by laboratory demonstrations carefully designed for pedagogic effectiveness, not only encourages the acquisition of current procedures and current interpretations but demands an exclusive concentration upon them.

Kuhn is well aware, of course, that this account of scientific training clashes strongly with accepted wisdom; but instead of looking for compromise and accommodation he chooses actually to emphasise and intensify the key points of disagreement. He point-edly refrains from diluting his analysis with references to the acqui-sition of a general 'scientific method', or to the cultivation of general powers of reasoning. Nor is he even willing to allow that scientific knowledge is taught tentatively and provisionally, or that scepticism and open-mindedness are seriously cultivated by teachers, with the intention of ensuring that scientists remain flexible and receptive to new experience. On the contrary, he claims that training is un-usually authoritarian and dogmatic, precisely in order to produce the highest possible degree of commitment to paradigms and the least possible inclination to think and act outside them. 'Even a cursory inspection of scientific pedagogy', he tells us in one of his more notorious remarks, 'suggests that it is far more likely to induce professional rigidity than education in other fields, excepting, perhaps, systematic theology' (Kuhn 1963: 350).

Kuhn thus explains stability and commitment in science sociologi-cally, in terms of the existence of potent mechanisms of socialisation and social control. But in thereby dealing with one problem, he makes another more acute. If paradigms are indeed the inherited culture of science, and one strongly impressed and enforced, how is it that they are on occasion replaced and discarded? How was it, for example, that Ptolemaic astronomy was replaced by the system of Copernicus, or that Newton's mechanics eventually gave way to the mechanics of Einstein and Heisenberg? How are *scientific revolu-tions* to be understood and explained?

Kuhn offers an extremely interesting account of how these radical changes of scientific practice typically occur, again building upon his familiarity with specific historical episodes. He starts with the claim that a group of scientists engaged in normal science is a very sensitive detector of anomaly. Precisely because the group is so com-mitted to its paradigm and so convinced of its correctness, any results and observations which resist assimilation to it become of peculiar interest and importance. Most of these anomalous results are indeed satisfactorily explained as normal science proceeds: they may cease to be puzzling as paradigms are elaborated and given de-veloped interpretations; they may prove to be familiar phenomena in unfamiliar surroundings; or they may simply turn out to be spurious. But a residue of recalcitrant anomalies may nonetheless persist and accumulate. Such a residue, growing ever larger over time, and growing ever more formidable as it resists attempt after attempt to re-assimilate it, may eventually prompt the suspicion that something is amiss with the currently accepted paradigm, and set the stage for its demise.

A paradigm is never simply discarded at such a time. That would be to abandon research, the *raison d'être* of the scientific community. Rather, the community becomes more speculative and wide-ranging in its research, more tolerant of deviant and unorthodox suggestions. It is in search of an alternative paradigm, a new scientific achievement which can both assimilate the currently troublesome body of accumulated anomaly and serve, like its predecessor, as a concrete model for future work. With the advent of such an alternative, commitment becomes re-aligned, the detailed practice of research moves along different paths. Normal science is reconstituted around a new model and the previous paradigm, no longer needed, is finally set aside.

There are many significant aspects to this story of scientific revolution, but the key feature is the absence of any compelling logical justification for the transition. Kuhn is insistent that changes of paradigm must be made intelligible in terms of the social psychology of the scientific group, not in terms of purely logical considerations (Kuhn 1970: ch. 9). The anomalies which lie at the centre of the group's concern are not aspects of nature pure and simple. They emerge and become perceptible only in the course of conventional activity based upon the pre-revolutionary paradigm: they are perceived as deviations from that paradigm, and without it they do not exist. Moreover, as the record of the failures of one paradigm, set apart from its successes, they scarcely represent an unbiased choice of grounds upon which to compare that paradigm with another. Certainly, there is no compelling reason why comparison should not instead be made in terms of the positive successes of the alternative paradigms, or the clarity and consistency of the theories associated with them. That scientists do, as a matter of fact, evaluate alternative paradigms mainly in terms of the problems and anomalies currently at the centre of their attention attests to the status of that evaluation as a practical, corrigible judgement closely bound up with the immediate contingencies of their working environment and quite unintelligible as the outcome of a general formal logical procedure. Just as logic does not compel the group to accept the paradigm upon which normal science is based, so it does not compel its replacement with another in the course of a scientific revolution.

This last is an empirical generalisation: it is a claim which Kuhn can hope to substantiate by the citation of historical examples. But it does not encompass all that he wants to say. Kuhn wants to insist not only that the choice between competing paradigms is not determined by purely logical considerations, but that it *cannot* be. Just as logic cannot compel the acceptance of a paradigm, he wants to argue, so it cannot compel its replacement with another. At this point, he is obliged to leave the realm of history and involve himself in abstract arguments: he manages the transition with conspicuous success.

Kuhn emphasises two important general points about normal science as an *activity*. First, any form of normal science whatsoever is research into the characteristics of an incompletely known world. As such it will be marked by successful accomplishments and by failures; it will unearth explicable phenomena and so-far-inexplicable phenomena. And as this state-of-affairs is unavoidable it can scarcely be considered unsatisfactory in itself. But the so-far-inexplicable phenomena in a tradition of normal science just are its outstanding anomalies, the phenomena which opponents will hold up as counterinstances to the central theory of the tradition. As such, they are the ubiquitous counterpoint to any successful sequence of research: 'either no scientific theory ever confronts a counterinstance, or all such theories confront counterinstances at all times' (Kuhn 1970: 80). Clearly, then anyone of a mind to do so can, with complete logical propriety, defend normal research – any normal research, based on any paradigm – as completely consistent with what is known of the real world. The data can always be described in a way which makes them compatible with the presuppositions of the research tradition.

Kuhn's second point is much more radical, and although it strongly supports his main argument it is not an essential support to it. He notes that it is in fact peculiarly difficult to effect a complete separation between the activity of research and the independent data which putatively confirm or call into question its presuppositions. The data are products of the activity, artefacts of the scientific culture, and the presuppositions of that culture are actively involved in their production. The paradigm at the heart of normal science is generally sustained, and can always legitimately be sustained, by a practice which assumes its correctness and which adjusts to that assumption in what it treats as data. Normal science is to a great extent self-validating: it produces a world in which it is true (Kuhn 1970: ch. 10). Thus it is not simply that experience can be made out, without logical difficulties, as consistent with the pre-suppositions and practices of normal science: experience can be constituted to be so consistent. (Note how all this simply puts a much more radical gloss on a point made earlier: 'Unsuccessful use of the paradigm only indicates the incompetence of the scientist, or the inadequacies of his equipment, or the existence of some unknown source of disturbance of the conditions of observation or experiment'.)

Finally Kuhn offers arguments couched in an explicitly philosophical idiom. Instead of analysing scientific revolutions as transitions from one mode of activity to another, he treats them as moves from one scientific theory to another. And he treats theories formally, as systems of statements, just as most rationalist epistemologists currently do. Having accepted this idiom Kuhn goes on to show that the comparative evaluation of competing theories remains a formally intractable problem. There is no common measure for the merits of competing theories, no clear and incontrovertible basis upon which to make a rational choice between them. Success in problem-solving will not do, since reasonable men may differ on what is to count as a problem, what problems are to count as important ones, and even what counts as a solution to a problem. Success in theoretical explanation will not do, since men have always disagreed, within science as elsewhere, upon what is in need of explanation and what is 'natural' and not in need of explanation. Resistance to refutation will not do, since it is never fully clear whether some observed state of affairs should count as a refutation, and if so whether it refutes the whole of a theory or merely some minor component of it. And there is the further point that reasonable men disagree on the comparative importance of problem-solving success, explanatory success, resistance to refutation and so forth. The irresistible conclusion is not that scientific theories cannot be compared and ranked, but that there is no natural scale for their ranking, no common measure which all reasonable men will agree to use and agree how to use. This is Kuhn's famous thesis of the incommensurability of scientific theories. It is a thesis which, as he himself points out, makes it extraordinarily difficult to provide a logically satisfactory account of scientific progress, or even of the difference between revolutions in the scientific and the political spheres. Scientific revolutions cannot consist in transitions from one theory to another indisputably superior one. Instead: 'Like the choice between competing political institutions, that between competing paradigms proves to be a choice between incompatible modes of community life' (Kuhn 1970: 94).

It will be clear by now that Kuhn's work uncompromisingly and comprehensively undermines the rationalist account of science. It repudiates the power of an autonomous individual reason; it rejects an individualistic account of research; and it denies that scientific change is a gradual evolutionary progression. Given the general acceptance of liberal-rationalist modes of thought in our society, it is not altogether surprising that Kuhn's work has occasionally been interpreted as anti-scientific polemic, and that it attained a certain celebrity amongst radical critics of science when it first appeared in the 1960s.

In fact, of course, Kuhn had merely examined what he took to be man's finest intellectual achievement. Far from attacking science for its failure to meet the standards of rationalism, he destroyed the credibility of rationalist mythology by exposing its incongruity with science: science itself remained firmly fixed upon its pedestal.

Kuhn was misunderstood, I suspect, because the general standpoint from which he wrote had become unfamiliar to us, just as most standpoints which allow the fundamental criticism of liberal-rationalist modes of thinking have become unfamiliar. Many aspects of Kuhn's approach are redolent of *conservative thought*: they suggest a link with that long tradition of holistic, intuitive conservatism which had its finest flowering in the nineteenth century but which has been carried on into this century by writers such as Michael Oakeshott, or, specifically in the context of science, Michael Polanyi. Where the mythology of rationalism speaks of reason and the individual this old style of conservatism speaks of custom and community. And it speaks of custom and community not to undermine and condemn but to support and commend. The opposition between the light of an individually based reason and the benighting influence of socially based customs and conventions, an opposition which is fundamental to the rationalist myth, has no place in conservative thought; and it is just this distinction which must be set on one side if we are to understand Kuhn. Kuhn does indeed describe science as a tradition and its practices as customary activities. He does indeed insist that scientific knowledge must be based upon the authority which derives from communal consensus. But this account is not designed to show how far science falls short of being genuine knowledge; on the contrary, it is designed to show

how science attains that status. *The Structure of Scientific Revolutions* is quite straightforwardly an apologia.

Whether or not Kuhn's justification of science is well grounded and convincing is an issue too large and too exacting to be engaged with here. What can be said, however, is that his approach is perfectly plausible and intelligible. Judged by the standards of rationalism his account can indeed be nothing other than a criticism of research standards in science, and a calling into question of the status of scientific knowledge. But Kuhn is precisely a critic of the standards of rationalism themselves: he seeks to show that no body of putative knowledge could possibly meet such standards and that epistemological evaluations must accordingly be based upon other considerations; he suggests that the agreed judgement of an appropriately trained community might itself serve as a criterion of what is rightly called knowledge. It is a testimony to the deep entrenchment of rationalist ways of thinking that this aspect of Kuhn's argument has often been overlooked or misconstrued.

Kuhn suggests that a system of beliefs may be built up that takes account of custom as well as experience, the social as well as the natural, and may still deserve to be called natural knowledge. This will perhaps seem counter-intuitive: surely, in producing knowledge of nature, only nature should be taken into account. There are, however, ways of reconciling Kuhn's approach with our intuitions. Consider, for example, our habitual understanding of perception, say visual perception for the sake of simplicity. It is generally accepted that perceptions provide reliable information about our physical environment, that they are in some genuine sense representations of nature. Now the detailed study of perception reveals an elaborate machinery at work. When we see that the cat is on the mat, much more is involved than the cat, the light from the cat, and our simple awareness of the light. The lens of the eye is at work focusing the light: it is a lens of changeable shape, under muscular control and capable of a range of focusing effects according to how it is controlled. The lens, moreover, is a part of an optical system which varies from individual to individual in its effects. It is an optical system which directs light not upon a glass screen for viewing by the mind's own eye, but on the arranged rods and cones of the retina, where light is converted to nerve impulses to be passed, after elaborate processing, to the back of the brain. Between the lens of the eye and the back of the brain, so the psychologists and physiologists tell us, the initial information we receive is subjected to elaborate modifications and transformations; much information is lost, and a good deal is added, probably through the operation of both innate and learned or acquired processes. Finally, the brain makes its own adjustments, conditioned by memory and acquired schemata, before, at last, we see the cat.

Thus seen on the mat, we generally believe that the cat indeed is there. We think it reasonable that an individual should so believe, on the basis of perception. And we think it reasonable to call the perception, the basis of belief, in some sense a representation of reality. Nor is this intuitive mode of thinking disturbed by our awareness of the elaborate machinery of perception. It is not just the cat which causes the perception of the cat, yet what is perceived is the cat. It is not just the cat's being on the mat which inspires the belief that it is on the mat, yet that alone is what is believed, and rightly believed.

Kuhn's account of the production of knowledge may be set into analogy with this account of the production of an individual belief. The machinery of the body, so the psychologists and physiologists say, is deeply implicated in the production of beliefs, yet the beliefs so produced may still rightly be said to be about external nature. A community, so Kuhn says, is deeply implicated in the production of knowledge, yet the knowledge may rightly be said to be natural knowledge. Our conception of a well-grounded belief allows, as it were, for the rich sense in which it is a construct of an individual. In the same way, our conception of knowledge can allow for the rich sense in which it is the construct of a community. 'Scientific knowledge, like language, is intrinsically the common property of a group or else nothing at all' (Kuhn 1970: 210).

It might be said that whereas this analogy helps to illuminate Kuhn's approach to the problem of knowledge, it also exposes what is wrong with that approach. If the individual possesses an elaborate apparatus for processing information and generating perception and belief, what possible need can there be for any additional apparatus? Why should a community routinely filter out yet more information, and impose its own conventional patterns and structures upon what remains? The answer here is that knowledge is a public possession and must have the same general form for all its users: it must serve as the basis for communications amongst those who share it, facilitate their interaction, make it possible for them to act co-operatively upon their physical environment. Kuhn is excellent in his treatment of these points: again and again he emphasises

how neither formal logical reasoning nor other individually based
cognitive propensities suffice to produce the coherence and standardisation essential to a body of knowledge. Indeed, he presses the
issue further and points out that what is inherent in the individual is
not even sufficient to constitute the apparatus which produces individual perception and individual belief. In any competent scientist,
he says, the construction of this apparatus is profoundly conditioned by scientific training, so that public practice permeates
private experience and the individual tends to see or fail to see,
remember or forget, believe or withhold belief, in harmony with the
other members of his community.

Kuhn's account of knowledge, which often initially appears
perverse and wrong-headed, does not in fact place undue demands
upon the mind as far as the understanding of its basic tenets is concerned: indeed, once these have been thoroughly explored in the
imagination they can come to seem perfectly mundane and straightforward. An uncompromisingly individualistic account of knowledge fares much less well when explored in this way. Set an isolated
'rational' individual to monitor experience without bias or preconceptions and one brings into being, not a scientist, but a reincar-
nation of Funes the Memorious, Borges' fine conception, he who
remembers all and hence knows nothing. And how this imaginary
Funes is to be transformed into a scientist, without being set into a
social and cultural context and allowed to assimilate its customs and
conventions, is a daunting problem even for the most ingenious philosopher.

Considering how those major strategic choices might be made,
which have to be made if a science is to thrive and prosper, Kuhn
asks: 'What better criterion than the decision of the scientific group
could there be?' (1970: 170). The remark neatly encapsulates
Kuhn's epistemology, an epistemology which, it is argued above,
deserves to be reflected upon with the utmost seriousness. At the
same time, the remark indicates why Kuhn's epistemological views
are so frequently found unacceptable: it appears to imply that
whatever a scientific community has a fancy to assert must *ipso
facto* be accepted, that scientists can, as it were, pick and choose
what is to count as knowledge. Needless to say, this is not Kuhn's
view at all. Kuhn is not suggesting that scientists be given cognitive
authority to operate with just as they will. He is saying that because
a scientific community is trained and equipped in a certain special
way, and tends by virtue of how it is constituted to operate in a

certain way, its judgements are our best available criteria in fixing what is to count as knowledge. This is to impute a generalised trust-worthiness to a scientific community rather in the way that it might be imputed to the eye, or to a functioning scientific instrument.

It should be noted too that in presenting his social epistemology Kuhn does not pretend to be offering a fully worked-out solution to the problem of the basis of our knowledge. He merely offers a beginning, a starting-point for thought. Thus, he does not seek to foreclose the question of the basic structure of the natural world: 'It is not only the scientific community that must be special. The world of which that community is a part must also possess quite special characteristics' (1970: 173). And he clearly recognises that there is a great deal more to be said about the special character of scientific communities, and about its epistemological significance. This is surely correct. For even if it is the case that there is no epistemological criterion superior to that of the actual judgement of the scientific group, this criterion is clearly insufficient as a basis for the evaluations of scientists themselves as they set about establishing the credentials of knowledge-claims. A research community wherein scientists employed this and only this criterion of evaluation would be like a stock market where all participants were uncompromising chartists: it would be impossible.

It has at once been philosophy's loss and history's gain that only very occasionally since the 1960s has Kuhn returned to the epistemological questions raised by his work. But for all the scale and profundity of his vision Kuhn has always been somewhat uneasy in the role of a speculator, and positively averse to metaphysical posturing. He is very much imbued with the epistemological caution which runs through the Anglo-Saxon philosophical tradition, and achieves his highest levels of insight and penetration when he is analysing particular concrete episodes in the history of science. Indeed, in many ways it is ironical that a discussion of Kuhn's work should appear in a series upon the return of Grand Theory. His mental universe could scarcely be more distant from that of Althusser, or even Habermas. This, however, is precisely why Kuhn does deserve his place in this series. He has laid bare the defects of rationalism in an idiom acceptable to those who assume it or defend it. And thus in societies like ours, where the myth of rationalism thoroughly permeates everyday habits of thinking, his work has played a major part in clearing the path for more promising lines of thought.

Traditionally, we have sought to understand the advancement of scientific knowledge purely in terms of reason and experience – in terms of the general logical operations which any man may perform and the empirical observations which any man may make. As to the remainder of the human condition, that has been of interest only as a way of understanding the biases and distortions which impede progress. We are now well on the way towards discarding this intolerably narrow view, and recognising that to understand our knowledge and its basis we must achieve a more comprehensive self-understanding. We need, in particular, to understand ourselves not simply as organisms but as communities. This is because knowledge is, in its very nature, a collective creation, founded not upon isolated individual judgements, but upon the evaluations we make together in social situations, according to custom and precedent, and in relation to our communal ends. Even scientific inferences must be seen as instances of customary behaviour, and not treated purely as manifestations of the universal reason of the individual. It is not so much that custom must replace reason in our thinking, as that reasoning itself must be seen as a profoundly conventional activity. Our hitherto impoverished conception of reasoning must be enlarged.

Precisely this has been the aim, if not the achievement, of much of the Grand Theory of the Continental philosophers. It is good to note an increase of interest in these writers within the English-speaking world, and a growing understanding of their objectives. The result must be an enrichment of our own thought. At the same time it may be that we shall eventually offer our own distinctive contribution to their project. For it is scarcely likely that as we explore the work of Habermas or Althusser we shall lose our traditional concern for evidence and justification. And it is precisely in its comparative lack of this concern that the major weakness of the literature of Grand Theory currently lies.

FURTHER READING

Most of Kuhn's general philosophical and sociological thinking is to be found in *The Structure of Scientific Revolutions* (1970) and in *The Essential Tension* (1977), a collection of essays spanning a period of almost two decades. The detailed historical work in relation to which this material should be considered and appraised includes two readily available book-length studies, *The Copernican Revolution* (1957), and *Black Body Theory*

(1978). Kuhn's work on the history of thermodynamics is also of considerable interest although, possibly because it is difficult of access, it is now little cited: it may be approached via Kuhn 1961, or Barnes 1982: ch. 1.

There is an extensive body of commentary and criticism dealing with Kuhn's general ideas. Perhaps the best-known contributions of this kind are those included in Lakatos and Musgrave 1970. Gutting 1980 is a more recent collection of commentaries. More extended appreciations of the significance of Kuhn's work are Stegmüller 1976 and Barnes 1982: Stegmüller assesses Kuhn's philosophical importance in a book which although difficult is richly rewarding; Barnes concentrates upon sociological issues.

For a comprehensive and perceptive review of the many sources of Kuhn's inspiration, the 'influences' upon his thought as is sometimes said, Cedarbaum 1983 should be referred to. Fleck 1979 represents what is currently the single most interesting source; long out of print in its German original, this work has now become available in English translation, and remains an outstandingly useful contribution in its own right. Fleck represents an important link between Kuhn's work and the European sociology of knowledge tradition.

In order to assess the suggestion that Kuhn's work may be related to a tradition of conservative thought it is essential to refer to Mannheim 1953. Needless to say, to relate the work of an author to a particular tradition or a particular style of thought is neither to deny the possible relevance of other traditions nor to imply anything whatsoever concerning the personal convictions of the author himself.

6
John Rawls

by Alan Ryan

Academically respectable philosophers are generally obscure figures. They have specialisms just as natural scientists have; they are known to their colleagues in those specialisms and to few besides – just as natural scientists are; they beaver away like their colleagues in chemistry and physics; and like everybody else they are variably nice to their families and friends. They are almost never known outside their own subject; and they almost never go in for public pronouncements on the great issues of the day. Bertrand Russell used to do it, and was held to have ruined his reputation as a result, even though he used to go to some lengths to maintain that when he wrote on political issues it was 'not as a philosopher'. 'I wrote', said Russell, 'as a human being who suffered from the state of the world' (Schilpp 1943: 730). Nonetheless, the picture most people now have of the engaged philosopher owes a great deal to Russell.

This makes it all the more surprising that John Rawls's long and intricate book should have caught the attention of so many people outside the world of professional philosophers. *A Theory of Justice* is 550 pages long; it is written with tremendous clarity and care, but there's nothing about it to provoke instant excitement. Its clarity puts it in a different universe from the suggestive murkiness of Foucault, Gadamer or Habermas; there is no suggestion that enlightenment can only be achieved after a prolonged groping in the dark. But, unlike Russell, say, who was his equal in clarity, but who enlivened his dryest work with a constant crackle of humour, Rawls writes with Puritan plainness and sobriety, and, also unlike Russell, Rawls has neither been jailed for his opinions nor been accused of fomenting revolution; he has not fired off letters to presidents nor torn up his party card. His views are controversial, but he is not himself a controversialist.

Yet since *A Theory of Justice* appeared in 1971, it has sparked off more argument among philosophers, and has been more widely cited by sociologists, economists, judges and politicians than any work of philosophy in the past hundred years. Its first major review (Hampshire 1972) announced that it was the most significant work in moral and political philosophy to have appeared in a century; comparisons were made with Henry Sidgwick's *Methods of Ethics* – the book which may be said to have created modern moral philosophy – and with John Stuart Mill's *Utilitarianism* and *On Liberty*. Commentary on Rawls quickly attained the status of a 'Rawls industry'; but not even the most hostile critic ventured to suggest that these initial estimates of Rawls's importance were exaggerated.

As we shall see, writers such as Robert Nozick ask some very awkward questions of Rawls. Nonetheless, Nozick begins his scrutiny of Rawls's theory with the following tributes:

A Theory of Justice is a powerful, deep, subtle, wide-ranging, systematic work in political and moral philosophy which has not seen its like since the writings of John Stuart Mill, if then. It is a fountain of lovely ideas, integrated together into a lovely whole... It is impossible to read Rawls' book without incorporating much, perhaps transmuted, into one's own deepened view. And it is impossible to finish his book without a new and inspiring vision of what a moral theory may attempt to do and unite; of how *beautiful* a moral theory can be. (Nozick 1974: 183)

It is true, and I'll try to explain why, that Rawls's impact has been greater in America than elsewhere; but the astonishing thing is the way in which a sober-sided Harvard professor should have caught the intellectual imagination of such a wide audience. Part of the explanation is no doubt that large numbers of readers had been waiting for the book for thirteen years – ever since Rawls had suggested in an article in the *Philosophical Review* ('Justice as Fairness' Rawls 1958) that the way to develop a theory of justice was to ask ourselves what arrangements we would have agreed on if we had been devising the basic political and economic institutions of our society via a 'social contract' made under conditions which guaranteed that contract's fairness. But the impact on non-philosophers is hardly explained by that. Let me suggest what does explain it.

A *Theory of Justice* is a book about rights. American liberals have long been accustomed to arguing about rights, in part because of the place that the Supreme Court has in American politics, and because of the possibility of appealing to rights enshrined in the Constitution of the United States. Battles over capital punishment, like battles over school desegregation thirty years ago, are fought out in the courts as much as in Congress, and they are fought out by asking whether, say, the right not to be subjected to 'cruel and unusual punishment' which is enshrined in the original constitution or 'the right to the equal protection of the laws' which constitutes the 14th Amendment means that capital punishment is unlawful, or that all children have a right to attend the same schools.

A *Theory of Justice* sets out to discover what rights we have against each other; it sets out to find these rights from first principles – rights against our government such as the right to a fair trial or the right not to be forced to fight in an unjust war, civil and political rights such as the right to vote and the right to choose our own occupation, and economic rights such as the right to protection against poverty and exploitation. What is distinctive about it, and what accounts for its wide influence, is that in doing so, it defends what one might for shorthand call 'American welfare state liberalism' – the view that governments must open up to their citizens the widest possible range of civil rights and economic opportunities. It argues that any government which fails to conduct itself on democratic lines, fails to open up economic opportunities or to promote the welfare of its least advantaged subjects violates their moral rights and has no claims to their allegiance. The boldness of these claims is obvious. Welfare state liberalism turns out – if *A Theory of Justice* is right – to be a great deal more than merely the political platform of the New Deal Democratic Party, and something quite other than a political programme which happens to appeal to the so-called 'New Deal coalition' of Jewish liberals, labour leaders, and black civil rights activists. It turns out to be a form of politics which is uniquely just and uniquely rational. The plainness of Rawls's prose perhaps makes it harder to see just how ambitious a project he was embarked on, but there is no doubt in my mind that it was that which accounts for its impact on the liberal audience which took it up. And the ambition has touched at least two noteworthy subsequent attempts to provide a grounding for modern liberalism (Dworkin 1978b; Ackerman 1980).

The intellectual support for liberalism was all the more welcome because welfare state liberals are an intellectually hard-pressed group. They are traditionally abused from the left by socialists who think they hardly begin to understand the real problems of a capitalist society and hemmed in on two sides by different sorts of conservative. In the American setting, it has been the conservatives who have been the more vociferous – no doubt another reason for Rawls's appeal to American liberals, who must often have felt that the conservatives had always seemed to have the best of the arguments about rights.

On the one side, paternalist conservatives have always argued that if a government is – as they agree it is – obliged to look after the needy and entitled to use tax revenues to do so, it is entitled to set the terms on which it does so. A paternalist government should decide what books we may read, what religious views we may profess, and extend its interest in our welfare to our moral welfare as much as our physical well-being. The argument is spelled out by George F.

Will in *Statecraft as Soulcraft* (Will 1984) in avowed opposition to Rawlsian liberalism and to the more familiar American conservatism which owes more to Herbert Spencer than to Edmund Burke. Will stands on the Burkean claim that society is a contract for more than material purposes: 'it is a partnership in all science; a partnership in all art; a partnership in every virtue, and in all perfection' (Burke 1961: 110).

If the liberals try to argue that, although the government has every right to spend its tax revenues on the hard-up, it has no right to police our libraries and our bedrooms, they find themselves facing conservatives of a different sort, who argue that the only defence against interfering governments is complete *laissez-faire*. I cannot here settle the vexed question of whether such enthusiasts for *laissez-faire* are best described as conservative; F. A. von Hayek has often denied that he is a conservative, and has said that he is a liberal *pur sang* and some English conservatives would repudiate Hayek's 'free market liberalism' precisely because they agree that conservatism is about tradition and paternalism, not about individual liberty and free choice. But here the speech of the vulgar must be our guide; the defenders of *laissez-faire* are frequently, and reasonably, regarded as conservative because they treat the growth of the welfare state and government regulation of the economy as a series of more or less disastrous moves away from an earlier and more golden age of minimal government. If some defenders of universal *laissez-faire* would be better described as 'anarcho-capitalists' than as conservatives, the public perception of them is sound enough, since they stand up for the capitalist economy to which conservatives are committed, and regard governments who tax their subjects in order to pay for a welfare state as engaged in a form of official robbery.

Theorists of this persuasion stake everything on liberty, and understand individuals as essentially the proprietors of themselves and their abilities, free to dispose of their 'property in their own persons' (Locke 1967: 305) as they see fit. The resulting social theory is agreeably simple, and uniquely calculated to keep government at arm's length in all spheres of life. Everyone must fend for himself with whatever property in his own talents he has been given by nature and whatever other property he can lawfully acquire; no doubt the rich ought to be *charitable* to the poor, but governments must not try to run a welfare state, for just as censorship violates a man's right to put what he likes into his own mind, so a welfare state violates a man's right to do as he likes with his own property. Small wonder that liberals often look wishy-washy and insecure, faced with the certainties of energetic paternalists on the one hand and the cool clarity of the descendants of Herbert Spencer on the other. *A Theory of Justice* promises relief by showing the liberal's position to be the consistent outcome of an argument from more or less uncontroversial premises. If its arguments are sound, liberalism is not a patched-up compromise between conservatism and socialism, but a distinctive creed with solid foundations.

A Theory of Justice asks us to engage in a thought experiment. Rawls asks us to imagine ourselves trying to arrange social and economic institutions in the company of others whose consent we have to obtain – in short, he asks us to imagine that we are drawing up a social contract. But there is one crucial feature of this situation: we are to imagine that we know nothing about our tastes, talents and interests, and do not know what social and economic position we shall occupy, nor in what society we shall live. This feature is what Rawls calls 'the veil of ignorance' (Rawls 1971: 136–42); the thought is that an acceptable theory of justice ought to tell us what rights we possess by telling us what rules we *would* have drawn up to govern the way we co-operate with one another, if only we'd known none of those things which usually get in the way of complete impartiality.

In setting up his theory in this way, Rawls has 'returned to Grand Theory' thrice over. Against those philosophers, dominant in the 1950s and 1960s, who restricted philosophy to the analysis of concepts, Rawls has set philosophy back on the path followed by his predecessors like John Stuart Mill. *A Theory of Justice* stands up for controversial political positions. Rawls's views are not extravagant or extreme, but they are certainly controversial. For instance, he holds that elected officials are under an altogether stricter obligation to obey the laws and uphold the constitution under which they were elected than the rest of us are (Rawls 1971: 112, 344) – a view which President Nixon flouted in practice, and, more interestingly, which his defenders objected to as a matter of theory. Rawls offers a defence of civil disobedience which would make politically motivated disobedience a much more acceptable part of our political life than either the American Supreme Court or the English judiciary seem likely to contemplate (Rawls 1971: 363–8). And his views about the subservience of economic institutions to 'social justice' place him firmly on one side of what is currently the most fiercely contested dividing line in politics in Britain today.

A Theory of Justice has also returned to *Grand* Theory in setting itself the task of providing a systematic and comprehensive theory of justice, starting from minimal first principles and ramifying out into principles to cover every case. This goes directly against the most common tendency in recent moral and political philosophy, which has generally argued that there is little room to *systematise* our ideas about social and political values, and that all we can do is 'trade off' one social value against another in an intuitive way (Barry 1965: 3–8). Rawls has tried to produce a theory of justice which will rank the components of justice in a determinate and rationally supported way. The similarity between Rawls's work and that of Kant extends not merely to the way they both espouse a 'hypothetical' social contract theory (cf. Rawls 1971: 12 and Reiss 1972: 73–87), but to the almost 'architectural' quality of the resulting theory, with its hierarchical structure of the principles of practical reason, first principles of right, and their personal and institutional implications all neatly labelled and rationalised (Rawls 1971: 109).

Rawls's third return to Grand Theory is perhaps his most surprising one: the intellectual apparatus which Rawls has called upon to sustain all this is the theory of the social contract. To go back to contractual ways of thinking is in the most literal sense a return, for while the social contract provided the theoretical framework in which Hobbes, Locke, Rousseau and Kant all wrote in the seventeenth and eighteenth centuries, it is usually supposed that the theory was dismantled by Hume – and the wreckage buried by Bentham in the early nineteenth century (Hume 1963; Bentham 1949). It is a mark of the distinction of Rawls's work that none of his critics is prepared to stand up and say that *A Theory of Justice* is simply archaic. They are unanimous in accepting that Rawls has at least uncovered *something* which the crude dismissals of Bentham and his fellow utilitarians hid from sight.

The reason behind Rawls's appeal to contractual ways of thinking is his perception of the central weakness of the commonest – that is, broadly utilitarian – ways of thinking about social welfare. Many people think at first sight that it is obvious that the only way to run a society is to maximise the welfare of its inhabitants. Rawls points out that this is at odds with our views about justice. There will be many occasions when we could increase the total welfare of society if we were willing to sacrifice one person for the benefit of all the rest – but most of us would think the sacrifice of an innocent simply unjust. The fundamental principle to which Rawls is committed is that nobody is merely a means to the ends of society at large; to put it differently, he insists on the *separateness* of persons, on the fact that we are not simply units of account in working out the total welfare. It is this separateness to which contractual ways of thinking do justice and other ways of thinking do not (Rawls 1971: 27).

It is this emphasis on the need to secure each individual against any temptation to sacrifice him or her for the general good which explains the place of two distinctive features of Rawls's theory. The first of these is the way in which he makes the rules governing the distribution of our fundamental freedoms take absolute priority over all other social rules; this, the principle of 'the priority of liberty' (Rawls 1971: 244ff), causes all sorts of difficulties for Rawls but it faithfully reflects one of the theory's crucial motivating ideas: that a theory of justice is in part a theory about the absolute impermissibility of coercing people in various ways. The second feature, that for which Rawls is best known, is his attempt to exploit the so called 'maximin' principle familiar from the theory of games, in explaining what 'fair shares' from the results of any co-operative enterprise must look like. It is a well-known theorem in the theory of games that when playing against an opponent in conditions of uncertainty, the best strategy to adopt is that of ensuring that the worst outcome of the game is as good as possible. We should play in such a way as to minimise our maximum losses or maximise our minimum gains, whence the abbreviated tag of 'maximin', or 'minimax'. It is a disputed question whether this analysis *does* apply in the context of Rawls's own analysis of justice. Behind the veil of ignorance, when we are trying to draw up terms for a social contract, we are not really playing *against* anyone. The justification of 'maximin' is that our opponents are trying to ensure that we end up with the worst outcome; it is this which makes it rational to ensure that their success is as painless to use as possible. We shall shortly see what this implies for Rawls's theory; but here we should notice how well Rawls's defence of his 'maximin' conception follows from the thought that a theory of justice has a substantial *defensive* component. If questions of justice arise in the context of co-operative enterprises, as Rawls says, they also arise only against a background in which it is likely that those with whom we co-operate are unwilling to let us have more than they have to to secure our co-operation. It is a theory of justice for people in competitive conditions.

A person who is fearful that others may wish to sacrifice him for their benefit and who is asked to construct a set of rules for governing their conduct will look most attentively at what happens to the *worst-off* person in the society whose rules he is thinking of. It is this that makes the most attractive principle for distributing the fruits of economic and social co-operation something like: distribute the benefits of co-operation in such a way that the worst-off person does as well as possible. If nothing is gained from an unequal distribution, things should be equally distributed; but if an unequal distribution would make things better for the worst-off person – perhaps by creating incentives which made everyone much more prosperous – then an unequal distribution is better than an equal one, and among all the possible unequal distributions the best is that which makes the worst-off person as well off as possible. (The intuitive thought is simple enough; if I do not expect to become a doctor, or suppose that there's no way of telling whether I shall become one or not, there's no reason for me to vote for an economic system in which doctors get high salaries, unless I think that this will improve medical services and benefit the non-doctors. But if I do expect this to improve medical services and so to benefit me, even if I turn out not to be a doctor, it would be silly to vote against high salaries for doctors simply because I knew I might not turn out to be one.)

This principle is what Rawls calls the 'difference principle'. It is clear how it resembles the principle of 'maximin' – the principle of maximising the benefits to you of the least favourable outcome of a competitive game. Nonetheless, it is not obvious that this is what rational contractors would choose in a condition of ignorance. It is vital to Rawls's own formulation of his theory that they should choose his maximin conception; and, equally, his utilitarian critics have perceived that it is a point in favour of utilitarianism if the theory of rational choice leads to it even in Rawls's own schema. It is at any rate hard to see why Rawls's contracting parties should be so adamantly opposed to thinking about anyone but the worst-off person. Since nobody has any reason to suppose that he or she is going to be the worst-off person, it is irrationally cautious to choose rules which are exclusively determined by the aim of making the worst-off person as well off as possible. If we turn out not to be the worst-off person, we may have made unreasonably large sacrifices of our welfare for the sake of the worst off. On the face of it, the principles which ignorance would dictate would have a strong utilitarian component – that is, if we were rational, self-interested, willing to keep our promises, but otherwise uninterested in other people's welfare (the conditions Rawls lays down) and ignorant of our future talents and place in society, we would vote for rules which would make the average person as well off as possible. We might be a shade more cautious, and vote for rules which had an 'insurance' component and made sure the worst-off person did not do too badly. But we would have no reason to vote to make the worst-off person as well off as possible, if this threatened to take a large slice out of the welfare of the average person. To argue for 'maximin' Rawls either needs some independent reason for supposing that extreme caution is part of rationality – which means going well beyond anything obtainable from the theory of games – or he needs to appeal more directly to our moral intuitions.

It seems to me – though not, it must be admitted, to most of his critics – that Rawls does the latter; in effect, he appeals to what one might call the psychology of the moral outlook to suggest that nobody who cared much for justice would be able to look the worst-off person in the eye and say that the society he lived in was just if all he could point to was the fact that the average standard of well-being was high. There is more than a hint of Rousseau rather than Kant in this, and it is a far cry from the view defended by Nozick that all I need ever say to the worst-off person is that I only used what I had a title to and therefore never violated his rights (Nozick 1974: 225–6).

But this principle is for Rawls subordinate to another and more important one. This is the principle that all members of society are to have the greatest freedom consistent with a like freedom for all. Here, there is no question of distributing benefits unequally. It is a matter of giving everyone a number of absolute immunities against the tyranny or coercion of others and a number of positive political rights in addition. The right to a fair trial, to freedom of speech, to freedom of occupation and to vote all belong in this category of rights to *the most extensive liberty consistent with a like liberty for all* (Rawls 1971: 60). This principle takes what Rawls calls 'lexical' priority over the difference principle; that is, before we may think about economic matters we must first attend to these civil liberties (ibid.: 61). Even if we could make the worst-off person better off by curtailing civil liberties – by abolishing elections for the sake of economic stability, say – we must not do so, for doing so would violate the personal integrity which it is the whole point of this theory to respect.

This is a good point at which to see how Rawls's account of our civil liberties extends into a defence of civil disobedience as a proper element in the political process, for this is the aspect of his theory which seized the attention of many Americans in the bitterest years of the Vietnam War. Rawls gives an account of how justice requires governments to be democratically elected and to govern with due respect for the convictions of the minority; law has no claim on us at all unless it is made by due process. But even if a government is properly constituted and generally governs according to both the letter and the spirit of the law, any political system will have lapses from grace. This poses the problem of how we are to behave if a government violates our considered convictions about what constitutes tolerable policy or legislation. Even under a just constitution, citizens who are concerned about the justice of the government they live under will think that their *ultimate* duty is to preserve the rule of justice, and that this takes priority over the obligation to obey any particular law or command. There cannot be any duty merely to obey every rule or every order handed down by their government. Citizens who are sincerely convinced that some act of government violates justice in a serious way, certainly may and sometimes must disobey the law as a way of calling attention to the violation and asking for reconsideration.

To do this they must act non-violently, and they must be ready to submit to whatever legal penalties there are for breaking the laws they break. It is important to see that it can only be in some political systems that *civil* disobedience is possible – that is, only in some societies will there be a consensus on what governments ought and ought not to do, and only in some societies will there be such a universal anxiety that people should be able to obey the law in good conscience, that what the disobedient are doing will make the right sense to their opponents. Only where the rest of us are desperate not to trample on the consciences of others will civil disobedience make much sense. Gandhi, for instance, thought that, no matter what the appearances, the British really shared his followers' sense of justice, and could be *civilly* disobeyed. Rawls never quite says whether America is the scrupulous sort of place he has in mind, or whether it had ceased to be so during the Vietnam War. But at a time when the government seemed to be fighting an open war against the VietCong and a covert one against its own young people, Rawls's reminder of the creative place of dissent in our politics and his insistence that the good citizen owes disobedience as well as obedience to his government, was both a noble and a healing gesture.

Not only do questions of civil liberties take priority over questions of welfare, they also play their part in dictating how the 'difference principle' is to be implemented. So it is not surprising to find Rawls insisting that when we implement the difference principle in economic matters we must make sure that all positions are open to everyone on the basis of equal opportunity (Rawls 1971: 61). That is, the civil liberties which take priority over everything else represent the idea that each person has a basic moral equality with everyone else – the positive face of the proposition that no one is to be merely a means to the ends of others – and since that is so, the only fair terms on which access to positions of advantage can be distributed are those which permit equality of opportunity.

What is surprising in Rawls's theory is not so much what it asserts as what it denies. The main thing it denies is that we should try to distribute income and wealth according to desert. Most people would think that desert is the central notion in justice; Rawls sweeps it aside. People's successes and failures spring from characters and talents they have done nothing to deserve (Rawls 1971: 103–4). They are certainly *entitled* to whatever income they earn by doing the jobs to which they have been appointed; but this entitlement only rests on our having observed the rules of appointment and performance, not on desert – much as I am *entitled* to occupy the house I have bought in a fair market, regardless of whether I deserve it. It is only the system of rules under which I gain my entitlements that is subject to further question – the question whether they work for the greatest benefit of the worst off.

Again, Rawls's account of justice has no room for the thought that even if we do not *deserve* our talents, we still have a right to what we can get from exercising them simply because they are *ours*. As he puts it, from the standpoint of justice our talents form part of a common social pool; it is the task of the theory of justice to discover what rights each of us should have over the results of using those talents. To put it another way, Rawls treats property rights as entirely a matter of convention; neither 'our' abilities nor what we can get for their exercise 'belongs' to us by natural right. About all kinds of property right we must ask: what conventional rights would the theory of justice require us to create? Rawls's theory does not merely support the thought that those who are asked to contribute by way of taxation to the operations of the welfare state have no right to complain about the use of 'their' income; it supports the more radical thought that it is not in any deep sense 'their' income at all. Many people do not much like the idea that we have *no* such basic ownership of *any* of our talents, and Robert Nozick for one has made a great deal of play with the grimmer implications of a wholesale denial of such a proprietorship (Nozick 1974: 206–7). For instance, it is as much an arbitrary matter that an intelligent, energetic and good-looking woman has those agreeable qualities as that Henry Ford II happens to be born the son of Henry Ford I; but do we suppose that the intelligent, agreeable and good-looking woman is either to be deprived of her advantages or else forced to use them in such a way as to benefit the worst off – say by marrying a man who is (again through no fault of his own) boring, lethargic and ugly and therefore much in need of a boost to his level of well-being? Indeed, Nozick asks, where does this leave Rawls's insistence on our not being mere means to the ends of others? What is left of me if all my qualities and aptitudes are simply part of the social pool?

Rawls has many resources for disarming his critics. To Nozick, he can properly reply that external property belongs in a morally less serious category than do our own abilities, and these in a less serious category again than do our personal affections. Moreover, the transfer of external property, particularly in the form of money, from one person to another can generally be relied on to do some good. To have someone married to you by force destroys just about all the value of the marriage relationship. To account for such obvious points, there is no need to resort to the thought that we have proprietorial relationships to our personal qualities, talents and the like.

On more straightforward economic issues Rawls is equally well placed to fight off critics who claim that he licenses something like the continuous interference of a socialist command economy. Although he often claims that justice is consistent with an economy run on welfare state capitalist lines *or* on welfare state socialist lines – since property rights are not part of our basic rights, there's no overriding argument in favour of the private ownership of things like construction companies, railways, or department stores – the theory of justice rules out most of socialism as currently practised. We cannot have direction of labour except in a military emergency. Since Rawls claims that we can restrict freedom for the sake of freedom but not for the sake of prosperity, the priority of liberty straightforwardly rules out a command economy. Since the same principle dictates that we must give people open access to occupations, most directive planning is ruled out too. Market socialism is consistent with Rawls's theory, but it is a socialism which no socialist country practises and which no country with a capitalist 'social market' economy seems tempted to try (cf. Ryan 1984). Moreover, even if the private ownership of businesses is not demanded by Rawls's theory, the private ownership and unconstrained multiplication of consumption goods plainly are, since only thus can people have secure freedom of choice of lifestyle. This, too, is at odds with the practice of most socialist regimes.

It is no part of my argument that Rawls is safe from his critics just because he is not a committed socialist. What the previous paragraph does show, however, is that Rawls is safe from those critics who maintain that what purports to be a defence of liberalism actually collapses into a wholesale collectivism; and it is part of my argument that it is a virtue of Rawls's theory that it leaves open the question of whether socialist economic arrangements are consistent with a proper concern for justice and liberty.

This, of course, is not what his critics on the left believe. They do not form a monolithic group, so I cannot pretend to sum a general view. But there are what one might call two representative objections to the theory. The first is the objection that it leaves out too much of the real force of egalitarianism. On Rawls's view there is no limit to the degree of inequality in society which is 'just'; so long as inequalities are necessary to make the worst off as well off as possible – or, rather, better off than the worst off would be in any other system we might reach – their extent is neither here nor there. No one brought up on writers like R. H. Tawney (Tawney 1932) would accept that. Genuine egalitarians want to close the gap between the best off and the worst off even if in worldly terms the worst off do somewhat less well than they otherwise might as a result. It is not clear to me how hard this criticism bites on Rawls's theory of justice. It must do so to some degree, since Rawls's theory explains the place of equality in economic life in terms of the self-interest of the worst off and cannot therefore treat equality as a moral and political value with a life of its own. But it may not bite hard, since by the time Rawls himself has argued for the virtues of a society in which envy can have no place, he has begun to sound a good deal more like Tawney himself (Rawls 1971: 536ff).

Rawls's Marxist critics, on the other hand, have less difficulty in establishing their distance from him. Marxism takes almost the polar opposite of stances at all levels. Methodologically, Marxism is hostile to 'rational man' theories, and hostile to 'state of nature' theories; against Rawls all Marxists argue that he performs the characteristic sleight of hand of apologists for capitalism by building in to human nature the features of competitors in the capitalist market place. Thus, it is not a truth about human nature that we need to be offered incentives to develop our talents, only a truth about men in competitive conditions who will give nobody anything for nothing (Lang 1979: 123ff; Macpherson 1973: 87ff). But only by building in such false assumptions can Rawls motivate his theory. The retort, of course, is that the record of Marxist attempts to run society on other assumptions about human nature has been so depressing that it seems safer to believe that human nature is more or less as Rawls's theory supposes it to be, and that the picture of men building a decent society on the basis of mutual advantage before they go on to create relationships of a more fraternal and altruistic kind is politically prudent as well as morally compelling.

Morally (if one can use that term of a Marxist view), Marxism and Rawls's theory are equally at odds. There is no room in Rawls's theory for such a notion as 'alienation' – the idea that men have created a world which now oppresses them as an alien power demands a theory of history and a philosophy of human nature quite at odds with the world of prudent calculators in a timeless bargaining situation. There is room in Rawls's theory for the other concept on which Marx's condemnation of capitalism rests, the concept of exploitation, but Rawls would not analyse exploitation in the same way, and the result would be very different from Marx's own concept of exploitation. Rawls would think of exploitation as a matter of well-placed bargainers driving iniquitous bargains with poorly placed bargainers while Marx tried to show that exploitation occurred not in exchange, but in production. Again, the morality appealed to by Rawls is individualistic, and supposes that the significant actors on the moral stage are individuals who mind about the conscientiousness of their actions; Marxists look rather to classes and consider the extent to which their actions promote their interests and the purposes of history, and place more store by solidarity than by justice. To say whether Rawls has adequate defences against all this is quite impossible. It is even truer here than it usually is that the issues at stake go so deep that they involve the adoption or rejection of something like an entire Weltanschauung rather than a particular theory. What one can say is that, insofar as Rawls claims that the ultimate test of his theory lies in its appeal to the reflective intuitions about justice which he takes all his readers to share, the conviction of highly intelligent and open-minded Marxists that they share no such thing is at any rate disturbing.

Even if one is neither a conservative nor a Marxist, one may have doubts about the solidity of the theory. One important doubt is about the priority of liberty over other values, and the doctrine associated with it, that liberty can only be restricted for the sake of liberty. In a general way, it is easy to see Rawls's point – liberals would hardly be liberals if they were willing to sell their freedom for a two percent rise in GNP. On the other hand, liberals would hardly be liberals if they thought that a commitment to democracy entailed that we should institute majority rule tomorrow afternoon in a society where we knew for certain that the first thing the majority would do would be to pass anti-semitic legislation and the second thing would be to pass a law restricting voting rights (Rawls 1971: 228ff).

But Rawls goes further than that, and in doing so surely makes a mistake. The thought that liberty can only be restricted for the sake of liberty hardly survives reflection on the criminal law – it is not for the sake of the liberty of my fellows that my freedom to hit them on the head is curtailed, it is for their safety, and it is not for the sake of their liberty that my freedom to steal their goods is curtailed either (Hart 1975). Conversely, Rawls himself agrees that there will be conditions where the absolute priority of liberty makes no sense; if people are so hard up that they cannot use their freedom, then we may curtail liberty for the sake of making their freedom more valuable to them by increasing their prosperity. At this point, one may feel that the theory is beginning to lose its simplicity and elegance, and that we are slipping back towards the view that all we can do is trade off various values against each other – Rawls like a good liberal is insisting that we exact a high price for losses of liberty, but not doing anything more distinctive than that.

In short, Rawls's theory offers a large and tempting target to critics. People who dislike the methodology complain that we cannot find out what our rights and duties *are* by asking what they *would have been* if they had been created by contract. Critics on the Left complain that the attempt to make civil rights sacrosanct in a way economic welfare is not ignores all those countries where survival, let alone comfort, demands tough, illiberal governments, which can force birth control, efficient irrigation, sensible farming methods and the other requisites of development upon a backward population. Critics on the Right who care less for the Third World than for the rights of Westchester County, either conspire with the left to argue that the various emergency clauses which Rawls allows to override the absolute priority of liberty can be invoked so often that they let governments do anything they like, or else throw up their hands in horror and refuse to believe that Rawls is so wicked as to think that we don't deserve our riches and don't really own our own abilities.

But reading Rawls is a particularly salutary experience for British readers. British politics is unaccustomed to a strenuous insistence on people's rights – our liberalism does not rest on the thought that people have absolute freedom of religious profession, free speech and the like, but on the thought that it does more harm than good to push dissenters around; and our welfare arrangements rest on a vague feeling that we ought to be nice to those worse off than us. To come across a writer arguing for 500 pages that even if it did do some good, we *must* not push dissenters around, and that regardless of our feelings about them, the hard-up have a *right* to be as well off as possible is a useful shock to our insular and excessively casual modes of thought.

FURTHER READING

Before the publication of *A Theory of Justice* (1971), Rawls had written several articles which were much discussed; in addition to 'Justice as Fairness' (1958), there was 'The Sense of Justice' (1963a), 'Constitutional Liberty and the Concept of Justice' (1963b), and 'Distributive Justice' (1967); since the publication of *A Theory of Justice*, Rawls has contributed to a symposium on the book in the *Journal of Philosophy* (1972) and has expanded some of its arguments in 'Fairness to Goodness' (1975) and in his Dewey Lecture 'Kantian Constructionism in Moral Theory' (1980). His reply to Hart's doubts about the 'priority of liberty' comes in 'The Basic Liberties and their Priority' (1982).

The critical literature is enormous; in *Political Theory*, 1977, there is a ten page bibliography of articles from the period 1971–6 (Fullinwider 1977). Happily, fourteen of the most interesting of them are reprinted in Daniels 1975. Two book-length studies of Rawls are Barry 1973 and Wolff 1977. But the impact of Rawls is visible in most recent work in political theory, for instance in Dworkin 1978, Miller 1977, Fried 1978 and Walzer 1983. Nozick 1974 remains the best route into the strengths and weaknesses of Rawls's work as well as an outstandingly interesting book in its own right.

Much of the work on Rawls has been concerned with the coherence and validity of the attempt to derive rights from a contractual framework, and has been highly critical. One essay which has attempted to rescue the insights of contractualism is Scanlon 1982; another balanced essay in the same vein is Hart 1979. Lastly, Parfit 1984 ought to be mentioned as a defence of utilitarianism which concedes Rawls's claim that the separateness of persons would be an argument against utilitarianism and proceeds to argue that persons are not, in a deep sense, separate after all.

7

Jürgen Habermas

by Anthony Giddens

For many years there has been a gulf between German and Anglo-Saxon social theory. German thinkers have always been fond of constructing arcane philosophical systems of awesome complexity. As Professor Skinner points out in his Introduction, until recently most social thinkers and philosophers in the English-speaking world have, by contrast, been highly suspicious of Grand Theory. If they are today more receptive to it, it is in some considerable part a result of the writings of Jürgen Habermas. Habermas is very much a 'grand theorist' in the traditional German manner. But he has made a conscious attempt to connect British and American trends in social science and philosophy with those deriving from German social theory. Those weaned upon Anglo-Saxon social thought can find much in Habermas's work that is recognisable to them, and this helps make what he is trying to accomplish more easily accessible than it would otherwise be.

Habermas is a relatively young man for someone who has attained a widespread international eminence. He is only in his middle fifties, and still at the most creative stage of his career. He is the most prominent latter-day descendant of what has come to be known as the 'Frankfurt School' of social theory. The Frankfurt School was a group of philosophers associated with the Institute of Social Research in Frankfurt, originally founded in the late 1920s. It included among its number Max Horkheimer, for many years the administrative director of the Institute, and a remarkable thinker named Theodor Adorno. But the member of the group who became most famous – or infamous, according to one's point of view – was Herbert Marcuse, the leading figure in the New Left in the late 1960s. The members of the Frankfurt School were Marxists, or regarded themselves as such; however they were very far from being Marxists of an orthodox persuasion. They regarded Marxism as a flexible, critical approach to the study of society, not as a fixed and inviolable set of doctrines. They were prepared to jettison ideas that to most other Marxists are essential to what Marxism is as a body of thought and a guide to political practice. Thus they held, for example, that the working class has become integrated into capitalist society, and is no longer a revolutionary force. Nothing might seem more obvious to those not persuaded of the attractions of Marxism, but to many more orthodox Marxists it was – and still is – shockingly heretical. The Frankfurt School argued that capitalism has changed so much since Marx's time that many of Marx's concepts have to be discarded or at least radically altered. These are

Habermas's views too. He also regards himself as a Marxist, although his detractors on the Left would claim that he has departed so far from Marxism that he has lost touch with it altogether. Habermas claims that he is engaged in a 'reconstruction of historical materialism', producing a version of Marxism relevant to today's world: although no doubt he would not say so, he is trying to be a Marx for our times. The ideas he has come up with are inevitably very controversial, and do not lend themselves to easy summary, but there can be no doubt of their originality and importance. In spite of his direct links with the Frankfurt School, Habermas cannot be seen merely as the purveyor of received notions: he has created a system of thought – whatever one might think of it – which is highly distinctive.

This system moves on several levels, and is encyclopaedic in scope. I will try to sketch in some of its main themes, concentrating upon these to the exclusion of others that in a longer appraisal would no doubt be regarded as equally important. The guiding thread of all Habermas's work, according to his own testimony, is an endeavour to reunite theory and practice in the twentieth-century world. In the nineteenth century, Marx believed that his theory provided both an analysis of capitalist society and the means of changing it in practice, through the revolution of the proletariat. The revolution has not come about, and will not do so, Habermas accepts, in the manner anticipated by Marx. Habermas agrees with the Frankfurt School that the Soviet Union is at best a very deformed version of a socialist society. We cannot use the Eastern European countries either as a model of what the desirable form of society should be like, or as indicating the likely direction in which the capitalist societies will move in the future. But for these reasons Marx's conception of the unity of theory and practice is hopelessly inadequate in the late twentieth century. It needs to be rethought in several quite fundamental respects. These concern both philosophical limitations of Marx's thought and more concrete innovations that need to be made in characterising the nature of modern capitalism.

On the philosophical level, Habermas sees Marx's writings as deficient in respects shared by many non-Marxist forms of philosophy from the nineteenth century through to the present day. Although there are many ambiguities in Marx's work, for the most part he thought of what he was doing as science. According to Habermas, this will not do at all, for reasons which, once understood, allow us to develop a critique of a good deal of modern philosophical thought, and of the broader culture of society too. There are two things wrong with regarding the study of human social life as a science on a par with the natural sciences. One is that it produces a mistaken view of what human beings are like as capable, reasoning actors who know a great deal about why they act as they do. The other is that it contributes to a tendency which Habermas sees as general in modern intellectual culture, an overestimation of the role of science as the only valid kind of knowledge that we can have about either the natural or the social world (Habermas 1974: 195–252).

The second of these points is very important for Habermas, and connects with his analysis of ideology. But let me take them in succession. Treating the study of society like a science led Marx, and later Marxists, Habermas says, to a characteristic dilemma. If capitalism changes – as Marx himself wrote – according to 'iron laws' which have all the determinism of laws of natural science, where is there any room for the active interaction of human beings in their own fate? Why should anyone bother to become a Marxist at all? For if human behaviour is governed by ineluctable laws, there is nothing we can do to shape our own history by actively intervening in it. When understood as a science, Marxism ignores what Habermas calls the 'self-reflection', or 'reflexivity' of human agents. That is to say, it cannot cope with one of the defining features which make us human. This is the fact that we are capable of reflecting upon our own history, as individuals and as members of larger societies; and of using precisely that reflection to change the course of history. This insight is lost in all forms of philosophy and social theory – usually referred to as 'positivism' – which try to fashion the social upon the natural sciences.

Now Habermas is not the first to make this kind of criticism of positivism. It has often been associated with those belonging to what Continental philosophers call the 'hermeneutic' tradition. Hermeneutics means the theory of interpretation. Those who have written in the hermeneutic tradition – who include H.-G. Gadamer, whose work is also discussed in this book – have stressed that to understand human behaviour we have to interpret its meaning (Gadamer 1975a). Rather than seeing human conduct as governed by laws, or as caused, like events in nature, we have to grasp the intentions and reasons which people have for their activity. According to those in the hermeneutical tradition, the study of human conduct is essentially quite different from studying events in nature. Therefore, they say – in complete contrast to those I have just discussed – natural science is irrelevant as a model for how we should study human behaviour. One of Habermas's most interesting contributions to philosophy is his attempt to reconcile hermeneutics and positivism and thereby overcome this division between them. There *are* circumstances in which human social life is conditioned by factors of which those involved know little – in which social forces resemble forces of nature. To that degree, the advocates of a natural science model are correct. But they are wrong to suppose that such social forces are immutable, like laws of nature. The more human beings understand about the springs of their own behaviour, and the social institutions in which that behaviour is involved, the more they are likely to be able to escape from constraints to which previously they were subject.

In order to illustrate this, Habermas makes what has become a celebrated comparison between psychoanalysis and social theory (Habermas 1971a, chs 10–12). Psychoanalysis involves a hermeneutic element. After all, the task of the analyst is to interpret the meaning of what the patient thinks and feels. Interpretation of meaning – as in decoding the content of dreams – is inherent in psychoanalytic therapy. But the analyst reaches the limits of interpretation where repressions block off access to the unconscious. Psychoanalytic language then tends to shift to talk of 'unconscious forces', 'unconscious constraints' and so on. It tends to become more like the language of the natural sciences. Why? Because the analysis at that point becomes concerned with things that happen to the individual, rather than things which the individual is able autonomously to control. It is in such circumstances, and only in such circumstances, Habermas argues, that concepts analogous to those of natural science are relevant to the explication of human conduct. The more successful the psychoanalytic procedure is, the less these kinds of concepts are appropriate, because the individual is able to expand the scope of rational control over his or her behaviour. The appropriate language then becomes hermeneutic. Note a further very important consequence of all this. Psychoanalytic therapy aims to change behaviour, by the very process of transmuting what happens to the individual into what the individual makes happen. Habermas suggests this is the same role as that which a critical theory of society should fulfil. Marxism is inadequate as a basis for accomplishing social change, insofar as it is solely concerned with 'iron laws', 'inevitable trends', etc. It is then only the science of human unfreedom. A philosophically more sophisticated critical theory must recognise that an emancipated society would be one in which human beings actively control their own destinies, through a heightened understanding of the circumstances in which they live.

It is very important, according to this standpoint, to see that there is no single mould into which all knowledge can be compressed. Knowledge can take three different forms, according to differing interests which underlie its formulation. These three 'knowledge-constitutive interests' each correspond to an aspect of human society. All societies exist in a material environment, and engage in interchanges with nature – this relation involves what Habermas calls generically 'labour'. Such interchanges promote an interest in the prediction and control of events. It is precisely this interest which is generalised by positivism to all knowledge. Insofar as Marxism relapses into positivism, it supposes that social life is governed by developments in the 'forces of production', operating mechanically to influence social change. But all societies also involve 'symbolic interaction' – the communication of individuals with one another. The study of symbolic interaction creates an interest in the understanding of meaning – always the main preoccupation of hermeneutics, which has mistakenly sought to generalise this to the whole of human activity. Finally, every human society involves forms of power or domination. The third knowledge-constitutive interest, that in emancipation, derives from a concern with achieving rational autonomy of action, free from domination – whether it be the domination of nature over human life, or the domination of some individuals or groups over others. Each of the knowledge-constitutive interests is linked to a particular type of discipline, as the table indicates. An interest in prediction and control is the pre-eminent concern of the 'empirical-analytic sciences' (which includes sociology as well as natural science). An interest in the understanding or interpretation of meaning is the prime guiding theme of the

Aspects of human society	Knowledge-constitutive interest	Type of study
Labour	Prediction and control	Empirical-analytic sciences
Interaction	Understanding of meaning	Historical-hermeneutic disciplines
Domination (Power)	Emancipation	Critical theory

'historical-hermeneutic disciplines'. Concern with the emancipation of human beings from systems of domination is the interest to which 'critical theory' is attached.

The foregoing ideas are set out principally in Habermas's work translated under the title of *Knowledge and Human Interests* (Habermas 1971a). Since the time of its first publication in 1968, Habermas has substantially revised and expanded upon the ideas contained therein. In the psychoanalytic encounter, the communication between therapist and patient is 'systematically distorted': repressions block and deform what the patient says to the analyst. But what is the positive goal of psychoanalysis as envisaged here? What would 'undistorted communication' be like, and how might this be connected to the ambitions of critical theory? In his more recent work, Habermas has devoted a good deal of attention to exploring possible answers to these questions, and has written extensively upon problems of communication and language in general. Two ideas are particularly important in grasping his views on these matters. One is the notion that all human linguistic communication involves 'validity-claims', implicitly made by all speakers. The other is the contention that an 'ideal speech situation', is presumed in the use of language (Habermas 1979: ch. 1).

According to Habermas, when one person says something to another, that person implicitly (sometimes explicitly) makes the following claims: (1) That what is said is intelligible – that is to say, that it obeys certain syntactical and semantic rules so that there is a 'meaning' which can be understood by the other. (2) That the propositional content of whatever is said is true. The 'propositional content' refers to the factual assertions which the speaker makes as part of what he or she says. (3) That the speaker is justified in saying whatever is said. In other words, certain social rights or 'norms' are invoked in the use of speech in any given context of language-use. (4) That the speaker is sincere in whatever is said – that he or she does not intend to deceive the listener. Thus put, the argument sounds very abstract, but what Habermas has in mind can readily be illustrated by means of an example. Suppose, in answer to an enquiry from a traveller, a ticket clerk at the railway station says 'That'll be £10 for a cheap day return'. The passenger might not initially know what a 'cheap day return' is, and if so may appear puzzled. In then explaining what the phrase 'cheap day return' means, the clerk is justifying the first claim – that what he or she said was intelligible and meaningful, even though the traveller was first of all perplexed by it. It is implicit in what the clerk says that the factual content of the statement is true – that it actually does cost £10 for the ticket (the second validity-claim). The passenger is also likely to take it for granted that the clerk has the right to make such an authoritative pronouncement about the railway fare (the third validity-claim); and that the clerk sincerely believes what he or she says (the fourth validity-claim). Note, however, that there may be circumstances in which any or all of these last three validity-claims may be contested by the passenger – in which case the clerk would be expected to justify or back up the statement that was made. Suppose, for example, the passenger suspected that the person standing on the other side of the counter was someone temporarily standing in for the usual clerk, because the real clerk was away from work. The passenger might then be inclined to check on the factual validity of the statement, and perhaps question the individual's right to be distributing tickets when not authorised by the railway to do so.

Undistorted communication is language-use in which speakers can defend all four validity-claims – where what is said can be shown to be meaningful, true, justified and sincere. Compare communication between analyst and patient, which may be 'systematically distorted' in various ways. What the patient says in free association may not be intelligible, either to the patient or, initially, to the analyst. Its factual content may be in some part false (as in fantasies). The patient may make claims in an unjustified way – for example, blaming others for acts for which they could not reasonably be held responsible. Finally, the patient may either consciously or unconsciously attempt to deceive the analyst in order to resist or evade the implications to which the process of analysis is leading. The aim of psychoanalytic therapy can thus be construed as that of making it possible for the patient to escape whatever psychological limitations inhibit the successful justification of validity-claims in day-to-day discourse.

Habermas argues that, of the four validity-claims, only the second and third can actually be defended *in* discourse – that is to say, by means of the speaker elaborating verbally upon whatever he or she says. The meaningfulness of speech can only be justified by the speaker actually showing that an utterance is intelligible – which is usually done by means of expressing that utterance in a different way. A speaker can only show himself or herself to be sincere by demonstrating sincerity in action (fulfilling promises, honouring commitments, and so on). Truth and justification, however, can be 'discursively redeemed': the speaker can elaborate upon why a given claim is true, or is normatively justified. Habermas's theory of truth has been quite widely influential in the philosophical literature, and leads on directly to his concept of an ideal speech situation, so it is worth sketching out what it involves.

For Habermas (following, in this respect, Strawson 1964) 'truth' is a quality of propositional assertions contained within language-use. Truth is a validity-claim which we attach to the factual content of statements. The simplest way to understand how Habermas develops this view is to begin from what is sometimes called the 'redundancy theory' of truth. According to the redundancy theory, the term 'truth' is a superfluous one, empty of any significance which is not already carried in the assertion of a factual proposition. Thus I might say, 'This table is three feet long'. If I say instead 'It is true that this table is three feet long', the words 'It is true' seem to add nothing to the statement that the table measures three feet. 'It is true' is redundant. Now in a certain sense Habermas agrees with this. In ordinary conversation we would say, in response to a question about the table's measurements, 'This table is three feet long', not 'It is true that this table is three feet long'. But in Habermas's view this is not because the concept of truth is a redundant or unnecessary one. It is because in most contexts of communication the claim to truth is implicit in what the speaker says. It is only when that claim is questioned by another person that the speaker is likely to invoke 'truth' and cognate terms. 'Truth', in other words, is a term brought into play in factual disputes or debates, and the concept of truth can only be properly understood in relation to such processes of argumentation. When we say something is true, we mean we can back up what we say with factual evidence and logical argument – that a claim can be 'warranted' as Habermas says (this time following Toulmin (Toulmin 1964)). Truth refers to agreement or consensus reached by such warrants. A statement is 'true' if any disputant faced by those warrants would concede its validity. Truth is the promise of a rational consensus.

It follows from this that truth is not a relation between an individual perceiver and the world – although it depends upon evidence based on perceptions. Truth is agreement reached through critical discussion. Here Habermas's standpoint seems to face a major difficulty. How are we actually to distinguish a 'rational consensus' – one based upon reasoned argument – from a consensus based merely upon custom, or power? We may gauge the seriousness of the difficulty by considering the problems that have arisen from Kuhn's use of the concept of paradigms in *The Structure of Scientific Revolutions* (Kuhn 1970). Kuhn proposes that a field of study only becomes a science when it acquires a paradigm – when there is a consensus among its practitioners about the basic premises and methods of their activity. But as Kuhn's critics quickly pointed out, the existence of a science cannot *only* depend upon the attainment of a consensus, or else science would be little more than a form of 'mob rule' (Lakatos 1970).

Although Habermas does not directly analyse the controversies surrounding Kuhn's writings, his response to the difficulty is certainly relevant to them. A rational consensus – in any area of factual discussion, including but not limited to science – is one reached purely 'by the force of the better argument'. A claim to truth, in other words, is an assertion that any other person able to weigh the evidence would reach the same conclusion as the individual making that claim. This in turn means that the notion of truth is tied to presumptions about the circumstances in which it is possible for arguments to be assessed in such a way that (1) all pertinent evidence could be brought into play, and (2) nothing apart from logical, reasoned argument is involved in an ensuing consensus. It is these circumstances which Habermas calls an ideal speech situation. An ideal speech situation is one in which there are no external constraints preventing participants from assessing evidence and argument, and in which each participant has an equal and open chance of entering into discussion.

Plainly, most actual conditions of social interaction and communication are not like this. What, then, is the point of attaching so much importance to an ideal speech situation? The answer to the question is twofold. First, for Habermas the ideal speech situation is not an arbitrarily constructed ideal. It is inherent in the nature of language. Anyone who uses language thereby presumes that they can justify the four types of validity-claim, including that of truth. A single utterance holds out the possibility of the existence of a form of social life in which individuals would live in free, equal and open communication with one another. Second, since this is the case, it follows that the ideal speech situation provides a critical measure of the insufficiencies of currently existing forms of interaction and social institutions. Any consensus based either on the sheer weight of tradition, or on the use of power or domination, would be exposed as deviating from a rational consensus. The ideal speech situation hence supposedly provides an 'objectively given' basis for critical theory.

For Habermas the concept of 'rationality' has less to do with the foundations of knowledge than with the manner in which knowledge is used (Habermas 1984: I, ch. 1). To say either that a statement or an action is 'rational' is to claim that the statement or action could be in principle justified in procedures of argumentation. Argumentation, in Habermas's term, is a 'court of appeal' of the rationality inherent in communication, making possible the continuance of communicative relations when disputes arise, without recourse to duress. It is on the basis of the notion of communicative rationality that Habermas attempts to counter relativism, and in terms of which he seeks to interpret the over-all evolution of human society. There may be no universally valid foundations of knowledge – in this respect, as in various others, what Habermas has to say parallels the views of Popper. But procedurally the canons of rationality – that is to say, the modes of reaching warranted conclusions – are the same everywhere.

According to Habermas, we are therefore able to rank both individuals and over-all cultures on a scale of evolutionary development, in which the criterion of evolutionary advancement is 'cognitive adequacy'. By 'cognitive adequacy' Habermas means the range and depth of the defensible validity-claims which they incorporate. In formulating these ideas, Habermas draws heavily from the writings of Piaget (Piaget 1965). Piaget distinguishes three stages in the cognitive development of children, which progressively expand their learning capacities. These correspond, Habermas suggests, to three main phases of social evolution: the 'mythical', 'religious-metaphysical' and the 'modern'. For Piaget, cognitive development is associated with a 'de-centring' process, in which the child gradually moves away from a primitive concentration upon its own immediate concerns and needs, towards an expanded awareness of the world and of the needs of others. Something similar is the case with social evolution. Small-scale, traditional cultures are dominated by myth. Myths are concretised and particular modes of thought, tending to see both other cultures and the material world from the vantage-point of the society in question. They are characteristic of societies which have not developed distinct intellectual arenas within which argumentation can be carried on. The pervasiveness of tradition means that most social activity is organised according to principles sanctified by time, not worked out on the basis of rational discussion and understanding. In Habermas's view, the development of more encompassing religions, more broadly founded than myth, signifies a movement towards the expansion of rationality. The formation of the major 'world religions' – such as Buddhism, Hinduism, Islam or Christianity – tends to be associated with the differentiation of science, law and art as partly separable spheres of activity.

Never loath to utilise a wide variety of intellectual resources, Habermas at this juncture makes appeal to the writings of Max Weber (Habermas 1984: I, ch. 2). But he does so with a critical eye. Weber placed a strong emphasis upon what he called the 'rationalis-ation' of culture, furthered by the world religions, and finding its maximal development in modern Western capitalism. Weber stead-fastly refused to identify the expansion of rationalisation with heightened rationality; a more rationalised form of social life has nothing to commend it over a less rationalised one. For Habermas, of course, this is not acceptable. Where 'rationalisation' means the furthering of procedures and opportunities for argumentation, its development is convergent with the growth of rationality. Weber did not indicate clearly enough the ways in which the rationalisation of the modern West differs from that characteristic of preceding civilisations. According to Habermas, the West alone is marked by the pre-eminence of 'post-conventional' cognitive domains. 'Post-conventional' forms of institutional order are those which have not only freed themselves from the dominance of traditional codes of conduct, but have become organised according to warranted prin-ciples. The most notable institutional sectors in which this process first comes to the fore are those of science and law.

For Habermas, therefore, there is a real sense in which West is best. In advocating such a view, he self-consciously stands in oppo-sition not only to relativism – in whatever sense may be attributed to that term – but also to those schools of social thought which hold the development of Western capitalism to be fundamentally a noxious phenomenon. But he by no means accords unequivocal approval to Western society. On the contrary, modern capitalism as he represents it is a form of society riven by tensions and conflicts. Habermas seemingly still wants to retain elements of the Marxist notion that capitalism is a type of society whose transcendence holds out the possibility of the achievement of a superior type of social order. But both his analysis of the nature of modern capitalism, and the avenues of social change to which it leads, differ very substantially from the classical Marxist conception.

An updated critical theory, Habermas suggests, involves seeing the wider role which science has played in developments since Marx's day – meaning by 'science' here the natural sciences. We live in a society in which science and technology have become inextricably fused, in which science ranks foremost among what Marx called the forces of production. But science has also in a certain sense become extended to the realm of politics. In the capitalist societies, science and technology are harnessed to the aim of delivering stable and extended economic growth. The scope of politics becomes basically reduced to a question of who can run the economy best – a matter of technical decision-making. We can see again that orthodox Marxism offers no critical alternative in this respect. For the chief goal of the Soviet Union is to catch up with, and surpass, the West in terms of economic development. What Habermas calls rather inelegantly the 'scientisation of politics' has proceeded just as far in the East European societies as in the West.

In Habermas's view, the fact that politics has become a sort of technology like any other is one of the chief ideological features of modern capitalism. What other writers have seen as the end of ideology – the draining away of over-all values and ideals in favour of pragmatic, technocratic government – Habermas regards as the very core of what ideology is. For politics should concern struggles over just those values and ideals which can make life meaningful for us. The repression of meaning in positivism, in the more technical spheres of philosophy and social theory, has as its counterpart the repression of meaning in many spheres of modern life.

This is a theme central to Habermas's analysis of the tensions and conflicts involved in capitalist society today. Habermas retains sufficient of the Marxist view to hold that capitalism is still a class society, divided between dominant and subordinate classes. But just as the proletariat is no longer the harbinger of revolution, class conflict is no longer the main source of tension threatening the stability of capitalism, or offering the most likely source of the transformation of the society. Marx's view of class conflict, in Habermas's eyes, was more or less valid for nineteenth-century capitalism. In the nineteenth century, economic life was not yet very highly structured, and was dominated by wide fluctuations of prosperity and slump; capitalists and workers faced one another in the market place as potentially violent antagonists. We live now in an era of technocratically managed capitalism. There still are economic cycles, but they have been substantially diminished by the intervention of governments in economic life. The strains produced by class division have correspondingly been alleviated by the introduction of standardised modes of industrial bargaining and arbitration.

Marx lived and wrote in the phase of 'liberal capitalism' – in which the role of the State in economic life was a restricted one, and where competitive markets held sway. Capitalism today is 'organised capitalism'. Various factors are involved in the transition from the one to the other, including particularly the expanded part played by the State in regulating economic activity, and the stabilising of class relations which results from the existence of standardised modes of industrial arbitration. Competitive markets have been undercut by the increasing dominance of the very large corporations, and by the co-ordination with State planning that a much more highly centralised economy permits. By means of price guarantees, subsidies, the balancing of budgets and forms of fiscal control, together with direct ownership of industry in the shape of the nationalised sector, the State helps to sustain conditions for the stable accumulation of capital. State intervention in economic life, when conjoined to the integration of science with technology, means that Marx's theory of surplus value is no longer applicable in current conditions. Marx based the core of his analysis of capitalism upon the theory that only labour-power creates value, and that profit derives from the surplus of value which capitalists are able to wrest from workers. But government control of education, science and technology injects a new influence, making it possible to affect the value of commodities in ways which cannot adequately be analysed according to the theorems of classical Marxism.

In Marx's time, Habermas accepts, class conflict was a major source of social tension and potential social transformation. But over the course of the past century or so, the disruptive consequences of class division have become moderated. There has come into being in Western countries what he terms a 'class compromise', a compact between the labour movement, big business and government. Unions and business leaders tend to negotiate wage increases and other contractual conditions in a direct way, rather than leaving them open to be determined by the market. There are no longer anything like fully competitive labour markets, any more than there are competitive product markets. Organised labour, in the shape of socialist parties, also has an important political role in the modern

State. Partly as a result of this, organised capitalism is also aptly called 'welfare capitalism'. A range of welfare schemes protect the less privileged from the vagaries of the market – illness and injury benefits, unemployment payments and so on. Class relations thus no longer have the hard edge they did in the nineteenth century; and the labour movement is not today the leading agency of social change. In reaching this conclusion, Habermas's views are in line with those of the Frankfurt School, referred to briefly earlier.

However, here Habermas's ideas take an interesting twist. The tensions involved in class division do not merely disappear, he suggests, they are displaced elsewhere, and reappear in different guise, shaping new forms of oppositional movement. Contemporary capitalist societies are still subject to economic crisis, but conflicts on the purely economic level are less important than those which occur in other institutions. Because economic life is today in considerable degree administered by government, in conjunction with the larger corporations, economic crises rapidly tend to become political ones. In Habermas's view, these are more threatening to the system than are economic problems, because the technocratic character of modern politics cannot generate deep and abiding loyalty to the political order. Politics having become a largely pragmatic affair, the mass of the population feels no real commitment to the political system, and readily becomes alienated from it if that system fails to maintain its narrow brief – i.e., to guide sustained economic growth. In such circumstances, which Habermas believes to be becoming more and more widespread, the political system faces what he terms 'crises of legitimation'. That is to say, because of its confined, technocratic character, the political order lacks the legitimate authority which it needs to govern. Rather than economic contradiction, the tendency to legitimation crisis is for Habermas the most deep-lying contradiction of modern capitalism. Just as class division and economic instability gave rise to the labour movement in the nineteenth century, so this emerging contradiction tends to spawn new social movements in the twentieth century. These are movements which attempt to inject back into political life the values it has lost – to do, for example, with the relations between human beings and the natural world, and human individuals with one another. Such relations involve fundamental moral values, and there are limits to the degree to which they can be subordinated to technocratic imperatives. At those limits, oppositional movements arise which fight back, to recover lost values or change existing ones. Ecological and religious revivalist movements are given by Habermas as examples, as is in some part the women's movement.

The scope of Habermas's writings is extraordinary, ranging as they do from the most abstract problems of philosophy through to quite concrete analyses of social and political issues. It would be out of the question to attempt an overall assessment of them in as concise an account as this. There is no doubt that Habermas has shifted intellectual ground over the course of his career, and this presents commentators on his work with some considerable difficulties. He has admitted to having abandoned some of the notions involved in *Knowledge and Human Interests*, but the discrepancies between the theorems advocated there and his later interpretations of cognitive development and social evolution seem greater than he has publicly accepted to date. Since his work does range so widely, Habermas is often tantalisingly sketchy just at the points where the reader is likely to require special reassurance about the plausibility of what he has to say. Why are there only three aspects of social life which generate knowledge-constitutive interests? Is the idea of knowledge-constitutive interests in fact compatible with the orientation of Habermas's later work on validity-claims, which do not seem to be tied to such interests? Why does Habermas refer so little to the psychoanalytic model of critical theory in his more recent writings? How can he depend so much upon Piaget's writings in developing a theory of social evolution, when the empirical basis of those writings is notoriously insecure? None of these questions, or ones of equivalent importance that could be posed, are to my mind satisfactorily discussed in Habermas's works.

But rather than pursuing any such queries further, let me conclude by briefly taking up again the relation between Habermas and Marxism, which I have used as the main organising thread of this essay. Habermas's ideas evidently stand at a very substantial distance from Marxism in its original form. How far has he succeeded in reuniting theory and practice in a way relevant to the demands of our era? And do we really need a Marx for our times at all? Perhaps Marxism is best forgotten about altogether, as a nineteenth-century theory whch is today simply archaic? So far as the first of these questions goes, it would seem that considerable scepticism is in order. The practical implications of Habermas's writings are not in fact at all easy to discern – although they would presumably involve lending support to the new social movements to which I have just referred. But it seems very doubtful whether any such movements would be capable of playing the sort of world-historical role that Marx envisaged for the proletariat. Moreover, Habermas never lets us know – or at least has not so far let us know – how his views relate to traditional conceptions of socialism. Although it is clear that the East European societies are not regarded by him as exemplars for others to follow, it is by no means apparent how much – if anything – Habermas wishes to retain of a vision of socialism comparable to that held by Marx.

Critical theory as Habermas portrays it has certainly lost the direct tie which Marx saw between the rise of the proletariat and the inevitable demise of capitalism. In Habermas's works it is apparent neither what social forces will overthrow capitalism, nor what type of society will supplant it. In my opinion, however, it would be a mistake to see this as wholly a defect in what Habermas has to say. Rather, it should be regarded as signalling a shortcoming in Marx and in Marxism. For in Marx the so-called 'union of theory and practice' was bolstered by a sort of historical guarantee. The triumph of the proletariat, in other words, was supposed to be the necessary culmination of the whole sweep of world history, which had prepared the way for socialism. If Marxism means a dogmatic certitude in the true course of history, the last thing we want is a Marx for our times. In the shape of Stalinism, a version of this doctrine has already made a dreadful impact in the present century. Habermas's work, informed by a radical defence of human freedom, and by an attempt to confront honestly some of the perplexities of the modern world, is happily fundamentally different from any such view.

FURTHER READING

Habermas's writings do not make easy reading, and it is best to start from one of the various secondary discussions of his work which now exist. One of the most accurate and accessible is to be found in Part Two of Held 1980. This book also contains the most useful general account of Habermas's forerunners in the Frankfurt School. A somewhat more difficult, but interesting and illuminating discussion appears in Jay 1984 (Chapter 9). The most comprehensive account of Habermas's ideas is given in McCarthy 1984. Of Habermas's own books, probably the most important are *Knowledge and Human Interests* (1971a), *Legitimation Crisis* (1973) and *The Theory of Communicative Action* (2 vols., Vol. I 1984, Vol. II forthcoming in English translation). These works should be read in the order listed to get an understanding of the progression of Habermas's views, as well as the changes which they have undergone.

A very large critical literature on Habermas exists, but the reader should pick a way through it with care. There are many critical analyses, particularly earlier ones, which are only poorly informed about the scope of Habermas's work. Some of Habermas's main writings are still unavailable in English, and this has tended to limit the usefulness, and compromise the accuracy, of the critical attacks to which he has been subject. Easily the most comprehensive and penetrating critiques of Habermas are those in Thompson and Held 1982. Among the best of the others are Hesse 1979; Paul Ricoeur 'Hermeneutics and the critique of ideology', in Ricoeur 1981; and Keane 1975. Geuss 1981 is interesting but some of the author's interpretations of the views he criticises have to be regarded as highly questionable.

8

Louis Althusser

by Susan James

A history of Marxist theory in Britain from 1925 to the mid-sixties would be a slim volume: not only did Stalinism muffle discussion of unorthodox ideas by members of the Communist Party, but social theory as an academic subject was also overwhelmingly liberal in its concerns, so that, with some honourable exceptions, academics either ignored Marxism, or treated it as a highly stylised foil for views they found more congenial.

During the sixties, however, this pattern altered, as Marxism came to play a central and flourishing part in academic courses in the arts and social sciences. The causes of this transformation (in some ways a disquieting one to those accustomed to regarding the intelligentsia as the victims and propagators of bourgeois ideology) are complex and diverse. An important catalyst in the process was the enthusiastic reception of the works of a series of European Marxists, all of whom offered fresh and stimulating insights into the tradition inaugurated by Marx and Engels. As beneficiaries of this wave of innovation, British academics were able to address a range of questions inspired and fuelled by Marxism, and to incorporate these into their teaching.

Although the European writers who played such a crucial role in reviving Marxism in this country dealt with a disparate set of issues, they were united by a comparative lack of interest in the strategic problem of how capitalism was to be abolished and transcended. Unlike many of their predecessors, they saw Marx's work not so much as a source of predictions about the future, nor as a manual for revolutionaries, but rather as the genesis of a rich and suggestive explanatory theory. And among the progenitors of what Perry Anderson has called 'Western Marxism' (Anderson 1976), perhaps the most influential of all was Louis Althusser, whose work, regardless of its polemics and lacunae, has largely reshaped the preoccupations of Marxist social theory. As well as refocusing attention on the texts of Marx, Engels and Lenin, it initiated a renewed and intense debate about Marx's central doctrine of historical materialism.

Althusser was born in Algeria in 1918, joined the French Communist Party in 1948, and until 1980 taught philosophy at the Ecole Normale Supérieure in Paris. His enormous intellectual reputation as a grand theorist, which reached its height by about 1970, is founded on two collections of essays, the first of which – *Pour Marx* – was published in 1965. In the same year Althusser gave a series of seminars with Etienne Balibar, which appeared in 1968 as *Lire le*

Capital, a major statement of his view which has remained the single most important work of the Althusserean corpus.

These essays, as well as a number written more recently, are variations on a common theme: the claim that, despite all the attention it has received, Marx's doctrine has so far been radically misunderstood and underestimated. This is partly to be explained, in Althusser's view, by the fact that even Marx did not altogether grasp the significance of his own work, and was only able to express it obliquely and tentatively. As Althusser recounts,

Contrary to certain appearances, or at any rate to my expectations, Marx's methodological reflections in *Capital* do not give us a developed concept, or even an explicit concept of the object of Marxist philosophy. They always provide a means to recognise, identify and focus on it, and finally to think it, but often at the end of a long investigation, and only after piercing the enigma contained in certain expressions. (Althusser and Balibar 1970: 74)

This problem must therefore be overcome. But Althusser argues that it has been compounded by the desire of Marx's commentators to treat his work as a coherent whole, when there is in fact a radical 'epistemological break' within it. While the early works are bound by the categories Marx inherited from German philosophy on the one hand and classical political economy on the other, *The German Ideology* marks a sudden departure: 'something new and unprecedented appears in Marx's work – the seeds of a theory which grows to maturity in *Capital* itself' (Althusser 1976b: 106). Only a careful and sensitive reading will reveal this shift; and only once we are aware of it will we be able to understand Marx's achievement.

Althusser's project is thus to bring us face to face with this extraordinary theory, display its originality, and, most important of all, exhibit its power. To realise such an ambition he must of course show that Marxism can withstand the criticisms commonly directed at it, and since many of the emphases and details of Althusser's argument are to be explained by his desire to rescue Marx from his detractors, it is helpful to bear this condition in mind. In what are perhaps the fiercest passages of *Reading Capital* Althusser denounces a series of interpretations of Marx's work – historicism, idealism, economism ... All are relentlessly condemned on the grounds that they fall short of the insight that Marx constructed a revolutionary view of social change, which Althusser calls 'the science of history' or historical materialism (Althusser and Balibar 1970: 166).

This discovery of a 'continent of knowledge' is comparable, so

Althusser argues, to Thales' contribution to mathematics or Galileo's to physics, in that it established an altogether new kind of theory with a structure quite unlike that of its predecessors (Althusser and Balibar 1970: 166–7). First of all Marx's theory is built on new concepts (such as the forces and relations of production) which have no counterpart in the classical theory of political economy. Even where Marx appears to adopt existing terms (such as surplus value, which seems to combine Ricardo's notions of rent, profit and interest), their relations with other concepts in the theory, and hence their meanings, are significantly different. In addition to its novel structure, however, historical materialism has an explanatory power quite unlike that of classical political economy; for while the latter attempted to explain economic systems as a response to individual needs, Marx analysed a much wider range of social phenomena in terms of the parts they play in a structured whole. *Capital* therefore provides us not just with a model of the economy, but with a way of accounting for the structure and development of a whole society. Most radical of all, moreover, Althusser claims to find underlying this discovery a revolutionary epistemology centring around the rejection of the established distinction between subject and object, which makes Marx's theory quite unlike those of his predecessors, and incompatible with them (Althusser 1972: 185).

Although he has revised his view of the chronology of the epistemological break in Marx's work, and of the extent to which traces of an earlier philosophical stance can be found in later texts, Althusser has held fast to the claim that there is such a transition (Althusser 1976b: 107–18). At the root of this change, he argues lies Marx's rejection of the view held by the classical economists that the needs of individuals could be treated as a fact or 'given' independent of any economic organisation, and could thus serve as a premise for a theory explaining the character of a mode of production. As is well known, Marx argued on the contrary that people's needs are largely created by their social environments and therefore vary with time and place. But Althusser suggests that his opposition to the traditional conception of needs went deeper than this; for as well as giving up the particular conception of needs underpinning classical political economy, Marx abandoned the very idea that there could be an account of what people are like which was prior to any theory about how they come to be that way, and which could thus form an independent starting point for a theory about society (Althusser 1976c: 205).

If the relations between the individual and society are as close as Marx believes, it would be pointless to try to build a social theory on a prior conception of the individual. So Althusser claims that, instead of explaining society by appealing to one kind of factor (individuals), Marx breaks it up into related units called, in Althusserean parlance, practices (Althusser 1969: 166–7). The advantage they have over individuals is that, although each practice only contains a part of the complex phenomenon which is society, each one is a whole in the sense that it consists of various different *kinds* of parts, all of them interrelated. For example, economic practice contains raw materials, tools, individual persons etc., all united in a process of production (ibid.).

Society is conceived as a collection of interconnected wholes – economic practice, ideological practice and politico-legal practice – which together make up one complex whole (Althusser 1969: 199). This analysis is crucial to Althusser's interpretation of historical materialism and is used to defend Marx against the charge of being a vulgar materialist – of positing a distinction between 'base' and 'superstructure' and trying to explain all aspects of the superstructure by appealing to features of the base. Apart from the inherent implausibility of this view, Althusser argues that it is a gross error to attribute it to Marx. For just as he criticises the suggestion that a social theory can be founded on a historical conception of human needs, so he repudiates the idea that we can use an independently defined notion of economic practice to explain other aspects of society. On the contrary, we have to recognise that all practices are dependent on each other, and are interdefined (ibid.: 205).

As an example of this interconnection Althusser points out that among the relations of production of capitalist societies are the buying and selling of labour power by capitalists and workers. These relations, which are part of economic practice, can only exist in the context of a legal system which establishes individual agents as buyers and sellers. And this arrangement, in turn, may have to be maintained by political or ideological means. We can therefore see that certain aspects of economic practice depend upon the so-called superstructure, as well as the other way round, and Althusser emphasises that it is a serious mistake to neglect this aspect of Marx's theory. 'The whole superstructure of the society considered is thus implicit and present in a specific way in the relations of production, i.e. in the fixed structure of the distribution of the means of production and economic functions between determinate categories of production agents' (Althusser and Balibar 1970: 177–8).

Practices are therefore interdependent. But as well as showing us how societies are organised, an analysis couched in these terms might enable us to understand social change, and thus provide a theory of history. We have seen that Althusser invokes certain aspects of political and ideological practice to explain the reproduction of the relations of production. Conversely, the failure of these mechanisms would explain the emergence of new production relations, which in turn would have consequences for other aspects of society. The model for this part of Marx's theory therefore seems to be a system in which an imbalance between two parts may lead to compensatory adjustments at other levels, or may sometimes lead to a major reorganisation of the whole.

In developing this idea Althusser relies on the Marxist concepts of contradiction and non-contradiction, which he claims are in turn illuminated by the notion of a complex structured whole. These ideal types stand at opposite ends of the spectrum of possible relations between practices: practices are contradictory when they grate on one another, so to speak, and non-contradictory when they support one another. Althusser is not in the least apologetic about describing the two relations metaphorically. Philosophy, he says, is bound to be metaphorical, since this is the only way of breaking the bounds of established usage and grasping ideas which are not already intuitively familiar. He then gives a more extended account of the roles of contradiction and non-contradiction and elaborates these descriptions in the course of discussing an example – Lenin's analysis of the Russian Revolution.

Lenin wishes to explain why it was that, although the 'peaceful mask' of capitalism had been torn off in all the countries of Western Europe by the end of the nineteenth century and popular discontent was widespread, it was only in Russia that a successful revolution occurred (Althusser 1969: 94–100). He suggests that this was due to the fact that Russia was the 'weak link' in a 'collection of imperialist states', by virtue of the fact that it contained 'all the contradictions which were then possible within a single state' (ibid.: 95). The explanation of the revolution is consequently traced to two sets of circumstances. The first are conditions within Russia, such as large-scale exploitation in cities, suburbs, mining districts, etc., the disparity between urban industrialisation and the medieval condition of the countryside, and the lack of unity of the ruling class. The second deals with the relation of Russia to the rest of the world, and includes the existence of an elite of Russians, exiled by the Tsar, who had become sophisticated socialists, as well as those aspects of foreign policy which played into the hands of revolutionaries.

Althusser uses this case to support his claim that Marx held a complex view of social change, and did not regard it as the outcome of a single contradiction between the forces and the relations of production. He appeals to the differences between events in Russia and the other parts of Western Europe to show that while a contradiction between the forces and relations of production may be a necessary condition of a situation in which revolution is 'the task of the day', it is clearly not sufficient to bring about a revolution proper (Althusser 1969: 99).

If this contradiction is to become '*active*' in the strongest sense, to become a ruptural principle, there must be an accumulation of 'circumstances' and 'currents' so that whatever their origins and sense (and many of them will necessarily be paradoxically foreign to the revolution in origin and sense, or even its 'direct opponents') they '*fuse*' into a '*ruptural unity*' when they produce the result of the immense majority of the popular masses *grouped* in an assault upon a regime which its ruling classes are *unable to defend*. (Ibid.)

And then he claims that the list of circumstances above were among the factors needed to produce the revolution in Russia. Furthermore, these circumstances are said to be essentially heterogeneous, so that they cannot be seen as aspects of one large contradiction; each is a contradiction within a particular social totality.

If, as in this situation, a vast accumulation of contradictions comes into play *in the same court*, some of which are radically heterogeneous – of different origins, different sense, different *levels* and *points* of application – but which nevertheless 'merge' into a ruptural unity, we can no longer talk of the sole, unique power of the general contradiction. (Ibid.: 100)

Althusser therefore concludes that Marx's concept of contradiction is inseparable from that of a social whole, and borrows a Freudian term to describe the relations between various states of affairs. Changes in social structure are said to be *overdetermined* by numerous contradictions (ibid.: 101).

This interpretation has two important consequences, both of which Althusser presents as strengths of Marx's theory: first, it allows that many kinds of circumstance can contribute to the course of events, and secondly it enables us to understand how these may combine to bring about dramatic and unexpected social changes, or 'ruptures' (ibid.: 100).

Althusser's reading, if it is correct, certainly exonerates Marx from the charge of vulgar materialism. However, as the argument stands it seems to have overshot the mark by removing from true Marxism any kind of materialism at all; for social changes are determined by various kinds of events, all of which have the same causal status. Needless to say, this is not what Althusser intends, and he redresses the balance by stipulating that economic practice, while integrated into the complex whole, does nevertheless play a major part in determining the relations between other spheres. Its influence derives from the fact that the complex whole, in addition to containing contradictory and non-contradictory relations, is what Althusser calls a structure in dominance: one of its aspects dominates the others, in the sense that it has more effect on them than they have on it, and therefore stands out as being of particular significance (Althusser and Balibar 1970: 106). This most prominent aspect of society (which is held to be religious in feudal formations and economic in capitalist ones) (Marx 1974: 81n) is called the 'dominant instance', and Althusser argues that it in turn is determined 'in the last instance' by the economy. That is to say, the economic practice of a society determines which other aspect of it dominates that society as a whole (ibid.: 224).

The idea of determination in the last instance is therefore vital to Althusser's analysis of historical materialism. And since it also links this to his interpretations of the subject and of ideology, it is especially important to try to understand what makes it convincing. Why, in Althusser's view, must there always be a dominant instance determined by economic practice? The answer is to be found, I think, in the underlying belief that any mode of production which distributes wealth away from its producers will not survive unless it can somehow be made acceptable. The *dominant* instance of a society is then that aspect of it which sustains the existing economic system by controlling and justifying its allocation of income and resources. And granted that particular modes of production will be more effectively legitimated by some practices than by others, the exact character of an economy will determine which instance is dominant.

Because Althusser discusses these ideas eliptically and presents his arguments in a highly schematic fashion, it is difficult to know whether he intends them to be taken *au pied de la lettre*. But whether he does or not, it seems reasonable to ask why a society should contain only *one* dominant instance, rather than having a mode of production legitimated in several equally influential ways. It is true that Marx speaks of single practices as central and Althusser may well believe that, as far as exegesis is concerned, no more need be said. However, if his aim is to defend as well as interpret Marx's theory this point becomes more pressing. Some assurance that societies have and must have this structure is surely required, and none is given.

This analysis of practices therefore has a number of limitations. It is interesting, nevertheless, partly as a relatively sophisticated attempt to rework the materialist strand of Marx's theory, and partly because Althusser uses it as the basis for a radical view of social explanation which he claims to find in Marx's mature work. So far, we have seen Althusser argue that in order to understand the structure and development of the social world we should appeal to the properties and relations of practices. But he also makes the stronger claim that all satisfactory explanations *must* be of this type, and in doing so excludes a number of alternatives. In particular, he is anxious to rule out one intuitively familiar form of explanation: the idea that we can explain social phenomena by appealing to a certain range of properties of individual persons, such as their beliefs, desires, preferences and judgements. In Althusser's view this is always an error because individuals are themselves, in all their aspects, determined by social practices.

Much of the time we treat social phenomena as the outcome of clusters of individual actions, and explain these actions in turn as the fruit of people's beliefs and desires, and the expression of their choices and decisions. According to a common view, individual actions, when they are seen in this light, cannot be caused by external factors such as political propaganda, schooling or religious doctrines. *Some* individual properties may be explicable in this manner – for example, my preference for a particular soap powder may be the effect of subliminal advertising. But not *all* my choices, decisions, and judgements can be so explained, because if they were they would not *be* choices, decisions or judgements. Furthermore, because we regard these capacities as an essential part of what it is to be human, we find it hard to imagine someone who lacked them and yet was unmistakably a person. Being able to choose, decide and so forth are conditions of being an agent. And being an agent is a defining characteristic of a normal adult.

Althusser, however, is not impressed by this picture, and argues against it that all our desires, choices, intentions, preferences and judgements are, after all, the effects of the social practices in which we live. We may *think* that they are not. But this is not conclusive proof that we are right. In order to sustain this counter-intuitive view, Marxist history must, he argues, offer an explanatory account of the course of social events which portrays individuals not as actors, but as the supports of social practices. History must be, in Althusser's phrase, a process without a subject (Althusser 1976b: 94–9, 201–7).

By 'the abolition of the subject' Althusser means the abolition of the intentional subject whose desires, motives and beliefs are cited as the explanation of social events and states of affairs. Rather than being regarded as actors who make their own history, individuals are to be seen as the 'supports' of social practices who maintain and reproduce them. As Althusser puts it:

The structure of the relations of production determines the places and functions occupied and adopted by the agents of production, who are never anything more than the occupants of these places, insofar as they are the supports (*Träger*) of these functions. The true 'subjects' (in the sense of constitutive subjects of the process) are therefore not these occupants or functionaries, are not, despite all appearances, the 'obviousness' of the 'given' of naive anthropology, 'concrete individuals', 'real men' – *but the definition and distribution of these places and functions.* (Althusser and Balibar 1970: 180)

This is not to deny, of course, that individuals are causal subjects: they fill various social roles, engage in the work of production, and thereby bring about changes in the social world. But, in keeping with Marx's rejection of *homo oeconomicus*, their intentional properties are to be regarded as consequences, rather than causes, of social practice.

This conception of individuals as determined by social practices is familiar enough, but it remains to see how Althusser fills it out. First of all, because conditions vary from society to society, the social practices in which particular individuals engage will depend on time and place. This much is uncontentious, and provides a defence of the claim that the properties of individuals are not constant, so that – as Althusser puts it – each class has 'its' individuals, whose beliefs and behaviour are founded upon their experiences (Althusser 1976a: 53). However, Althusser also argues that, as well as the manifestations of subjecthood changing from society to society, the concept of subjecthood itself also changes. What it is to be an individual subject fluctuates from ideology to ideology.

Where only a single subject (such and such an individual) is concerned, the existence of the ideas of his belief is material in that *his ideas are his material actions inserted into material practices governed by material rituals which are themselves defined by the material ideological apparatus from which we derive the ideas of that subject* ... It therefore appears that the subject acts in so far as he is acted by the following system: ... Ideology existing in a material ideological apparatus, prescribing material practices governed by a material ritual, which practices exist in the material actions of a subject acting in all consciousness according to his belief. (Althusser 1971: 158–9)

A central part of our view of individual agents is our conviction that there is an explanatory link between belief and action. But Althusser argues that this, too, is the fruit of practice:

The ideological representation of ideology is itself forced to recognise that every 'subject' endowed with a 'consciousness' and believing in the 'ideas' that his 'consciousness' inspires in him and freely accepts, must '*act* according to his ideas', must therefore inscribe his own practice as a free subject in the actions of his material practice. If he does not do so, 'that is wicked' ... In every case, the ideology of ideology thus recognises, despite its imaginary distortion, that the 'ideas' of a human subject exist in his actions, or ought to exist in his actions, and if that is not the case, it sends him other ideas corresponding to the actions (however perverse) that he does perform. (Althusser 1971: 157–8)

Within bourgeois society the human individual is generally regarded as a subject with a certain range of properties including that of being a self-conscious agent. However, people's capacity for perceiving themselves in this way is not innate; it is acquired within a framework of established social practices which impose on them the role (*forme*) of a subject (Althusser 1976a: 95). Each set of social practices not only determines the characteristics of the individuals who engage in it but also supplies them with a conception of the range of properties they can have, and of its limits.

Before we can assess this view, we need to have some idea of how it is that society makes individuals in its own image, and this brings us to the most ambitious and least satisfactory part of the theory that Althusser claims to find in Marx's work. Althusser first argues, as we have seen, that many of our roles and activities are given to us by social practice: the production of steelworkers, for example, is a feature of economic practice, while the production of lawyers is part of politico-legal practice. But other properties of individuals, such as their beliefs about the good life or their metaphysical reflections on the nature of the self, seems to escape these categories. Such things as our values, desires and preferences are inculcated in us, so Althusser claims, by ideological practice, which has the defining property of constituting individuals as subjects (Althusser 1971: 160). This practice consists of Ideological State Apparatuses (ISAs), an assortment of institutions including the family, media, religious organisations and – most important in capitalist societies – the educational system, together with the received ideas they propagate (Althusser 1971: 135–9, 161–70). Some of these apparatuses can be identified as the origin of particular *types* of individual traits. The source of other characteristics, however, cannot be so closely pinned down. There is no particular Ideological State Apparatus which induces in us our belief that individuals are self-conscious agents. Rather, we learn it in the course of learning what it is to be a daughter, schoolchild, black, steelworker, councillor, or whatever.

Despite their many institutional forms, ideologies all constitute subjects in the same way: they all utilise a single functional mechanism, and have an immutable structure 'present in the same form throughout ... the history of class societies' (ibid.: 152). To illustrate this Althusser provides a single, farcical example. He imagines Christian religious ideology (personified in the Voice of God) addressing a string of instructions to an unsuspecting subject. 'This is who you are: you are Peter! This is your origin, you were created by God for all eternity, although you were born in the 1920th year of Our Lord! This is your place in the world! This is what you must do! By these means, if you observe the "law of love" you will be saved, you, Peter, and will become part of the Glorious Body of Christ! Etc....' (ibid.: 166). More seriously, however, Althusser points out that, before individuals can identify themselves as Christians, say, they must already be subjects. And it is by seeing themselves somehow mirrored in ideologies that people are said to acquire their identities (ibid.: 168).

Suggestive as this account may be it leaves many questions unanswered, and Althusser's discussion of ideological practice has been widely attacked by his critics. It is not just that we find it so exceedingly hard to imagine how the various properties of individuals, in all their diversity, could be determined – though this problem is extremely important. It is also difficult to reconcile Althusser's view of ideology with his belief that Marx's science of historical materialism is both interesting and true.

Althusser supposes, as we have seen, that all class societies depend on ideological practice, since without it they would be unable to reproduce themselves and would immediately collapse. And yet ideologies sustain what Althusser calls 'imaginary relations' and serve to mask the exploitative arrangements on which class societies are based (ibid.: 152–6). If we now stop to ask why these arrangements *have* to be masked – why people cannot knowingly be exploited – a problem arises. As some of Althusser's opponents have pointed out, he seems to assume that if people understood the system in which they were living they would not put up with it.

This in turn, however, is to assume that humans have a natural capacity to recognise and reflect on their interests – in short, it is to reinstate exactly the kind of starting-point Marx is supposed to have avoided in a conception of human nature which is prior to and independent of historical materialism (Connolly 1981: 48–56).

As a rebuttal of Althusser's account of the relations between individuals and structured totalities, this objection is incomplete. Ideologies *may* be needed to neutralise human characteristics which are prior to all practices. But might they not also serve to overcome properties of the individual members of a society which are themselves the *result* of other social practices? If this were so, the existence of ideologies could be explained without resorting to an 'anthropological dimension'. Furthermore, an Althusserean who faces this criticism directly will surely reply that there is no question of individuals who have certain 'real interests' being 'duped' by ideology: to talk in this way is to revert to the very problematic Marx was striving to transcend. The function of ideological practice is not to 'deceive' ready-made subjects, but to constitute individuals as subjects. So although a different totality might produce subjects who were neither exploiters nor exploited, such individuals cannot be produced within capitalist societies. For they would have to have escaped the very apparatuses which constitute subjects, and thus would not *be* subjects at all.

This is a strong answer to the question in hand, but it releases a sea of epistemological troubles. First, as we have already noticed, Althusser's account must somehow explain the enormous variety of beliefs and judgements, many of them damaging to the *status quo*, that are found in capitalist societies (and others for that matter). He might perhaps attribute its incompleteness to the fact that he is a 'bourgeois' subject, who can only glimpse an alternative view of the individual: but this defence is still a problem, for even a glimpse suggests that the ISAs of the capitalist totality may be more or less effective, and this variation will have to be explained. Furthermore, the Althussereans' analysis of ideology emphasises the claim that ISAs constitute subjects, at the expense of the view that they legitimate a mode of production. Their reply, as I have imagined it, turns away the suggestion that ISAs somehow 'persuade' people into views and roles which do not reflect their own interest, on the grounds that these apparatuses constitute subjects rather than manipulating them. But social practices only need legitimating if there is some chance that they may be rejected. So it seems that this is a further reason for Althusser to allow that the process of constitution may be more or less successful. On the face of it, two lines of defence seem to be open to him. One alternative is to distinguish the constitution of individuals as intentional subjects who reason, choose and decide, from their constitution as capitalists, workers or lumpenproletariat, and to argue that it is the particular roles of a society which give rise to the need for legitimation. But it is unlikely that Althusser would welcome such an option because, as we saw, he is anxious to reject this very distinction. The other alternative is to claim that the very constitution of individuals as intentional subjects serves to legitimate capitalist modes of production, for only if individuals perceive themselves as free agents will these alienating arrangements seem tolerable. The constitution of subjects, and the simultaneous constitution of the occupants of particular roles would then both be seen as forms of legitimation. This approach to the problem looks the more promising of the two, but it prompts an absolutely central question: What is the status of Althusser's claims about the relation between individuals and structured totalities? How does he know – or how do *we* know – that they are right?

Althusser's answer to this most pressing query has developed in the course of his work. Early on he was anxious to combine the view that our beliefs about the social world are determined by the structured whole with the claim that historical materialism has achieved the status of a science, a body of knowledge which gives us a true account of the world. Later, however, he conceded that this attempt had been unsuccessful, and his earlier rigorous separation of science and ideology misguided (Althusser 1976b: 119). If we are constituted as subjects by the totalities we inhabit, then our beliefs about the divide between science and ideology (Althusser's included) will be determined too, and we cannot expect to arrive at an impartial, objective view of it. Whereas Marx is usually thought to have envisaged a classless society in which people will no longer be deluded by false consciousness, Althusser has posited a determinism so strong as to be inescapable.

Having arrived at a form of relativism deeply uncongenial to Marxism, neither Althusser not his followers have been able to develop their position any further. Their failure to do so has prompted contemporary social theorists not so much to repudiate an Althusserean view outright as to move on to explore other approaches. In many cases, however, the directions they have taken owe a great deal to Althusser, and his philosophical concern with the determinist face of Marxism has provoked a wide range of new work. In social theory it has contributed to a revival of interest in the relations of 'structure' and 'agency' (Giddens 1979 and 1984; Elster 1983), and within Marxist circles has provoked fresh discussion of the doctrine of historical materialism itself (Anderson 1983; Cohen 1978).

That Althusser's writing should have had this impact on professional philosophers and social theorists is hardly surprising. But it is perhaps harder to understand why he should have won such a widespread reputation and become, for a time, one of a small band of leading European intellectuals. The explanation of this phenomenon is, of course, bound to be complicated. But part of it lies in the enthusiasm of other Marxists for the polemical strategy underlying Althusser's approach. To begin with, his emphasis on Marx's materialism excited the sympathy of those who, while committed to Marxism as a general political philosophy, were hostile to the 'humanist' interpretation which focused on its Hegelian aspects. For many people this was no Marxism at all, and Althusser promised a return to something more traditional. This attempt to rejuvenate an old-fashioned commitment also gained in attractiveness from Althusser's close concentration on Marx's texts. It suggested, first of all, a way to escape from the fruitless and divisive discussions of the role of the party which had long dogged Marxist circles in Europe. But it also offered to put Marxists back in touch with their roots, so to speak; to redirect their attention to the writings of Marx, Engels and Lenin themselves, in the hope of gaining a fresh perspective from which to view contemporary issues.

In this Althusser was undoubtedly successful. As he said, summing up his own contribution in characteristically pugilistic terms, 'a "front" was opened'; and it continues to be held (Althusser 1976b: 147).

FURTHER READING

The central claims of Althusser's work are best approached by way of *For Marx* (1969) and 'Ideology and Ideological State Apparatuses' (1971), which serve to introduce the themes of his most important essays – those in *Reading Capital* (Althusser and Balibar 1970). The position he there defends is in turn refined in 'Elements of Self-Criticism' (1976b), where he modifies a number of his key doctrines. The idea of history as 'a process without a subject' receives further attention in 'Reply to John Lewis' (1976a).

The philosophical context of Althusser's work is illuminated by Poster (1975) and Anderson (1976). Callinicos offers a shrewd account of the political circumstances which gave rise to Althusser's view (Callinicos 1982), and has also written an excellent, brief account of his position (Callinicos 1976).

On more specific aspects of Althusser's interpretation of Marx, there is a large literature. The idea that economic practice is 'dominant in the last instance' is expounded and elaborated by Balibar (Althusser and Balibar 1970) and Poulantzas (1973). Althusser's conception of history as a process without a subject is sympathetically viewed by Derrida (1981b), violently attacked by Thompson (1978), and defended against this onslaught by Anderson (1980). It is further discussed by Lukes (1977) and James (1984). The related idea that ideological practices constitute subjects is interestingly criticised by Benton (1977) and Connolly (1981), and is further analysed by Hirst (1976), Rancière (1974) and James (1984). Althusser's claim to have unearthed the *science* of Marxism is critically treated by Balibar (1978).

Finally, a retrospective account of Althusser's influence and his place in French Marxism is the subject of a book by Benton (1984).

9
Claude Lévi-Strauss

by James Boon

> Is mine the only voice to bear witness to
> the impossibility of escapism?

The quotation from *Tristes Tropiques* which heads this essay is indicative of Claude Lévi-Strauss: world-weary, yet enchanted by evidence of remotest human differences; dubious of progress, yet sceptical of regaining anything lost; devoted to systematic analysis of all social, religious, economic and artistic order; and capable of sustained prose of classical balance, baroque counterpoise, and stately pace, marked by open-ended ironic returns. *Tristes Tropiques* was Lévi-Strauss's retrospect on a career already *en marche* and his prospectus for the programme of life's work to which he had become resigned and which he has since achieved as Professor of Anthropology at the Collège de France since 1960, elected to the Académie Française in 1973.

Tristes Tropiques was an autobiography dissolving its 'self' in the act of discovering a cross-cultural, transhistorical 'language', a method. It was a quest *en texte* that metaphorically figured the world's forms, experienced across its tribal vestiges, its colonial margins, and its wartime outcasts in their degraded circumstances. *Tristes Tropiques* was the news that there was no 'news', only repeated transformations. Its narrator – first a voluntary exile, then a forced one – constructed chapters, each in a contrasting tonality, that moved from jaded inter-war Europeans, to bustling New World cities hollowly echoing Old World aspirations, to dispirited settlements remaining from old colonial boomtowns, to not-quite-lost tribesmen descended from large-scale pre-Columbian cultures. It was a book of recollections in which fragmentation and refugee-dom took over. *Tristes Tropiques* revealed a world without destiny, without ultimate aim, a world of remnants. Historical consciousness, an ideology favouring certain privileged societies, alone pretended otherwise.

Tristes Tropiques renounced 'seeking in vain to recreate a lost local colour with the help of fragments and debris' (1977: 33). Manifestly, it was the travel book to end all travel books. Towards putting 'an end to journeying', it mocked its own mission:

Then, insidiously, illusion began to lay its snares. I wished I had lived in the days of *real* journeys, when it was possible to see the full splendour of a spectacle that had not yet been blighted, polluted, and spoilt... Once embarked upon, this guessing game can continue indefinitely. When was the best time to see India? At what period would the study of the Brazilian savages have afforded the purest satisfaction, and revealed them in their least adulterated state? Would it have been better to arrive in Rio in the eighteenth century with Bougainville, or in the sixteenth with Léry and Thevet? For every five years I move back in time, I am able to save a custom, gain a ceremony or share in another belief. But I know the texts too well not to realize that, by going back a century, I am at the same time forgoing data and lines of inquiry which would offer intellectual enrichment. And so I am caught within a circle from which there is no escape: the less human societies were able to communicate with each other and therefore to corrupt each other through contact, the less their respective emissaries were able to perceive the wealth and significance of their diversity. In short, I have only two possibilities: either I can be like some traveller of the olden days, who was faced with a stupendous spectacle, all, or almost all, of which eluded him, or worse still, filled him with scorn and disgust; or I can be a modern traveller, chasing after the vestiges of a vanished reality. I lose on both counts... (1977: 33)

Degradation is the condition of understanding. *Tristes Tropiques* stands in the great Ruskinesque tradition of transvaluing decay. Out of ruins it garnered, if not hope, at least meaning, or signification. It is lyric and mordant, an enigmatic composition more properly accompanied by a descant than by commentary.

In tones of Rousseauesque regret rather than Nietzschean *ressentiment*, Lévi-Strauss resigned himself to the universe of message. What communicates is already corrupted; no pristine purity can speak. Epistemologically and methodologically, one 'knows' not in isolation or directly, but only thanks to the mediation of contrastive others. The circle and cycle through history from culture to culture is full and closed. In this tragicomedy there is no exit, only transpositions of equivalent terms: theme through variations, the same song in different keys plus occasional improvisations, over and over again.

Tristes Tropiques portrayed all cultures – the narrator's own foremost among them – as failures in destiny's eyes. Yet it celebrated the way every culture elaborates value out of precisely what another culture has rejected. Lévi-Strauss approaches human forms as language-like social facts, consensual values, dialectical selections. One summary statement in *The Way of Masks*, written twenty years after *Tristes Tropiques*, argues against interpreting any forms, including artistic creations, simply by what they represent in themselves or by their aesthetic or ritual use:

A mask does not exist in isolation; it supposes other real or potential masks

always by its side, masks that might have been chosen in its stead and substituted for it.... A mask is not primarily what it represents but what it
transforms, that is to say, what it chooses *not* to represent. Like a myth, a
mask denies as much as it affirms. It is not made solely of what it says or
thinks it is saying, but of what it excludes.

Is this not the case for any work of art? ... Contemporary styles do not
ignore one another. Even among peoples called primitive, a certain familiarity is established in the course of wars followed by pillage, intertribal cere-
monies, marriages, markets, occasional commercial exchanges. The
originality of each style [and each culture], therefore, does not preclude bor-
rowings; it stems from a conscious or unconscious wish to declare itself different, to choose from among all the possibilities some that the art of
neighboring peoples has rejected. This is also true of successive styles [from
one period to another]. (1982: 144)

Tristes Tropiques had construed societies, cultures and historical
periods on the whole as dialectical in just this way: significant for
what they suppress as well as evince, each style saying something
'which the preceding style was not saying but was silently inviting
the new style to enunciate' (ibid.). As in Freud, and perhaps Marx,
but not Darwin, everything possible is already prefigured, covertly.

Tristes Tropiques, then, presumed to embody – critics would say
to expropriate – the ethnological calling, declaring it the guilty conscience of Europe's excessiveness, a guilt that the rest of the world is
fated to share:

...Western Europe may have produced anthropologists precisely because
it was a prey to strong feelings of remorse, which forced it to compare its
image with those of different societies in the hope that they would show the
same defects or would help to explain how its own defects had developed
within it. But even if it is true that comparison between our society and all
the rest [*toutes les autres*] whether past or present, undermines the basis of
our society, other societies will suffer the same fate. (1977: 443)

It was and is a book of its culture (France, the West) and against it; a
book of its century and against it; and also against those few other
centuries of the West's political mission to dominate the world's differences. Lévi-Strauss ingeniously, perhaps winkingly, matches
formulas for distinguishing temporal eras to formulas for distinguishing Amazonian societies, in a book designed to convert both
cultures and histories into a catalogue of variations.

The Nambikwara had taken me back to the Stone Age and the Tupi-
Kawahib to the sixteenth century; here [among rubber-producers in the

seringal] I felt I was in the eighteenth century, as one imagines it must have been in the little West Indian ports or along the coast. I had crossed a continent. But the rapidly approaching end of my journey was being brought home to me in the first place by this ascent through layers of time. (1977: 423)

It was written in 1954. Its success in France may be explained by the expanded horizons it offered readers after their wartime claustrophobia, by restoring to comparative studies, ethnology, and worldwide discovery literature inflections from French moral philosophy. Lévi-Strauss had already produced a study of Nambikwara social organisation, based on his ethnographic expeditions in the mid-1930s in Brazil's Amazon basin when he was teaching sociology at the University of São Paulo. He had achieved professional prominence from incisive articles on social structure, linguistic models of cultural phenomena, and difficult issues in comparative method (collected in 1958 in *Structural Anthropology*). Deported from Vichy with other Jewish intellectuals, he had spent time at the New School for Social Research with fellow refugees in New York, where Franz Boas's ethnographic collections were displayed in the American Museum of Natural History. Lévi-Strauss worked with surrealist André Breton, befriended linguist Roman Jakobson, and after the war served as French cultural attaché. Back in France he worked for the Musée de l'Homme and taught comparative tribal religions at the Ecole Pratique des Hautes Etudes. In late 1953, still a 'simple director of studies at the Ecole', he was offered a Full Professorship with tenure at Harvard by the late Talcott Parsons, but declined, unwilling to 'lead to the end of his career an expatriot's life' (Lévi-Strauss 1984: 258).

In 1949 Lévi-Strauss had completed his monumental volume on varieties of exchange systems implicit in different societies' marriage and descent rules. *The Elementary Structures of Kinship* eventually gained controversial renown as a landmark in the general theory of social structure; it remains ardently debated today. In good anthropological fashion the work emphasised societies lacking both centralised agencies of legitimate force and market-based redistribution, where kinship was the encompassing order and/or the template of polity. *Elementary Structures* established Lévi-Strauss as a major heir to Emile Durkheim's work on social solidarity, the division of labour, and primitive religion and to Marcel Mauss's sensitive analyses of non-rationalised systems of ritualised economic exchange. He drew on American anthropology, such as Robert Lowie's systematic comparisons of variant social organisation and kinship nomenclatures; and he developed, critically, efforts by such British structural-functionalists as A. R. Radcliffe-Brown to refine abstractions of rules implicit in fields of social relations. Following many leads in Dutch, British, American and French anthropology, *Elementary Structures* emphasised the importance of an apparent ethnographic curiosity: certain societies make their broadest divisions *by definition* reliant on each other for basic social needs. Here base units (those engaged in production) are socially incomplete, dependent on partner units to reproduce themselves. The most striking cases are organised like multi-party systems constituted in and of the fact that one party must find its spouses among another party. Such societies cannot be construed as an amalgamation of even ideally independent units. Both competition and co-operation are institutionalised across exchange relations; one unit's rival is also its benefactor: those who take are, directly or indirectly through the workings of the whole system of exchanges, those who provide. This paradox forms part of an unprettified 'reciprocity' that Lévi-Strauss has called 'the essence of social life'. Both anti-Hobbes and non-utilitarian (since there is no way totally to divorce self-interest from social interest), this image of solidarity has fundamental implications for political theory and the philosophy of social practice. Lévi-Strauss's *Elementary Structures* effectively posed something like a 'social unconscious' lurking behind all varieties of human public and private life: the 'need' to relate somewhat 'out' (non-incestually), but not too far out, not randomly.

One theme has remained primary in all Lévi-Strauss's works, including his magnum opus on mythology: cultures encode proprieties by imagining their transgressions. Both marriage systems and mythic systems are about proper communication – a kind of combined ethics and aesthetics – balanced against certain threats and risks. The ultimate threat against orderly communication is non-circulation (incest in the realm of social exchange; silence or non-questions and non-answers in the realm of language). The more immediate risk to balanced order is non-return on an investment: for example, no spouse received in return by a social unit that gives up an offspring as another's spouse, or no answer returned on a question posed. Throughout his work Lévi-Strauss draws parallels among ritual recognition of nature's alternation of seasons, the circulation of spouses in society, and the exchange of words in conversation: three realms of proper 'periodicity' in the perpetuated give-and-take called 'culture'. Catherine Clément has handily summarised his views on the 'incorrect distance' that myths envisage in counterdistinction to desirable equilibrium, first citing Lévi-Strauss's central discussion of incest and riddles, a leitmotif in his work on mythic logics:

'Like a solved riddle, incest brings together terms that are supposed to remain separate: son and mother or brother and sister, as does the answer when, against all expectation, it links up with its corresponding question' [Lévi-Strauss 1973a: 33]... The prohibition of incest has an ecological moral. The consequences of incest, of solving the riddle, are decay and flood. By contrast the consequences of estrangement, of chastity, of leaving the answer without a question, is sterility (animal and vegetable). As always in myths there are two opposing dangers: the danger of too much and the danger of not enough, the danger of excess and the danger of lack. 'To the two prospects that may beguile his imagination – the prospect of eternal summer or an eternal winter, the one profligate to the point of corruption, the other pure to the point of sterility – man must resolve himself to prefer the balance and periodicity of the alternation of seasons...' [Lévi-Strauss 1973a: 35]. (Clément 1983: 134–5)

Since *Tristes Tropiques* Lévi-Strauss has continued his detailed analyses of kinship and marriage, ritual and social classifications, and particularly myths in which communication balance-against-excess predominates. Two additional collections of essays have appeared – *Structural Anthropology II* and recently *Le Regard éloigné*, which defends an ethic and aesthetic of mutual distancing. *Paroles données* offers summaries of his courses from 1951 to 1982 at the Ecole Pratique des Hautes Etudes and the Collège de France. But his major work has been a succession of interrelated volumes, each in its way an expansion on different implications of *Tristes Tropiques*: *Totemism*, *The Savage Mind*, the four volumes of *Mythologiques*, and *The Way of the Masks*. The principal predecessors to this corpus remain Durkheim and Mauss, particularly their classic essay on primitive classification, and the works of Franz Boas on Northwest Coast Indian cultures; but Lévi-Strauss has seasoned his accounts with dazzling insights from hosts of social theorists, philosophers, scientists, and literary figures. In all his works he empathises more with the systems he analyses than with their enactors. Critics unsympathetic to this characteristic analytic remove in linguistics, musicology, iconography and similar endeavours consider Lévi-Strauss's work to be overly intellectual, cold, aloof, even sterile. Moreover, his organisation of studies around an encyclopedic range of variations has run counter to the 'ethnographer'-centred works and professional identity that gained ascendency in British and American anthropology through the influence of Bronislaw Malinowski, Margaret Mead and many others.

We shall sample some issues and demonstrations from this difficult corpus below. It is worth noting beforehand that Lévi-Strauss's life's work has unfolded with uncommon consistency and extraordinary controversiality. He has combined tour de force reviews of world ethnographic evidence with polemics designed to make tribal studies, comparative ethnology and mythological analysis play second fiddle to no discipline. He has challenged and responded to challenges from social theorists, existentialists, phenomenologists, psychologists, functionalists, formalists, various fellow anthropologists, and many sentimentalists both past and present. Reactions, both friendly and hostile, to Lévi-Strauss have been complicated by difficulties in translation, by possible misunderstandings on the part of commentators who have explicated his views (particularly, in Britain, Rodney Needham and Edmund Leach), and by internecine wars among French intelligentsia, launched by the celebrated dispute between the Sartre of *Critique de la raison dialectique* and the Lévi-Strauss of *La Pensée sauvage*. Lévi-Strauss has seemed almost to invite controversiality, perhaps because rival approaches are, like contrasting styles and cultures, another source of differences and therefore grist for structuralism which, without oppositions to analyse systematically, would have nothing to say.

1968 was a pivotal year in political perceptions of methods and -isms. Structuralists – a label resisted by most scholars so designated, including Lévi-Strauss – stress systematic order in various dialectic rhythms, promote analytic rigour, and equate the manifest (including manifestos) with the superficial, insisting that profound values (including truths) are inevitably concealed. The political context of 1968 intensified alarm about whether structuralism was compatible with various Marxisms and whether it ultimately drained the 'human' out of humanism. Anything devoted to 'order', even covert marginalised orders of the social and linguistic unconscious, tended to be indicted as part of the establishment's will to oppress and repress. As Clément artfully writes in her narrative recall of the psychologist Jacques Lacan and other so-called structuralists: everything was 'swept away in May 1968 in favor of a return to history, to events, to randomness' (1983: 133). Because it was precisely any positive, absolute sense of history, events and even randomness that Lévi-Strauss had set critically in question, the consequences of 1968 for the reception of his works were extreme. Thus, structuralism, variously defined vis-à-vis Marxism, literary formalism and other movements, has been 'under suspicion' at least since 1968. By now, however, those challenging it are in turn suspect; so the cycles continue. As usual, many foes have actually internalised certain structuralist assumptions. We are all, as the saying goes, structuralist nowadays.

Several broad components of Lévi-Strauss's approach – very different from the structuralisms of Piaget, Chomsky, Dumézil and others – should be mentioned before sketching some intricacies of his work. Like Boas, Edward Sapir and other predecessors, he was stimulated by modern linguistic convictions that every language is both a self-sufficient communication system and a variation on more abstract principles, ultimately on 'language' in general. He incorporated many ideas and methods from Ferdinand de Saussure's models of languages as systems of signifiers–signifieds, Roman Jakobson's poetics of message-making, and other structural linguistics, adapting them to studies of social system, ritual and mythic data. His structuralism is characterised by a doubled trajectory of obsessive attention to ethnographic detail (everything a potential 'sign'), plus bolder generalisation, even grand universals, about human rules such as the incest taboo. He has become the purveyor of Grand Theory par excellence. For example, all societies restrict allowed sexual partners and back up these rules with other classifications; the more interesting point, however, is that all societies (universalisation) do so variably (significant differences).

Lévi-Strauss employs technical terms, such as Saussurian distinctions between *langue* (the systematic basis of a language act's communicability) and *parole* (the continuously altering language acts themselves). A related distinction opposes synchronic analysis (abstracting a system, a *langue*, as if it were timeless) to diachronic analysis where temporal duration is factored in. ('Diachrony', which must be understood in counter-distinction to 'synchrony', should not be confused with 'history'.) Also important are notions of 'binary oppositions' and 'distinctive features' that effect selective connections of relationships across different sectors of rule and meaning. These important analytic devices enable structuralism to approach everything in experience as 'matter for' communication codes. Such codes interrelate values and practice; they establish terms of exchange among different social divisions and cultural categories; and they constrain the possibilities of translation across languages and cultures. In the extreme, structuralism equates life, or knowledge of it, with language (or with structuralism's disputed view of language). It is intent on how things signify, on the way societies produce meaning, not truth. Meanings produced are conventionally called 'cultures'.

Lévi-Strauss developed his method explicitly against functionalist notions of societies as ideally stable isolates, whose different parts interlock and reinforce each other in machine-like or organism-like fashion. He has rejected some views of Durkheim and certain followers who made metaphors of organicism and mechanism central in conceptualising societies. Yet he has praised Durkheim's emphasis on contradictions that sustain social and cultural divisions; here Durkheim foreshadowed structuralism. Standard functionalist theories consider contradictions in any system as potential obstacles to its proper functioning, which must be corrected, repaired, purged, or cured. This is a therapeutic model in which contradiction is not so much integrated as released and tensions felt by the actors thus eased. In contrast, structuralist theories consider contradiction unavoidable; this much they share with various schools of dialectic, including Hegelian and Marxist ones. Systems, such as sets of mythic variants, operate not despite contradiction but by means of it (an example will be given below). Systems exist *for* differential communication, not for stability. In the advanced structuralism of Lévi-Strauss's *Mythologiques*, one need imagine no social stability nor even equilibrium. Rather one traces cultural codes that achieve relative and transient order out of relative randomness through continuous adjustments, shifts, and ongoing fluctuations. Although Lévi-Strauss has questioned the adequacy of conventional causal models in theories of change (compare Michel Foucault), he has not, as is often charged, ignored history. (Indeed *Structural Anthropology* began with a chapter declaring ethnology and the historiography of founders of the *Annales* School to be ideal alliance partners.) He has, however, proposed that 'history', like everything else, can only be known and transmitted through codes of contrasts. History is not a privileged form of consciousness and offers no exclusive access to either truth or freedom. For Lévi-Strauss, time, like space, exists at the human level *for variation*.

The fabric of Lévi-Strauss's corpus

Lévi-Strauss seldom converts his investigations into conventional didactic formats. Instead, he writes retrospects of his discovery process. His books are kaleidoscopic extensions of their subject matter; they contain spirited puns and unremittingly erudite allusions. This serious playfulness has made Lévi-Strauss notorious among literal-minded readers suspicious of *doubles entendres* (his *entendres* may be even trebled or quadrupled, although he avoids graphic antics and 'letterplay' favoured by post-structuralists writing in the wake of Mallarmé). His works have been declared harder to pin down than the myths they analyse. They sustain, with added precision, the play of contrastive relations across sensory orders that myths, ritual and social regulations are shown to contain.

Readers of the French editions of Lévi-Strauss receive fairer warning of his quality of mind and prose. The self-conscious titles are matched by emblematic covers devised to expand the arguments' relevance. Translation kills the puns; and original cover illustrations have been removed in English versions. The most notorious example is *La Pensée sauvage* (both 'savage thought' and 'wild pansy'), whose original floral cover illustrated an appendix (both deleted in *The Savage Mind*) offering European examples of concrete symbols for abstract classifications, complementing the book's elucidation of tribal logics and practice. For reasons equally obscure, complex cover illustrations of *Mythologiques* have been removed from English editions. We thus lose this level of demonstration along with the rhyme that orchestrates the tetralogy's titles into a cycle (Lévi-Strauss compares them to Wagner's *Ring*). Upon completing the pathbreaking series, he claimed that he had always intended that the uncultured *cru* of *Le Cru et le cuit (The Raw and the Cooked)* would modulate into variant cooking customs, then dress codes, winding eventually back to the natural *nu* of *L'Homme nu (The Naked Man)*. He thus wrapped up, between *le cru* and *le nu*, over two thousand pages interrelating tribal techniques and ethics in areas of cooking, food production and preparation, hunting, warfare, domestic consumption, menstruation, age grading, costume creation and exchange, and related cultural arts. The entire

set of *Mythologiques*' titles bears scrutiny: one is a juxtaposed opposition *(Le Cru et le cuit)*; one names a transforming process linking
honey (beyond the raw) to ashes (beyond the cooked) *(Du Miel aux
cendres)*; one is a classic just-so formula *(L'Origine des manières de
table)*; and the last is a modified noun, in fact *the* modified noun
(L'Homme nu). Each title's form encapsulates distinctive mythic
operations and narrative emphases. *Mythologiques* is simultaneously an elaborately contextualised comparative analysis of
select components of New World aboriginals and an intricate
typology of different myths, different modes of ordering variants,
plus critiques of the history of reductive explanations of mythology
and related cultural forms.

The volumes' most sustained generalisation is that myth is to
semantics or meaning *(sens)* as music is to sound *(sons)*, and that
complementary spheres of human order are myth, music, mathematics, and language, four autonomous varieties of 'meta-codes'
or codes of codes. Music thus joins a series of metaphors that Lévi-
Strauss has developed for structuralist analysis itself. Over the years
he has also likened structuralism to mathematics (algebraic models),
language (linguistic models) and myth (structuralism as the 'myth of
mythology', exponential to myth as myth is exponential to
language). When Lévi-Strauss draws an analogy between myth and
music (one bundles semantic features, the other sonic features), he
characteristically develops the point by reversing the equation:

Myth coded in sounds in place of words, the musical work affords a table of
decodings [*une grille de déchiffrement*], a matrix of relationships that filter
and organise lived experience, substitutes itself for that experience and
procures the beneficent illusion that contradictions can be surmounted and
difficulties resolved. (Lévi-Strauss 1981/1971: 590–1; my trans.)

Lévi-Strauss views all cultural forms as 'necessary illusions', systems
of signification substituted for experiences that cannot be communi-
cated, cannot be 'known', directly, however they are lived.

Musical analogies work at many different levels in *Mythologiques*. For example, the striking 'Overture' to *The Raw and the
Cooked* includes a musicological parallel for its implicit typology of
narrative forms and the pattern of emergence, development, and
eventual exhaustion detected in cycles of myths. Lévi-Strauss contrasts dominant tendencies in Bach and Stravinsky (whose works
emphasised what he calls 'code'), Beethoven and Ravel (who emphasised 'message'), and Wagner and Debussy (who emphasised

'myth'). Works of the first pair tend 'to expound and to comment on the rules of a particular musical discourse; the second group tell a tale; the third group code their messages by means of elements that already partake of the nature of narrative' (Lévi-Strauss 1969b: 30). Lévi-Strauss then winks at his own analogy in a witty footnote (mysteriously deleted from the first English translation of the 'Overture' in *Yale French Studies* that influenced many critics before they ever saw the volume):

Needless to say, I took the first six names that came to mind. But this was perhaps not entirely an effect of chance, since it turns out that when one lists these composers in chronological order [Bach, Beethoven, Wagner, Debussy, Ravel, Stravinsky], the special functions to which they relate form a closed cycle [code, message, myth, myth, message, code], as if to demonstrate that in the space of two centuries tonal music has exhausted its internal possibilities of renewal. (Lévi-Strauss 1969b: 30)

Both playfully and profoundly, Lévi-Strauss views everything as pulsating cycles coding both affect and intellect, a rhythm repeated in his works' organisation.

A brief essay can merely allude to such reverberations in books Lévi-Strauss has called 'the negative of a symphony'. I wanted, however, to signal this macro-dimension of his corpus – frustrating to many, exhilarating to some – before breaking the old news that similar qualities exist on the micro-level as well. To illustrate well-known difficulties, I shall summarise several paragraphs from *The Savage Mind* (1966: 49–54) that typify most pages of his fifteen books. Densely woven data is laced with methodological guidelines, provisos, theoretical tenets, and assessments of rich New World variations in ritual taboos (particularly varieties of isolation during menstruation), posed against the West's movement toward conformity. This comparative theme of *Mythologiques* was rehearsed in *The Savage Mind* in an analysis first developed for a course in 1959–60 (Lévi-Strauss 1984: 268–72).

The ostensible subject is eagle hunting among North American aboriginal Hidatsa, who credit supernatural animals with teaching their men its special techniques. A long-standing ethnographic question has been attested by several investigators: Was this culture-hero the black bear or the wolverine (Latin name provided)? Lévi-Strauss considers the identification vital for interpreting Hidatsa hunting. Lacking direct evidence, he reviews the etymology of the Indian name for 'wolverine' and the folklore of neighbouring tribes concerning wolverines' gluttony and cunning in craftily avoiding being trapped; wolverines steal both trapped animals and the traps themselves. Lévi-Strauss then turns to the Hidatsa context: hunters here hide in pits waiting for eagles to take the bait. (He reserves additional vital facts for later: that the bait must be bloody and that the eagles themselves are strangled bloodlessly.) Hidatsa eagle hunters thus assume the location reserved in all other kinds of hunting for the trapped animal. Simultaneously hunter and hunted, the eagle hunter embodies a contradiction. Lévi-Strauss compares his paradoxical quality to the contradictory reputation of the wolverine: both hunter and hunted, unfearing of traps, trapping the trapped in turn.

We recall that for Lévi-Strauss the basic logical process behind myth (and ritual which relates to myth dialectically) is to *convert* contradictions, not so much to solve them as to surmount them (or 'motivate' them in the Saussurian sense) by restating their components in other terms. Lévi-Strauss suggests a totemic equivalence between the eagle hunter and the wolverine: wolverine is to Hidatsa nature as eagle hunter is to Hidatsa culture. He demonstrates an analogy between the contradictions each represents. 'Analogies of contradictory relationships', by the way, is one bare-bones definition of '*pensée sauvage*'.

Lévi-Strauss next broaches explicit hunting cosmology. Eagle hunting's special style ritually conjoins the distant extremes of the Hidatsa cosmos: *subterranean* hunters capture an *aerial* quarry, portrayed in myths as soaring the highest. Many obscurities in ritual and practice can now be clarified. Myths narrated during hunting expeditions portray wildcats and raccoons as culture heroes who bestow arrows and are forbidden as eagle bait. Eagle hunting is unique in eliminating intermediaries between hunter and game: eagles must be killed without arrows, and animals associated with arrows may not be used to lure eagles. More is afoot here than protecting valued plumage from bloodstains. A classification of hunting styles, creatures, and tools emerges. Lévi-Strauss could have set it out didactically; instead he coaxes it from data during the course of his prose. He might well have provided a diagram of pluses and minuses as an alternative projection of the same data, but in this case he did not.

Lévi-Strauss next reveals what may be the guiding anomaly of this entire analysis, although he does not here say so (I surmise as much from the way *Mythologiques* eventually developed; one can never know for sure in a structuralist study whether 'leads' were there at the start or discovered retrospectively). Contrary to all other Hidatsa hunting, and to most hunting rituals everywhere, menstruating women are considered beneficial rather than inauspicious in capturing eagles. Menstrual blood is both a metaphor for blood and organic decay (like bait) and a part (a metonym) of the ritual materials. One Hidatsa word means both a lover's embrace and the grasping of bait by eagles. Lévi-Strauss relates these points to Amerindian ideas of excessive unions, where components ordinarily separated by proper periodicities are dangerously conjoined. Eagle hunting and intercourse during menstruation are conceptualised in parallel, both tied to complex codes of orderly succession versus putrefication and rot – another fundamental topic of *Mythologiques*.

At this juncture Lévi-Strauss's analysis accelerates its pace and increases its sweep. It happens that eagle hunting is an indicator of differences between hunter-gatherers' and agriculturalists' ideologies of pollution. By construing 'eagle' not referentially but operationally as 'bloodless game lured in the presence of menstrual blood', interesting comparisons can be made with prominent Pueblo mythology. Lévi-Strauss investigates not what eagles mean to Pueblos but how whatever eagles might mean to Pueblos can clarify whatever eagles might mean to Hidatsa. His analyses remain equally removed – *éloigné* – from any particular case (including Hidatsa); they are essentially comparative. Because the Pueblo myths equate an eagle-girl protagonist and a ghost wife, Lévi-Strauss leaps to South American evidence also devoted to ghost wives, thus clarifying certain historical and geographical issues, without necessarily claiming that all the myths were borrowed from a common northern source. He concludes with his famous kind of disclaimer: 'The most that can be said ... is that analogous logical structures can be constructed by means of different lexical resources. It is not the elements themselves but only the relations between them which are constant' (1966: 53).

This kind of essayette represents, I suggest, the 'atom' of all Lévi-Strauss's works. Both their advantages and their limitations can be better appreciated if one concentrates on the strategies and logic of such paragraphs, rather than seeking some surefire Gallic gimmick, as so many commentators on his method have done. The pages are vintage Lévi-Strauss; no detail of evidence can be ignored; what is trivial in one case may be paramount in another (more echoes of

Freud), whether myth to myth or culture to culture (different levels of transformed selections). Moreover, one never knows what contents will signify until proceeding empirically.

Principles outlined in *Totemism* and *The Savage Mind* continue through *Mythologiques*. Ranging across the universe of Amerindian tribal values, the books gain critical leverage against standardised uniformity engendered in Western political, economic, and historical supremacy. In continuity with both Durkheimian sociology and Boasian ethnology, Lévi-Strauss remains pro-difference, pro-variegation over monoculture, pro-spices over bland cuisine, pro-cold societies over hot states, while perfectly aware that most trends are running against him and, more importantly, against *them*. He criticises Western science and philosophy for abetting forces of centralisation and standardisation that level differences. Paradoxically, however, he also congratulates the human sciences for coming to understand the significance of tribal and archaic codes, at last recognising that Western reason and rationality is itself just one variation in the human field of differential knowledge. Thus tribal-style logics ultimately win out in Lévi-Strauss's sense of the history of ideas in the human sciences.

Lévi-Strauss often concludes his books with a nod to the nothingness (*rien*) prevalent in existentialist values that he has rejected yet whose anxiety of the void he shares. He describes both his own studies and cultures themselves as means of setting in abeyance not *anomie* but *ennui*. He often *also* concludes his books (many have multiple endings) with mysterious hints of communication between the human and non-human worlds: knowing glances exchanged with a cat, conversations with hermetic lilies, genetic and topological codes interrelating all forms of life and structure, including human consciousness. Somewhere between the extremes of not-being and being (Lévi-Strauss theatrically invokes at the end of *L'Homme nu* Hamlet's false alternatives) – and somewhere within the full circle of relentless transformations without progress – pulse the variational forms that Lévi-Strauss's works pursue and in whose nature they participate. In this human condition of permuting messages, there is endless additional information, but never the total picture and no news. Lévi-Strauss's method promises no escape to freedom or even autonomy; such states themselves are deemed relative to one's position in a system. There is in his exquisite resignation no escapism. Only communicate.

FURTHER READING

Few scholars have ever achieved Lévi-Strauss's interdisciplinary impact, and perhaps no scholar has had more books written about his work during his lifetime. His career has been a phenomenon. Moreover, the literature on structuralism – for, against and ambivalent – and on approaches that define themselves against it would fill a good-sized public library. I restrict suggestions to several recent volumes that provide helpful orientations; their bibliographies contain abundant additional readings.

A useful guide to technical concepts in structuralism, semiotics and component fields is Ducrot and Todorov 1979. Constructive reviews on post-structuralism and structuralism are compiled in Harari 1979. Interesting essays extending Lévi-Strauss's ideas into classics, intellectual history, and comparative religion appear in Izard and Smith 1982. Two new volumes edited by Rossi (1982a, 1982b) revisit and sustain many vexed issues in kinship analysis, structuralist Marxism, and structuralist challenges to positivism. On relations between Lévi-Strauss and other varieties of symbolic analysis, structural-functionalism, and semiotics, see Boon 1982 and Singer 1984.

No book about Lévi-Strauss is an adequate substitute for books by Lévi-Strauss. His two most accessible full-length studies, apart from *Tristes Tropiques* (1977), are *Totemism* (1963b) and *The Way of Masks* (1982).

10

The *Annales* historians

by Stuart Clark

The idea that history is best seen as a narrative of the deeds of individual political actors was first seriously challenged during the French Enlightenment. Voltaire and Montesquieu were typical in arguing for what was called a more 'philosophical' account of the past. This eighteenth-century 'new history' was to be more concerned with the manners, customs and beliefs of whole peoples and with the broad patterns of their social and cultural development. In the last fifty years a new and more radical attempt has been made to displace political actions from the centre of historical attention, and again it has come from France. It has emerged mainly in the work of those historians associated since 1946 with the journal *Annales: Economies, sociétés, civilisations*, and since 1947 with the Sixième Section of the Ecole Pratique des Hautes Etudes in Paris – now an independent institution with its own title of Ecole des Hautes Etudes en Sciences Sociales. The most important single influence has been that of Fernand Braudel, sole editor of *Annales* from 1957 to 1968 and president of the Sixième Section from 1956 to 1972. Exercised through these commanding positions in French academic life and in dozens of occasional lectures and essays, this influence is nevertheless largely attributable to one remarkable piece of work – his *The Mediterranean and the Mediterranean World in the Age of Philip II*. First published in 1949 and again in a substantially revised version of 1966, it remains the most original as well as the most originative contribution to *Annales* history (Braudel 1972/3).

What is significant here is not so much any major revision of the techniques of empirical enquiry, although the relentless pursuit of the quantifiable which has become a hallmark of *Annales* represents just such a departure. Rather, it is the re-injection into supposedly doctrineless history – the *histoire historisante* of 'pure facts' which Braudel associated with the French methodologists Charles-Victor Langlois and Charles Seignobos – of a fresh commitment to an overarching social theory. In an inaugural address to the Collège de France in 1950 Braudel talked of this theoretical reorientation of French historiography and of its far greater relevance to post-war society. Searching for a formula to capture its essence he suggested that of all the innovations wrought by the *Annales* historians the most decisive was that of 'transcending the individual and the particular event'. Hitherto, the problems of history had been set (if at all) by the analytical philosophers. Attention was accordingly given to its logical status as a predictive tool, to the conditions of its objectivity, and other similar issues. But this was to conceive of the discipline merely in epistemological terms, and in particular as a more or less successful attempt to match present depictions with a past 'landscape'. Instead, Braudel argued, the problems of the historian lay in the 'landscape' itself; they arose from the very character of human affairs. Traditional history had, despite itself, rested covertly on twin beliefs in the dominance of exceptional actor-heroes and in the influence of the instant and the dramatic in men's lives. The threat of the contingent was overcome by the imposition of narrative order. It was the task of the new history, led so to speak 'by life itself', to uncover the impersonal forces which in reality fashioned men and their destinies and to plot the slower rhythms at which social time in fact moved (Braudel 1980: 6–11, 17; cf. Ricoeur 1980: 7–12).

Annales history has been governed, then, not by a choice between epistemologies but by a preferred philosophy of action, what Braudel has called 'a whole new way of conceiving of social affairs' (Braudel 1980: 33). In epistemological terms very much less separates it from the historical positivism it sought to replace. It is distinguished above all by a view of human experience in which the individual agent and the individual occurrence cease to be the central elements in social explanation. Since events are constituted largely by the force of many different conjunctural and structural circumstances, it follows that the historian's time cannot be that of the linear narrative and his interests cannot be limited by the merely political. Since these circumstances both outweigh the reasonings and choices of particular men and women and yet do so differently in different epochs, the historian must beware of both a traditional voluntarism and the anachronism which comes from assuming that the springs of action have themselves always been uniform – as though history could be reduced to 'a monotonous game, always changing yet always the same, like the thousand combinations of pieces in a game of chess' (Braudel 1980: 11).

It is to these principles that we can trace, above all, that celebrated people-less, almost immobile history of the 'eco-demographic' *ancien régime* which in the last thirty years has been one of the preoccupations of *Annales* (Le Roy Ladurie 1981: 1–27). However, French impatience with the conventional narrative history of politics has its origins before the war. It was in order to break down the intellectual walls which surrounded it that the medievalist Marc Bloch and his colleague at the university of Strasbourg, Lucien Febvre, founded the first *Annales* (the *Annales d'histoire economique et sociale*) in 1929. In their own discipline they were admirers of the warmer, more rounded vision of Michelet and they were scornful of what they regarded as the sterile positivism of official French historiography – the *histoire Sorbonniste*. But their inspiration was really derived from the other social sciences and from those, like Henri Berr, who believed in their essential interdependence. From Henri Wallon and Charles Blondel, Febvre derived a life-long interest in social psychology. From the human geographer Paul Vidal de la Blache (Braudel later called him 'the most influential of all'), he learned to recognise the different ways in which societies responded to physical environments. From the philosopher Lévy-Bruhl, he and Bloch developed the notion that beyond individual thinkers and their particular expressions of value and belief lay patterned systems of thought – 'mentalities' – which differed radically from age to age. Above all, following Durkheim, both historians accepted the primacy of the social and the collective in the lives of historical agents.

As a result, they came to think of the history of discrete events, linked only by their place in a chronological series, as hopelessly artificial and irrelevant. The manifesto which opened the new journal attacked the ideals of Von Ranke and the cult of detail with a venom worthy of Voltaire. Bloch's *Feudal Society* of 1939–40 was accordingly an analysis of the structural relationships which linked the society, the economy, the politics, the technology and the psychology of the feudal world. Febvre's classic study *The Problem of Unbelief in the Sixteenth Century*, published in 1942, related a particular intellectual event to the structural conditions for its occurrence – in this case its non-occurrence. He argued that it was anachronistic to attribute atheistic beliefs to Rabelais and his contemporaries since the absence of certain linguistic and conceptual tools from their mental resources imposed limits on their capacity to disbelieve.

The post-war *Annales* historians always acknowledged a debt to these pre-war pioneers. Conjunction with the other studies of society – Braudel's 'common market of the human sciences' – continued to be a preoccupation. Fresh intellectual inspiration came from the philosopher-economist François Simiand, the anthropologist Marcel Mauss and the sociologist Georges Gurvitch. But there was also a noticeable shift of interests and a hardening in the overall historical philosophy. Febvre and Bloch retained a lively interest in mentalities and in collective psychology. The classics of the second generation – for example, the studies of Beauvais and the Beauvaisis by Pierre Goubert, of Languedoc by Emmanuel Le Roy Ladurie, and of the Basse-Provence by René Baehrel, together with Braudel's *The Mediterranean* itself – were all firmly rooted in the analysis of socio-economic and, above all, demographic patterns. It is only recently that *Annales* historians have returned on any scale to the subject of mentalities.

For Febvre and Bloch too, events and structures were still complementary aspects of reality and factors like will and intention were recognised to be important. Febvre in particular set himself against any form of geographical determinism, following instead the 'possibilism' of de la Blache and stressing the idea that environments are as much vehicles of endowed meanings as brute facts about the external world. Those who came after tended to adopt a far more determinist position and neglected almost entirely the element of purposive human action in historical change. More than once Braudel has alluded to the contribution of the war itself in bringing this about. National disaster and the experience of captivity drove him decisively away from events and the historical perspective in which they mattered. No less than other intellectuals, historians were forced by catastrophe to think freshly about fundamental issues; but they did so in a manner which set them apart from the dominant existentialism of the post-war era.

We can see this above all in the view of change which has been the guiding principle of Braudel's own work. He has always argued that historical time may be divided into units of varying duration according to the rate at which change occurs in its various sectors. There is, first of all, the short time-span taken by events. This is the time sector of individual actors in their various engagements, the fast-moving time of micro-history, the time of the instant and the immediate. It is, of course, the concern of the traditional narrative – indeed, its only concern. Secondly, Braudel distinguishes an intermediate rate of change which he calls the time of *conjonctures*. This is the time taken by the broader movements of economies, social structures, political institutions and civilisations. Here the pace is slower and the durations are those of, for example, cyclical movements in prices and wages, the rhythms and phases of demographic, technological and social change, and the trends and tendencies of trade and exchange. Such phases last for five, ten, twenty, perhaps fifty years. Finally, there is the span of longest duration, *histoire de la longue durée*, where time is almost stationary and the historian needs the perspective of centuries – secular or multi-secular – in order to recognise and plot any change at all. This is the domain of man's biological, geo-physical and climatic circumstances, of 'man in his intimate relationship to the earth which bears and feeds him'. It is to these ponderous realities which time takes so long to erode that Braudel has given the name 'structures' (Braudel 1972/3: 20–1; Braudel 1980: 10–13, 27–34, 74).

This is the triple division which in reverse order governs his general vision of the Mediterranean world in the sixteenth century. The book opens with the *longue durée* of the environmental features of the sea itself, its physical surroundings and climate, together with the patterns of human movement, settlement and communication produced by them. It then proceeds to the demographic, economic and commercial trends of Philip II's reign and to forms of social grouping, institutions and warfare. It ends traditionally with 'events, politics, and people'. Braudel believes that this is a decisive reversal of priorities, and that the slow-paced history of structures is in particular capable of making a vital contribution to social theory. This is not simply because demographic cycles or patterns of climate, being immeasurable on a time-scale dealing with transience, have hitherto been invisible to historians. He is arguing for much more than a pluralistic view of time consequent upon a different choice of subject matter. Nor is it only a matter of using the long term, with its stress on continuity and recurrence, to bring the past into contact with the present – though Braudel does feel strongly about this too.

What really lies behind his enthusiasm for structural history is a view of social explanation, above all an emphasis on the determining effects of structures on those who inhabit them. Marcel Bataillon, the historian of Spain, who was one of the examiners when *The Mediterranean* was submitted as a *thèse* in 1947, wrote later that it was a study of chance and necessity in human lives. Braudel is certainly not doctrinaire on this issue, nor is he a believer in the 'imperialism' of one exclusively dominant factor in history. In his inaugural address of 1950 he insisted, 'There is no unilateral history.' He does not neglect, at least in principle, the possibility of interaction between history's various time layers. The historian deals with what he calls a 'dialectic' of the time spans and his eventual aim should be to balance the opposition between the instantaneous and the durable in a unitary account. In one of his most disarming remarks he adopts the imagery of the hour-glass to evoke the ever-reversible movement in explanation from events to structures and from structures to events (Braudel 1980: 10, 38, 50; Braudel 1972/3: 903).

In fact, this is a rather misleading image, for like the reference to a dialectic it suggests an equality between the counter-poised elements in historical explanation. And neither in his theory nor in his practice is Braudel prepared to concede such an equality. We need only turn to the many more disparaging images in which he has expressed his hostility to events. They are seen (ironically enough by the historian of the Mediterranean) as 'surface disturbances, crests of foam that the tides of history carry on their strong backs'. They have the evanescent quality of smoke and vapour; like single blooms they flourish for a day and then fade; they lie like dust on the more solid objects of the past. In an especially memorable passage Braudel compares them to a display of fireflies which he had once seen in Brazil: 'their pale lights glowed, went out, shone again, all without piercing the night with any true illumination. So it is with events; beyond their glow, darkness prevails' (Braudel 1949: 721; Braudel 1972/3: 21, 901; Braudel 1980: 10–11, 67).

Elsewhere Braudel describes the world of events as narrow, superficial, ephemeral, provisional and capricious. Above all, it is the world of illusion. He does not deny that like the other layers of history it has its own reality, but he argues that this is reality as it appears to agents, not reality as it *is*. This is the world of the consciousness of the individual, but the men and women who inhabit it are victims of false consciousness. The perspectives in which they view their lives are too short and constricted to allow them to discriminate properly between what is important and what is trivial. They themselves grasp the passage of time only 'narratively' from the headlong rush of day-to-day happenings, and most of what Braudel calls real history therefore escapes them. Naturally they think of their affairs in terms of the categories of intention, choice and self-determination. This is a world in which 'great men appear regularly organizing things, like conductors organizing their orchestras'. But they fail to recognise those forces which are separate from them but which fashion what they do – just as the destinies of Turks and Christians alike were unknowingly established by common patterns of climate, terrain and vegetation in the Mediterranean region; just as Philip II and his advisers were blind to the way their actions were responses to seismic shifts in its geo-history (Braudel, 1972/3: 901; Braudel 1980: 27–8, 74, 177).

The historian must pay attention to this world but he must never fall victim, as his traditional predecessors had done, to its illusions – like a 'slave to every overnight celebrity'. Rather he should mistrust the event, and caution us, as actors in our own world, against it. His history should never be merely 'that small-scale science of contingence', what Braudel elsewhere labels 'so-called' history (Braudel 1980: 18, 38, 57, 74). It must be the history of the long term, for only here are to be found, so to speak, the real actors, whose actions are just as authentic as those of ordinary agents but have results that are profound and lasting because they are determinative. Nothing is more revealing than Braudel's use of the vocabulary of agency when talking about impersonal forces in history. It has often been remarked that the heroes of his book on the Mediterranean are those personified entities – mountains, plains and peninsulas, the sea itself, even time and space – to which, anthropomorphically and even a little mystically, he attributes designs and purposes (Febvre 1950: 218; Hexter 1972: 518).

The language to which he invariably turns when describing the role of structures is that of inertia, obstruction and imprisonment. They 'get in the way of history, hinder its flow, and in hindering it shape it'. To include events in *The Mediterranean* at all, he wrote in the first edition, was to suppose that the lives of individuals could occasionally be liberated from these chains. For the most part men and women are indeed prisoners of the *longue durée* because all that they do is limited and constrained by the frameworks in terms of which they are obliged to act. 'For centuries', he writes, 'man has been a prisoner of climate, of vegetation, of the animal population, of a particular agriculture, of a whole slowly established balance from which he cannot escape without the risk of everything's being upset... There is the same element of permanence or survival in the vast domain of cultural affairs.' Such frameworks he regards as infrastructural, and the changes that occur in them are said to be ultimately responsible for what goes on in the other time sectors of history which gravitate round them. It is in this sense that demography reveals that civilisation is the child of number. The biological revolution of the sixteenth century was 'more important than the Turkish conquest, the discovery and colonization of America, or the imperial vocation of Spain'. Likewise, Braudel invokes what he calls the 'physics' of Spanish policy, rather than any explanation in terms of conscious decision, to account for Spain's orientation towards the Atlantic from the 1580s onwards (Braudel 1980: 31–4, 74, 85–6, 206; Braudel 1949: 721; Braudel 1972/3: 403, 19).

We can see then that this view of historical change is not merely multi-dimensional, as Febvre's was, but hierarchical. And in this hierarchy, structures are said to be the most decisive elements and events the least – they are no longer, so to speak, the background to history but its foreground. Braudel closes *The Mediterranean* with this statement: '...when I think of the individual, I am always inclined to see him imprisoned within a destiny in which he himself has little hand, fixed in a landscape in which the infinite perspectives of the long term stretch into the distance both behind him and before. In historical analysis as I see it, rightly or wrongly, the long run always wins in the end' (Braudel 1972/3: 1244). These assumptions have also governed much of the work of the second major *Annales* historian of the Braudel era, Emmanuel Le Roy Ladurie. In his seminal study *The Peasants of Languedoc*, published in 1965, Ladurie set out to deal with 'the activities, the struggles, and the thoughts of the people themselves' (Le Roy Ladurie 1974: 8), and indeed he devotes some incisive pages to the themes and institutions of their own culture. Yet for the most part we find them groping blindly for survival as prisoners of their productive practices. They emerge as victims of immemorial technological conservatism, their efforts to achieve real growth being blocked and ultimately defeated by the rigidity of their gross product. All the significant moments in their history between the fourteenth and eighteenth centuries are seen, in effect, as failures to surmount Malthusian obstacles. In his own inaugural address to the Collège de France in 1973 Ladurie reaffirmed his belief that the driving forces of mass history lay 'in the economy, in social relationships, and at a deeper level still, in biological phenomena'. Between 1300 and 1720 (he argued) the conditions of European rural life were determined inexorably by the laws governing the establishment of an ecological and demographic equilibrium (Le Roy Ladurie 1981: 3 and *passim*).

There is very much to admire in the achievements of the *Annales* historians and their work has made an enormous impact on the character of historical thought. Indeed, no comparable group of scholars has exerted a more decisive influence. They have broken for ever the timidity and suspicion with which areas of enquiry other than political were once regarded, and demonstrated beyond doubt that historians must learn from kindred disciplines if they are to deepen and enliven their understanding. Eclecticism has come to be respectable amongst them, while no aspect of human experience, however neglected or suppressed, is now free from the sort of energetic and innovative scrutiny for which the journal itself has become justly famous. It has been said that no history is less ethnocentric than Braudel's and the range of his interests and that of the journal's is often intellectually breathtaking. Historians now could not easily dispense with the *longue durée*, whether in the areas of application of Braudel and Le Roy Ladurie or in the study of mentalities. The notion of anachronism, on which historical thought may be said ultimately to rest, has been brought more sharply into focus as a result.

Nevertheless, the most significant aspect of the influence of *Annales* has been the way it has brought some of the fundamental issues of social theory to the attention of historians. It has not done so self-consciously. Those associated with it have been reluctant to indulge in abstract theorising. In a piece of finely judged obscurantism the first issue of the 1929 journal disavowed it altogether, and there is occasionally a sense of almost deliberate philosophical naivety about some of the later methodological statements (Aymard 1972: 496; Ricoeur 1980: 7, 24). However, the historian who wishes to follow Braudel is obliged to consider the extent to which reality is either a cultural construct or irreducible to the perceptions of agents; he must also debate the perennial problems of freedom and constraint in human behaviour; and he must tackle the apparent antithesis between the individuality of events and the generality of structures. Perhaps the best way of showing this and of pursuing further the character of *le monde Braudellien* is to set his advocacy of 'structural' history in the wider context of French structuralist thought.

At first sight this does not seem a very promising tactic. The relations between elements of a system which it is the task of the structuralist to uncover have, strictly speaking, a mathematical character – one which must hold good in an isomorphism between two or more of the system's cultural representations (Descombes 1980: 84–6). As Braudel himself warns, this pursuit of abstract, formal equivalences seems to go well beyond any historical concern for the durable infrastructures which constitute the foundations of human life (Braudel 1972/3: 1244; Braudel 1980: 43–4). At the other end of the scale, the sort of structuralism that Le Roy Ladurie has recommended to historians is, he admits, no more than a universal property of knowledge – that of searching beyond the surface appearance of cultural phenomena for the limited number of variables in terms of which they are related and transformed (Le Roy

Ladurie 1981: 5). Nevertheless, if structuralism ends (in principle) in mathematics, its origins lie in linguistics, specifically in the theories of Saussure. In associating the analysis of culture with semiology, these theories have implications for historians which are far more distinctive than Le Roy Ladurie's view allows, while yet remaining relevant to what Braudel calls 'the very sources of life in its most concrete, everyday, indestructible and anonymously human expression' (Braudel 1972/3: 1244). In fact, Saussurean structuralism, while not one of its direct inspirations, is, at least initially, significantly close to the spirit of *Annales* on a number of issues. And that the two ultimately diverge only redoubles its usefulness as a point of comparison.

The view of language which Saussure wished to combat – that it originates in a kind of nomenclature – is, after all, the one which sustained the naive positivism, much disdained by *Annales*, in terms of which the historian's discourse was traditionally thought to be a faithful record of a world of objective facts. The view which he wished to substitute – that language does not follow reality but signifies it – is shown by Roland Barthes in his essay 'Historical Discourse' as radically undermining this conception of history. Here the attempt to warrant the claim that 'this happened' in terms of a straightforward narrative of the 'facts' is shown to be no more than an assertion of authority on the part of the historian. The factual descriptions which result are therefore not the source of meaning – they presuppose it. Meaning creeps, as it were, shamefacedly back behind the supposedly primordial referents of traditional history as the (unformulated) foundation for its conception of reality. Barthes points accordingly to the philosophically crucial importance of those historians – he is surely thinking of the *Annales* group – who abandon the narrative of events for the analysis of structures and thus make 'not so much reality as intelligibility' the key historiographical problem (Barthes 1970: 153–5).

To this may be added Saussure's further argument that intelligibility is itself arbitrary. This results from the fact that nothing links signifiers (phonetic sequences) naturally either to the objects to which they refer or to the signifieds (concepts) with which they are combined to make linguistic signs. Only convention and usage govern the way the range of phonetic possibilities and the world of ideas are divided up in different linguistic systems; 'in a language there are only differences, and no positive terms' (Saussure 1983: 118). On this view, understanding is necessarily relativist and holist, for the meaning which an individual sign conveys can only be a function of its relationship to the total system of differentiation in which it exists and can only be grasped by reference to it. Here too there are affinities with the governing themes of *Annales* history – hostility to what is individual, awareness of the anachronisms which follow indifference to a whole set of circumstances, commitment to the 'totality' of the social fact, and so on. Finally, there is the impetus given by Saussure to the idea that linguistics is only one part of a semiology of human culture and that structuralist principles for studying linguistic phenomena are applicable *whenever* meaning is conveyed, whether verbally or non-verbally. The view that all social life is constituted by processes in which signs are exchanged and is in that sense always 'linguistic' has become fundamental to structuralism and its importance for our notions of culture cannot be exaggerated. Again, it relates to a central aim of *Annales* – the massive expansion of the historian's range of vision to include, in Febvre's epigrammatic formulation, anything which says things about men. Febvre's own list has itself a semiological flavour: 'Words, signs, landscapes, titles, the layout of fields, weeds, eclipses of the moon, bridles, analysis of stones by geologists and of metal swords by chemists, in a word, anything which, belonging to man, depends on man, serves him, expresses him and signifies his presence, activity, tastes and forms of existence' (Febvre 1973: 34).

Nevertheless, despite a general congruence between structuralism and the *Annales*, there remain important differences – differences which make Braudel's claim to be 'by temperament a "structuralist"' seem something of a special case (Braudel 1972/3: 1244). To begin with, it is by no means certain that his work does after all fulfil Barthes's expectations for the new history. Certainly he attacks as vehemently the realism of those historians for whom 'things just as they really are' could be pictured in narrative, as if caught by surprise, without the observer being implicated. For him, as for Barthes, this is a classic piece of mystification. However, the principle that reality presupposes meaning remains for Braudel a critical weapon. He is not interested in applying it to those users of language (in its wider sense) whom we call historical agents. Their meanings are not regarded as being implicated in what is to count as reality for them. Instead, he attempts a radical disjunction between what things meant for agents and what they reveal of certain conjunctural and structural realities known only to historians. Braudel's own realism therefore consists in a desire to show how the world *was* in times past, irrespective of how it was seen by those who lived in it. Of course, structuralists too have sought to uncover elementary relationships between cultural phenomena which are not perceived in the world of consciousness, and to give these the status of true, as opposed to manifest, realities (Braudel 1980: 43-4; Lévi-Strauss 1977: 57-8). But Braudel's preferred reality tends to lie outside signification altogether in the world of physical objects and relationships – geo-physical formations, patterns of climate, ecological systems, demographic mechanisms, and so on. Drawing on the distinction which, more than any other, has defined the structuralist enterprise, we might say that what has interested Braudel is nature rather than culture, 'things' rather than 'words'. The very choice of the Mediterranean as a focus of study is itself indicative. In an *Annales* review of 1963 he pointed out that, whereas Pierre Chaunu's 'Atlantic' was an arbitrary entity, 'a constructed human reality', his own 'Mediterranean' was 'an unmodified geographic whole.' (Braudel 1980: 92). It is noticeable too that Le Roy Ladurie has distanced himself from the Saussurean mainstream on the same grounds. In 1973 he spoke of his interest not in words, but in the things the words stand for; even when the latter come down to us as the collective representations of agents 'they have a basis in reality [and] cannot be reduced simply to the way in which people have spoken of them'. Since this reality is natural it is not surprising that his work has been presented on occasions as a history of nature; 'it is the geology of the layers of rock beneath our feet that has concerned me more than the admittedly fascinating geography of discourse, which is of course crucial to any serious cultural history'. For the structuralist who derives his inspiration from linguistics this must seem somewhat question-begging (Le Roy Ladurie 1981: 3-4; Ricoeur 1980: 29; Stoianovich 1976: 84).

As a further illustration of Braudel's priorities we may take the volume called *The Structures of Everyday Life* which he published in 1967 as the first part of his study *Civilization and Capitalism*. As in *The Mediterranean* he initiates the larger enquiry by considering its infrastructural and almost timeless features – in this case, the daily routines associated with foodstuffs, shelter, clothing, sources of energy, forms of transport, currencies and communications. These are as usual linked to the primary and pre-constraining realities of population change. Braudel says that 'Material life is made up of people and things', but people are in fact reduced to number, and number to an indicator of Malthusian advances and regressions. Moreover, the routines of material life themselves are regarded in terms of intrinsic rather than conferred properties. Braudel's interest in food is agronomic and alimentary – in productive techniques, yields, appetites, consumption, diets and calories – rather than cultural – in food behaviour, its grammar and conventions. When foodstuffs, especially the major food plants, are regarded qualitatively it is as measures of standards of living and levels of society. Tools are likewise viewed as indices of cultural sophistication against a single scale of attainment, not as signs conveying cultural messages among those who use them. Types of houses bear 'witness to the slow pace of civilizations'; Braudel accordingly monitors their material construction and physical layout in order to plot their progress. Sitting and squatting (and the relevant furniture) turn out to be cultural alternatives related to ways of life; but Braudel cannot resist the thought that in origin bodily comportments of this kind stem from 'an almost biological difference' (Braudel 1981: 31, 267, 290 and *passim*).

Braudel is not, of course, unaware that material life is the bearer of significations. Many of his examples, in a study immensely rich with detailed illustrations, show that its realities were constructed rather than given – that, for instance, types of food and drink were given qualities based on the social status of those who consumed them, or associated with religious categories of sacred and profane, and so on. The arbitrary influence of convention on styles of dress and furnishings even elicits from him the remark that here the historian's investigations take him 'not simply into the realm of material "things", but into a world of "things and words" – interpreting the last term in a wider sense than usual, to mean *languages*...' Man has to find food, shelter and clothing but he could choose to feed, live and dress differently (Braudel 1981: 333). Nevertheless, this remains an unexplored theme. One could not imagine Braudel examining eating habits as syntagmatic chains, as Barthes and others have done, or like Pierre Bourdieu constructing homologies between the interior layout of a dwelling and the moral and social structure of the community in which it occurs, or with Lévi-Strauss differentiating between two identical tools on the grounds that each of them is the product of a system of representations (Barthes 1967: 27–8; Bourdieu 1979: 133–53; Lévi-Strauss 1963a: 4). In addition, and this is rather more damaging, we do not find Braudel paying any attention to those aspects of their everyday routines which the men and women of the fifteenth to eighteenth centuries thought were important to material existence, but which we regard (on cultural grounds, it must be said) as having no objective reality. One looks in vain for an account of the fundamental impact on material practices of astrological prognostications, beliefs in the actions of spirits and demons, religious rites and observances, and many such ingredients of popular and elite culture in the *ancien régime*.

This is not the place to debate the merits of what is after all a matter of philosophical taste. What is important is the extent to which history of this sort is marked off from the main current of French structuralism by its pursuit of a 'reality' that does not lie in 'intelligibility'. In Saussurean linguistics and semiology no attention need be given to the problem of reference to a 'real' world. Outside meaning, this world is outside analysis; once construed it remains 'useless for checking the semiotic value of a sign' (Eco 1973: 69). Nor are there grounds for excluding any human activities from the embrace of signification and its arbitrariness, no matter how much they seem, like material life, to be constituted naturally. It is not surprising that cultural anthropologists, not all of them French, have been anxious to establish this point. Producing, consuming, wearing, building, exchanging – indeed all practical activity – 'unfolds in a world already symbolized' (Sahlins 1976: 123 and *passim*). Routineness, far from invalidating this claim, confirms it. It has been said that even at the level of sheer survival the symbolic order is evident (Boon 1982: 85, cf. 112–13, 117). Braudel, on the other hand, has preferred to regard the environmental and material aspects of experience as unappropriated by cultural forms, with the implication (heretical to structuralists) that some meanings at least might be initiated directly from nature. This in turn has been reflected in the actual character of his writing, which stands out as relentlessly descriptive and taxonomic. Structural enquiry must adopt a different mode, for the objects of its attention are never *mere* objects, distinguished in terms of inherent natural properties. They are essentially vehicles of communication whose identity is defined by differentiation, and they are grasped not descriptively but by a kind of 'deconstruction' of the system in which they belong (Descombes 1980: 77).

It is this preference for a natural rather than a cultural account of experience that also helps to underpin Braudel's determinism. The extent to which he sees the structures of *longue durée* as natural realities enables him to treat them as coercive frameworks in which words and deeds are necessarily imprisoned. This is a much more difficult argument to sustain once they are viewed as construed realities. For this brings them within the range of an enquiry in which all the systems in terms of which meanings are exchanged are regarded in the same way as the structural linguist regards language. And it is hard to see how a system which imparts meanings entirely arbitrarily to phonetic and mental sequences can be compared to a prison – even though, as Saussure repeatedly emphasised, its existence and most of the changes it undergoes are independent of anyone's will. Signs are not then (as Descombes puts it 1980: 103–9) 'at the service of the subject' but since the physical sounds and movements we make or the objects and processes we confront would be utterly bereft of any significance without them, this does not seem to be a burden. In this view, the structural features of language itself and of the other sign-systems that constitute what we call culture can only be seen, ultimately, as positive and permissive of words and deeds, not negative, regulative or preventive. They enable them to have meaning, perhaps authorise it, but they do not determine it – they are 'not so much the imperatives of culture as its implements' (Sahlins 1976: 122–3; cf. Giddens 1979: 70).

It must be admitted that on this issue Braudel is in good company. Some of the most lively contributions to French literary criticism in the structuralist and post-structuralist mode have been concerned with the severely restrictive character of language and with the predicament of the author as a victim of the codes on which his work depends. And the idea that cultural choice is pre-constrained is, of course, also central to the anthropology of Lévi-Strauss, despite his homage to Saussure. There is something familiar to readers of Febvre and Braudel in his stated intention to draw up 'an inventory of mental patterns, to reduce apparently arbitrary data to some kind of order, and to attain a level at which a kind of necessity becomes apparent, underlying the illusions of liberty' (Lévi-Strauss 1969b: 10; Rosen 1971: 269–94). It remains true, however, that, while using language for specific purposes is the occasion for many individual sorts of constraint, acknowledged or otherwise, the idea that the formal relationships which we identify when we call something 'linguistic' could themselves be constraining is foreign to structuralism. Braudel says at one point that 'mental frameworks too can form prisons of the *longue durée*' (Braudel 1980: 31) but his usual resort is to structural determinisms lying outside culture altogether – where man is more acted on than actor. In a sense, this is also true of Lévi-Strauss, whose search for universal laws of mind is necessarily a search for natural features of human brains. Yet this is regarded as going well beyond linguistic structuralism and as bypassing the semiologist's main interest in the conventions which enable objects and actions to become signs (Pettit 1975: 68; Culler 1981: 31–2). And as has been said, the arbitrariness of these conventions and the shifting nature of the semantic values they warrant are indications enough of their cultural rather than natural foundations.

The final feature of Braudel's history which distances him from mainstream structuralism is the sharp contradiction and hostility which he sees between events and structures. The practical objective of *The Mediterranean* may well have been 'a global history, ranging from stillness to the liveliest movements of men' but there have been some telling comments on its essential disunity (Braudel 1980: 93). Critics have been unkind enough to describe its form as at best 'Rabelaisian' and at worst 'invertebrate' (Hexter 1972: 523–9; Hughes 1966: 58). The lack of actual linkages between its three parts has fostered doubts about whether Braudel's triad of timespans could ever accommodate a truly rounded view of human affairs. The suspicion is that he may have confused what he himself admits to be an arbitrarily based taxonomy of rates of change with a coherent philosophy of history (Bailyn 1951; cf. Kellner 1979). Here too Saussurean principles may be invoked by way of comparison. For whether we are dealing with a strictly linguistic event, or any other kind of event treated 'linguistically', the nature of language teaches us that the concrete piece of behaviour and the system which enables it to mean something are mutually entailed in such a way that their unity is never in doubt. To communicate by particular forms of speech and action (*parole*) is itself to presuppose a general body of rules (*langue*); while such rules can only be said to exist in order to warrant specific instances of their use. Saussure's immensely influential principle was that individual units of signification only enjoy both their individuality and their power to signify by virtue of relations of difference with other units in the same symbolic system. In the very act of identifying just what they say we already commit ourselves, at least implicitly, to structures. For Braudel, on the other hand, looking at individual historical events is actually obstructive, for it prevents us from appreciating the deeper realities which have shaped the past – occurrence must accordingly give way to recurrence. In the legacy of Saussure both the finite events of speech and the other cultural activities we assimilate to them only exist at all as actualisations of the continuous, formal properties of language – here, we may say, occurrence *is* recurrence, and the event becomes a relation (Sahlins 1976: 21). It is relationships of this formal, logical kind – rather than spatial relationships between 'layers' or even temporal relationships between 'long' and 'short' time-spans – that might be said to bring together *histoire structurale* and *histoire événementielle* in a genuinely holistic explanation.

It has sometimes been suggested that *Annales* history was structuralist before the fact (Goubert 1973: 254; Burguière 1971: II–III; Le Roy Ladurie 1981: 5). Yet one has the impression that some of its aims could have been secured even more effectively if it had been more receptive to the central issue of signification. One thinks here of the early attacks on positivism and anachronism and the search for holistic understanding, but especially of Braudel's tireless campaign against the artificial autonomy of the historical individual (whether actor or event). At the same time, some of its less convincing features might have become redundant – above all, the idea that political history is irredeemably vitiated by superficiality, and the temptation to make judgements on evolutionist, even teleological, grounds about the stages reached by economies, societies and mentalities. The first of these has indeed been challenged from within the *Annales* group, notably by Jacques Le Goff (Le Goff 1971: 1–19). The second has been continuous from Febvre's account of the primitiveness and deficiencies of sixteenth-century thought (Febvre 1982: 335–464) through to Braudel's readiness to measure levels of material achievement in civilisations and to speak of 'the great forward impetuses of evolution' (Braudel 1980: 84). Neither commends itself to those for whom all forms of social life, including what is political, are related like parts of a language, and for whom in consequence all cultural unities are equally adequate and complete (Boon 1982: 126–8). One assumes that Lévi-Strauss would be shocked by Braudel's suggestion that 'Varieties of human experience are spread out over a single itinerary' (Braudel 1981: 182). There is a sense, then, in which the structural history of Braudel and the *Annales* owes more to their hostility to any form of phenomenology than to their anticipation of structural*ism*. In this respect it ought to be matched with the arguments of those thinkers – Foucault, Althusser, Lacan – for whom the 'abolition of the subject' has also been an intellectual goal.

In any case, structuralism has occasionally been notoriously unsympathetic to history – to diachrony. It is hardly to be expected that a historian like Braudel, for whom 'everything begins and ends with time' could have moved yet closer to it (Braudel 1980: 76). In fact, his repeated insistence that history is above all a speculation on the nature of time has constituted a spirited defence of diachrony against a prevailing antagonism. Besides, we have been talking only of the *Annales classiques* and the generation of Fernand Braudel. Today there is no longer such a unified school with a dominant approach to the past. Greater sensitivity to the conceptual implications of semiology has marked recent *Annales* scholarship. More attention is now devoted to the symbolic ordering of social life and to the history of mentalities. An issue of the 1971 journal devoted to 'History and Structure' was in fact given over entirely to studies of forms of signifying – myths, institutions, texts and images. Linguistics and anthropology have become more influential than geography or even demography. Above all, the study of the event has again become respectable, not as the foundation for the *récit événementielle*, but as the focus of a problem-centred history which spreads ever outwards, in the synchronic as well as the diachronic mode, from (the linguistic image is appropriate) 'text' to 'context'. This is a model familiar enough in Febvre's movement from the puzzle of the atheism of Rabelais to the intellectual milieu of his age. What is striking is that Le Roy Ladurie has recently completed no fewer than four studies in the same style – an evocation of life in the medieval village of Montaillou, an account of popular disturbances in the town of Romans in 1579 and 1580, a reading of an eighteenth-century dialect story against the background of village life in the Midi, and a review of Gascon witchcraft beliefs. This is not the bad old history of events; but neither is it 'history without people'. It may very well represent another equally challenging and equally influential shift in the social theory of *Annales* – this time towards rather than away from the spirit of Bloch and Febvre.

FURTHER READING

The social and intellectual circumstances surrounding the first *Annales* of Bloch and Febvre are best approached via Hughes (1966: ch. 2). Febvre's thought and writings are analysed in an *Annales* publication, Mann 1971, and some of his most forceful essays and reviews are translated in Burke 1973. More than in his book on Rabelais (1942, trans. 1982) Febvre's influence on Braudel can be traced to an earlier work, *La Terre et l'évol-ution humaine* (1922).

There are useful brief surveys of the themes of *Annales* history in Aymard 1972, in Iggers 1975 and in perhaps the most incisive of many review essays, Kedourie 1975. The best account, although somewhat contrived in places, is Stoianovich 1976, with a generally approving preface by Braudel. The relationship between *Annales* and analytical philosophy of history in France is dealt with in Paul Ricoeur's 1978–9 Zaharoff Lecture at Oxford University (1980) and those who wish to consider the yet wider context of French philosophical thought in general now have the benefit of Monte-fiore 1983 as well as of Descombes 1980. Intimations of future develop-ments are offered by Furet 1983 and, from a broader and more critical point of view, by Chartier 1982. Stone identifies a reaction against the *Annales* style in his 'The Revival of Narrative' (1979). Naturally, the journal remains its own best advertisement. Especially revealing are the 'Débats et combats' inaugurated at various intervals in its development, but a survey of any run of issues will demonstrate its extraordinary range and vitality. Its epigone might be said to be the journal *Review* published by the Fernand Braudel Center at SUNY, Binghamton, the first issue of which (1978) contains Peter Burke's 'Reflections on the Historical Revolution in France: The *Annales* School and British Social History'.

In the present context the first French edition of Braudel's *The Mediter-ranean* (1949) should be consulted for the concluding section to Part I, called 'Géohistoire et déterminisme'; otherwise the revised edition and its English translation (1972/3) are now standard. His second major work, *Civilization and Capitalism, 15th–18th Century*, is also available in trans-lation, its three volumes being entitled *The Structures of Everyday Life: The Limits of the Possible* (1981), *The Wheels of Commerce* (1982) and *The Perspective of the World* (1984). Matched with these vastly extended enquiries are several occasional writings of considerable theoretical interest, even though Braudel often evokes a position rather than argues for it. Among those collected and translated in Braudel 1980 are two indispens-able items – the inaugural lecture 'The Situation of History in 1950' and the *Annales* article of 1958 'History and the Social Sciences: The *longue durée*'. The characteristic preoccupations of Le Roy Ladurie may likewise be gleaned from two anthologies of his essays, lectures and reviews, *The Terri-tory of the Historian* (1979) and *The Mind and Method of the Historian* (1981).

Although reaction to Braudel's work has been very extensive indeed, there are, as yet, few substantial commentaries on it. The best starting point is an issue of volume 44 of the *Journal of Modern History* entitled 'History with a French accent'. This brings together in an ideal combination a typical set of reminiscences and personal views from Braudel himself, an account of *Annales* and *The Mediterranean* by one of his warmest admirers, H. R.

Trevor-Roper, and an energetic dissection of the genesis and contents of the book (using Braudel's own triadic methodology) by one of his sharpest critics, J. H. Hexter. Mention may also be made of Bailyn's early scepticism (1951), Kellner's striking attempt (1979) to argue that *The Mediterranean* is a piece of Menippean satire and Kinser's analysis (1981) of Braudel's notion of structure.

Bibliography

Ackerman, B. 1980. *Social Justice in the Liberal State* (New Haven, Conn.)

Althusser, L. 1969. *Pour Marx* (Paris 1965); trans. Ben Brewster as *For Marx* (London 1969)

  1971.'Idéologie et appareils idéologiques d'état', in *La Pensée* 151 (1970); trans. Ben Brewster as 'Ideology and Ideological State Apparatuses', in *Lenin and Philosophy and other Essays* (London 1971)

  1972. 'Sur le rapport de Marx à Hegel', in *Hegel et la pensée moderne: Séminaire sur Hegel dirigé par Jean Hyppolite au Collège de France 1967–8* (Paris 1979); trans. Ben Brewster as 'Marx's Relation to Hegel', in *Politics and History* (London 1972)

  1976a. *Réponse à John Lewis* (Paris 1973); trans. Grahame Lock as 'Reply to John Lewis', in *Essays in Self-Criticism* (London 1976)

  1976b. *Eléments d'autocritique* (Paris 1974); trans. Grahame Lock as 'Elements of Self-Criticism', in *Essays in Self-Criticism* (London 1976)

  1976c. 'Est-il simple d'être marxiste en philosophie?', *La Pensée*, October 1975; trans. as 'Is it Simple to be a Marxist in Philosophy?', in *Essays in Self-Criticism*, trans. G. Locke (London 1976)

Althusser, L. and Balibar, E. 1970. *Lire le Capital* (Paris 1968); trans. Ben Brewster as *Reading Capital* (London 1970)

Anderson, P. 1974. *Lineages of the Absolutist State* (London)

  1976. *Considerations on Western Marxism* (London)

  1980. *Arguments within English Marxism* (London)

  1983. *In the Tracks of Historical Materialism* (London)

Arendt, H. 1958. *The Human Condition* (London)

Ayer, A. J. 1967. 'Man as a Subject for Science', in *Philosophy, Politics and Society* Series III, ed. P. Laslett and W. G. Runciman (Oxford)

Aymard, M. 1972. 'The *Annales* and French Historiography (1929–1972)', *Journal of European Economic History* 1, 491–511

Bailyn, B. 1951. 'Braudel's Geohistory – a Reconsideration', *Journal of Economic History* 11, 277–82

Balibar, E. 1978. 'From Bachelard to Althusser: The Concept of Epistemological Break', *Economy and Society* 7: 3, 207–37

Barnes, B. 1974. *Scientific Knowledge and Sociological Theory* (London)

  1977. *Interests and the Growth of Knowledge* (London)

1982. *T. S. Kuhn and Social Science* (London)

Barnes, B. and Bloor, D. 1982. 'Relativism, Rationalism and the Sociology of Knowledge', in *Rationality and Relativism*, ed. M. Hollis and S. Lukes (Oxford)

Barry, B. 1965. *Political Argument* (London)

1973. *The Liberal Theory of Justice* (Oxford)

Barthes, R. 1967. *Eléments de sémiologie* (Paris 1964); trans. A. Lavers and C. Smith as *Elements of Semiology* (London 1967)

1970. 'Le discours de l'histoire', *Social Science Information* 6 (1967), 65–75; trans. Peter Wexler as 'Historical Discourse', in *Structuralism: A Reader*, ed. M. Lane (London 1970), 145–55

Bauman, Z. 1978. *Hermeneutics and Social Science* (London)

Bell, D. 1960. *The End of Ideology* (New York)

Bentham, J. 1949. *Principles of Morals and Legislation and A Fragment on Government*, ed. W. Harrison (Oxford)

Benton, T. 1977. *Philosophical Foundations of the Three Sociologies* (London)

1984. *The Rise and Fall of Structural Marxism: Louis Althusser and his Influence* (London)

Berger, P. and Luckmann, T. 1967. *The Social Construction of Reality* (London)

Bernstein, B. 1976. *The Restructuring of Social and Political Theory* (New York)

1983. *Beyond Objectivism and Relativism* (Oxford)

Betti, E. 1962. *Die Hermeneutik als allgemeine Methode der Geisteswissenschaften* (Tübingen 1962); trans. in Bleicher 1980

Bhaskar, R. 1978. *A Realist Theory of Science* (Leeds 1975); second edn Brighton 1978

1979. *The Possibility of Naturalism* (Brighton)

Bleicher, J. 1980. *Contemporary Hermeneutics. Hermeneutics as method, philosophy and critique* (London, Boston & Henley) 1970

1982. *The Hermeneutic Imagination. Outline of a positive critique of scientism and sociology* (London, Boston, Melbourne & Henley)

Blondel, E. 1974. 'Les guillemets de Nietzsche', in *Nietzsche aujourd'hui?*, Vol. 2 (Paris)

Bloor, D. 1976. *Knowledge and Social Imagery* (London)

Boon, J. A. 1982. *Other Tribes, Other Scribes: Symbolic Anthropology in the Comparative Study of Cultures, Histories, Religions, and Texts* (Cambridge)

Bourdieu, P. 1979. 'La maison kabyle ou le monde renversé', in *Echanges et communications: Mélanges offerts à Claude Lévi-Strauss*, ed. J. Pouillon and P. Maranda, 2 vols. (The Hague, Paris 1970), 739–58; trans. R. Nice as 'The Kabyle House or the World Reversed', in P. Bourdieu, *Algeria 1960* (Cambridge 1979), 133–53

Braudel, F. 1949. *La Méditerranée et le monde méditerranéen à l'époque de Philippe II* (Paris)

1972/3. *La Méditerranée et le monde méditerranéen à l'époque de Philippe II*, 2nd rev. and augmented edn, 2 vols. (Paris 1966); trans. S. Reynolds as *The Mediterranean and the Mediterranean World in the Age of Philip II*, 2 vols. (London 1972/3)

1980. *Ecrits sur l'histoire* (Paris 1969); trans. S. Matthew as *On History* (Chicago, London 1980)

1981. *Civilisation matérielle, économie et capitalisme, XVe–XVIIIe Siècle*, 3 vols. (Paris 1979); rev. edn includes rev. edn of Vol. I with the title *Les Structures du quotidien: Le Possible et l'impossible* (Paris 1979); Vol. I of this edn trans. S. Reynolds as *The Structures of Everyday Life: The Limits of the Possible* (London 1981) (Vol. II) *The Wheels of Commerce* (London 1982) and (Vol. III) *The Perspective of the World* (London 1984)

Brodbeck, M. 1968. 'Meaning and Action', in *Readings in the Philosophy of the Social Sciences*, ed. M. Brodbeck (New York)

Burguière, André. 1971. 'Présentation: Histoire et structure', *Annales. E.S.C.* 26: 3, I-VII

Burke, E. 1961. *Reflections on the Revolution in France* (New York)

Burke, P. (ed.) 1973. *A New Kind of History from the Writings of Febvre* (London)

1978. 'Reflections on the Historical Revolution in France: The *Annales* School and British Social History', *Review* 1, 147–56

Callinicos, A. 1976. *Althusser's Marxism* (London)

1982. *Is there a Future for Marxism?* (London)

Cavell, S. 1976. *Must We Mean What We Say?* (Cambridge)

Cedarbaum, D. G. 1983. 'Paradigms', *Studies in the History and Philosophy of Science* 14: 3, 173–213

Chartier, R. 1982. 'Intellectual History or Sociocultural History? The French Trajectories', in D. LaCapra and S. L. Kaplan (eds), *Modern European Intellectual History: Reappraisals and New Perspectives* (London)

Clément, C. 1983. *Vies et légendes de Jacques Lacan* (Paris 1981); trans. A. Goldhammer as *The Lives and Legends of Jacques Lacan* (New York 1983)

Cohen, G. A. 1978. *Karl Marx's Theory of History: A Defence* (Princeton)

Connerton, P. 1980. *The Tragedy of Enlightenment* (Cambridge)

Connolly, W. E. 1981. *Appearance and Reality in Politics* (Cambridge)

Culler, J. 1976. 'Presupposition and Intertextuality', *MLN* 91, 1380–96

1981. *The Pursuit of Signs: Semiotics, Literature, Deconstruction* (London)

Dallmayr, F. and McCarthy, T. 1977. *Understanding and Social Inquiry* (Notre Dame)

Daniels, N. 1975. *Reading Rawls* (Oxford)

Davidson, D. 1984. *Inquiries into Truth and Interpretation* (Oxford)

Derrida, J. 1973. *La Voix et le Phénomène* (Paris 1967); trans. D. B. Allison and N. Garver as *Speech and Phenomena, and Other Essays on Husserl's Theory of Signs* (Evanston 1973)

    1976. *De la Grammatologie* (Paris 1967); trans. G. C. Spivak as *Of Grammatology* (London and Baltimore 1974, 1976)

    1977. 'Limited Inc abc ...', *Glyph* 2, 162–254

    1978. *L'Ecriture et la différence* (Paris 1967); trans. A. Bass as *Writing and Difference* (Chicago 1978)

    1979. *Eperons: Les styles de Nietzsche* (Chicago and London 1979); trans. B. Harlow as *Spurs: Nietzsche's Styles* (Chicago and London 1979)

    1981a. *La Dissémination* (Paris 1972); trans. B. Johnson as *Dissemination* (Chicago 1981)

    1981b. *Positions* (Paris 1972); trans. A. Bass as *Positions* (Chicago 1981)

    1982a. 'Envoi', trans. P. Caws as 'Sending: On Representation', *Social Research* 49, 294–326 (Summer)

    1982b. *Marges de la philosophie* (Paris 1972); trans. A. Bass as *Margins of Philosophy* (Chicago 1982)

Descombes, V. 1980. *Le Même et l'autre* (Paris 1979); trans. L. Scott-Fox and J. M. Harding as *Modern French Philosophy* (Cambridge 1980)

Dijksterhuis, E. J. 1961. *De Mechanisering van het Wereldbeeld* (Amsterdam 1950); trans. C. Dikshoorn as *The Mechanisation of the World-Picture* (Oxford 1961)

Dilthey, W. 1958. *Der Aufbau der geschichtlichen Welt in den Geisteswissenschaften, Gesammelte Schriften*, Vol. 7 (Leipzig and Berlin 1927; second edn 1958)

Dreyfus, H. L. and Rabinow, P. 1982. *Michel Foucault: Beyond Structuralism and Hermeneutics*, with an afterword by Foucault (Hassocks, Sussex)

Ducrot, O. and Todorov, T. (eds.) 1979. *Dictionnaire encyclopédique des sciences du langage* (Paris 1972); trans. as *Encyclopedic Dictionary of the Sciences of Language* (Baltimore 1979)

Dunn, J. 1979. *Western Political Theory in the Face of the Future* (Cambridge)

    1980. *Political Obligation in its Historical Context* (Cambridge)

    1982. 'Understanding Revolutions', *Ethics* 92, 299–315

Durkheim, E. 1897. Review of A. Labriola, 'Essais sur la conception matérialiste de l'histoire', *Revue Philosophique* 44

Dworkin, R. 1978a. *Taking Rights Seriously* (London)

    1978b. 'Liberalism', in *Public and Private Morality*, ed. S. Hampshire (Cambridge)

Eco, U. 1973. 'Social Life as a Sign System' in *Structuralism: An Introduction*, ed. D. Robey. Wolfson College Lectures, 1972 (Oxford)

Elster, J. 1978. *Logic and Society* (New York)

　1979. *Ulysses and the Sirens* (Cambridge)

　1982. 'Marxism, Functionalism and Game Theory', *Theory and Society* 11, 453–82

　1983. *Sour Grapes* (Cambridge)

Febvre, L. 1922. *La Terre et l'évolution humaine* (Paris)

　1950. 'Un livre qui grandit: *La Méditerranée et le monde méditerranéen à l'époque de Philippe II*', *Revue historique* 203, 216–24

　1973. 'Vers une autre histoire', *Revue de métaphysique et de morale* 58 (1949); trans. Keith Folca as 'A New Kind of History' in Burke (1973)

　1982. *Le Problème de l'incroyance au XVIe siècle: La Religion de Rabelais* (Paris 1942); trans. B. Gottlieb as *The Problem of Unbelief in the Sixteenth Century: The Religion of Rabelais* (Cambridge, Mass. 1982)

Feyerabend, P. 1975. *Against Method* (London)

　1981. *Realism, Rationalism and Scientific Method*: Philosophical Papers, Vol. I (Cambridge)

Fish, S. 1980. *Is There a Text in this Class?: The Authority of Interpretive Communities* (Harvard)

Fleck, L. 1979. *Entstehung und Entwicklung einer Wissenschaftlichen Tatsache* (1935) trans. F. Bradley and T. J. Trenn as *Genesis and Development of a Scientific Fact* (Chicago, 1979)

Foucault, M. 1967. *Histoire de la folie* (Paris 1961); trans. as *Madness and Civilisation* (London 1967)

　1970. *Les Mots et les choses* (Paris 1966), trans. as *The Order of Things, An Archaeology of the Human Sciences* (London 1970)

　1971. *L'Ordre du discours* (Paris 1971), trans. as 'Orders of Discourse', *Social Science Information* 10: 2, 7–30

　1972. *L'Archeologie du savoir* (Paris 1969), trans. as *The Archaeology of Knowledge* (London 1972)

　1973. *Naissance de la Clinique* (Paris 1963), trans. as *The Birth of the Clinic* (London 1973)

　1977a. *Surveiller et punir: naissance de la prison* (Paris 1975), trans. as *Discipline and Punish* (London 1977)

　1977b. *Language, Counter-Memory, Practice*, ed. D. F. Bouchard (Oxford)

　1978. 'About the Concept of the "Dangerous Individual" in 19th-Century Legal Psychiatry', *International Journal of Law and Psychiatry* 1, 1–18

　1979. *La volonté de savoir* (Paris 1976), trans. as *The History of Sexuality*, Vol. I (London 1979)

　1980. *Michel Foucault: Power/Knowledge*, ed. C. Gordon (Hassocks, Sussex)

1981. 'Questions of Method: An Interview with Michel Foucault', *Ideology and Consciousness* 8 (Spring)

1982. 'The Subject and Power', Afterword in Dreyfus and Rabinow 1982

1983. 'Afterword (1983)', in Hubert L. Dreyfus and Paul Rabinow, *Michel Foucault: Beyond Structuralism and Hermeneutics* (Chicago, second edn 1983).

Fried, C. 1978. *Right and Wrong* (Cambridge, Mass.)

Fullinwider, R. K. 1977. 'A Chronological Bibliography of Works on John Rawls's "A Theory of Justice"', *Political Theory* 5, 561–70

Furet, F. 1983. 'Beyond the *Annales*', *Journal of Modern History*, 55, 389–410

Gadamer, H. G. 1967. *Kleine Schriften*, 3 vols. (Tübingen 1969); part trans. in Gadamer 1976

1975a. *Wahrheit und Methode. Grundzüge einer philosophischen Hermeneutik* (Tübingen 1960; fourth edn 1975); trans. W. Glyn-Doepel as *Truth and Method* (London 1975)

1975b. 'Hermeneutics and Social Science', *Cultural Hermeneutics* 2: 4

1976. *Philosophical Hermeneutics*, trans. D. Linge of extracts from Gadamer 1967 (Berkeley 1976)

1981. *Reason in the Age of Science* (Cambridge, Mass. & London 1981). Most of the essays in this volume were originally published in Gadamer's *Vernunft im Zeitalter der Wissenschaft* (Frankfurt 1976)

Gadamer, H.-G. and Boehm, G. 1976. *Philosophische Hermeneutik* (Frankfurt)

Geertz, C. 1980. *Negara: The Theatre State in Nineteenth-Century Bali* (New Jersey)

1983. *Local Knowledge* (New York)

1984. 'Anti Anti-Relativism', *American Anthropologist* 86, 263–78

Gellner, E. 1974. 'The New Idealism: Cause and Meaning in the Social Sciences', in *Positivism and Sociology*, ed. A. Giddens (London 1974)

Geuss, R. 1981. *The Idea of a Critical Theory* (Cambridge)

Giddens, A. 1976. *New Rules of Sociological Method* (London)

1979. *Central Problems in Social Theory: Action, Structure and Contradiction in Social Analysis* (London)

1982. *Profiles and Critiques in Social Theory* (London)

1984. *The Constitution of Society* (Cambridge)

Goubert, P. 1973. 'Sur trois siècles et trois décennies: Passage des méthodologies', in *Mélanges en l'honneur de Fernand Braudel*, 2 vols. (Toulouse 1973), Vol. 2, 251–8

Gutting, G. (ed.) 1980. *Paradigms and Revolutions: Appraisals and Applications of Thomas Kuhn's Philosophy of Science* (Notre-Dame)

Habermas, J. 1970. 'Der Universalitätsanspruch der Hermeneutik' in *Hermeneutik und Dialektik*, Vol. 1 (Tübingen 1970), trans. J. Bleicher as 'The Hermeneutic Claim to Universality', in Bleicher 1980

1971a. *Erkenntnis und Interesse* (Frankfurt 1968); trans. J. Shapiro as *Knowledge and Human Interests* (London 1971)

1971b. *Zur Logik der Sozialwissenschaften* (published in *Philosophische Rundschau* 1967; second edn Frankfurt 1971)

1973. *Legitimationsprobleme im Spätkapitalismus* (Frankfurt 1973); trans. T. McCarthy as *Legitimation Crisis* (Boston 1975)

1974. *Theory and Practice* (London)

1979. *Communication and the Evolution of Society* (Boston)

1980. 'The Hermeneutic Claim to Universality', in Bleicher 1980

1981. 'Modernity versus Postmodernism', *New German Critique* 22 (Winter)

1984. *Theorie des kommunikativen Handelns*, 2 vols. (Frankfurt 1981); trans. T. McCarthy as *The Theory of Communicative Action* (Vol. I, Beacon 1984; Vol. II forthcoming)

Hacking, I. 1982. 'Language, Truth and Reason', in *Rationality and Relativism*, ed. M. Hollis and S. Lukes (Oxford)

Hampshire, S. 1972. 'A New Philosophy of the Just Society', *New York Review of Books*, 24 February 1972, 38–9

Harari, J. (ed.) 1979. *Textual Strategies: Perspectives in Post-Structural Criticism* (Ithaca)

Hare, R. 1952. *The Language of Morals* (Oxford)

Hart, H. 1961. *The Concept of Law* (Oxford)

1968. *Punishment and Responsibility* (Oxford)

1975. 'Rawls on Liberty and its Priority', in Daniels 1975, 230–52

1979. 'Between Utility and Rights', in *The Idea of Freedom*, ed. A. Ryan (Oxford)

Hegel, G. W. F. 1977. *Phänomenologie des Geistes* (Bamberg and Würzburg 1807); trans. A. Miller as *The Phenomenology of Spirit* (Oxford 1977)

Heidegger, M. 1962. *Sein und Zeit* (Tübingen 1927); seventh edn trans. J. Macquarrie and E. Robinson as *Being and Time* (Oxford 1962)

1977. 'Brief über den Humanismus'; trans. F. A. Capuzzi as 'Letter on Humanism', in M. Heidegger, *Basic Writings*, ed. David Farrell Krell (New York 1977)

Held, D. 1980. *Introduction to Critical Theory: Horkheimer to Habermas* (London)

Hempel, C. G. 1965. *Aspects of Scientific Explanation* (New York and London)

Hermeneutik und Dialektik I. 1970. Festschrift für H.-G. Gadamer (Tübingen)

Hermeneutik und Ideologiekritik. 1971. Contributions by Karl-Otto Apel, Claus von Bormann, Rüdiger Bubner, Hans-Georg Gadamer, Hans Joachim Giegel, Jürgen Habermas (Frankfurt)

Hesse, M. 1979. 'Habermas's Consensus Theory of Truth', *Proceedings of* the 1978 Biennial Meeting of the Philosophy of Science Association 2, 373–96

Hexter, J. H. 1972. 'Fernand Braudel and the *monde Braudellien...*', *Journal of Modern History* 44, 480–539

Hirsch, E. D. Jr. 1967. *Validity in Interpretation* (New Haven 1967)

Hirst, P. Q. 1976. 'Althusser and the Theory of Ideology', *Economy and Society* 5, 385–412

'History with a French Accent', *Journal of Modern History* 44 (special edn)

Hollis, M. 1977. *Models of Man* (Cambridge)

1982. 'The Social Destruction of Reality' in *Rationality and Relativism*, ed. M. Hollis and S. Lukes (Oxford)

Hollis, M. and Lukes, S. 1982. 'Introduction' to *Rationality and Relativism*, ed. Hollis and Lukes (Oxford)

Hoy, D. C. 1978. *The Critical Circle: Literature, History, and Philosophical Hermeneutics* (London and Berkeley)

1980. 'Hermeneutics', *Social Research* 47: 4 (Winter), 649–71

1981a. 'Must We Say What We Mean? The Grammatological Critique of Hermeneutics', in *Contemporary Literary Hermeneutics and Interpretation of Classical Texts,* ed S. Kresic (Ottawa)

1981b. 'Philosophy as Rigorous Philology? Nietzsche and Poststructuralism', *New York Literary Forum* 8–9, 171–85

1982a. 'Deciding Derrida', *London Review of Books* 4:3 (18 February–3 March), 3–5

1982b. 'Forgetting the Text: Derrida's Critique of Heidegger', in *The Question of Textuality*, ed. W. V. Spanos, P. A. Bove, and D. O'Hara (Bloomington, Indiana)

Hughes, H. S. 1966. *The Obstructed Path: French Social Thought in the Years of the Depression, 1930–1960* (New York)

Hume, D. 1963. 'Of the Original Contract', in *Essays* (Oxford), 452–73

Husserl, E. 1970. *Die Krisis der Europäischen Wissenschaften und die transzendentale Phänomenologie* (The Hague 1954); trans. D. Carr as *The Crisis of the European Sciences and Transcendental Phenomenology* (Evanston, Illinois 1970)

Iggers, G. G. 1975. *New Directions in European Historiography* (Middletown, Conn.)

Izard, M. and Smith, P. (eds.) 1982. *La fonctionne symbolique* (Paris 1979); trans. John Leavitt as *Between Belief and Transgression: Structuralist Essays in Religion, History, and Myth* (Chicago 1982)

James, S. 1984. *The Content of Social Explanation* (Cambridge)

Jay, M. 1984. *Marxism and Totality* (Cambridge)

Keane, J. 1975. 'On Tools and Language: Habermas on Work and Interaction', *New German Critique* 6, 82–100

Kedourie, E. 1975. 'New Histories for Old', *The Times Literary Supplement*, March 7

Kellner, H. 1979. 'Disorderly Conduct: Braudel's Mediterranean Satire', *History and Theory* 18, 197–222

Kinser, S. 1981. 'Analiste paradigm? The geo-historical structuralism of Fernand Braudel', *American Historical Review*, 86

Kristeva, J. 1969. *Semiotikè* (Paris)

Kuhn, T. S. 1957. *The Copernican Revolution* (Cambridge, Mass.)

    1961. 'Sadi Carnot and the Cagnard Engine', *Isis*, 52, 367–74

    1963. 'The Function of Dogma in Scientific Research', in *Scientific Change*, ed. A. C. Crombie (London)

    1970. *The Structure of Scientific Revolutions* (Chicago 1962; second edn 1970)

    1977. *The Essential Tension* (Chicago)

    1978. *Black Body Theory and the Quantum Discontinuity, 1894–1912* (Oxford)

Laing, R. D. 1960. *The Divided Self* (London)

Lakatos, I. 1970. 'Falsification and the methodology of scientific research programmes', in Lakatos and Musgrave 1970

Lakatos, I. and Musgrave, A. (eds) 1970. *Criticism and the Growth of Knowledge* (Cambridge)

Lang, W. 1979. 'Marxism, Liberalism and Justice', in *Justice*, ed. E. Kamenka and A. Erh-Soon-Tay (London), 116–48

Laslett, P. 1956. 'Introduction' to *Philosophy, Politics and Society*, Series I, ed. P. Laslett (Oxford)

Le Goff, J. 1971. 'Is Politics Still the Backbone of History?', *Daedalus* 100, 1–19

Le Roy Ladurie, E. 1974. *Les Paysans de Languedoc*, 2 vols. (Paris 1965; second edn 1966; abridged edn 1969); trans. J. Day as *The Peasants of Languedoc*, from the abridged edn (Urbana, Illinois, 1974)

    1979. *Le Territoire de l'historien*, vol. I (Paris 1973); selections trans. S. and B. Reynolds as *The Territory of the Historian* (Brighton 1979)

    1981. *Le Territoire de l'historien*, vol. II (Paris 1978); selections trans. S. and B. Reynolds as *The Mind and Method of the Historian* (Brighton 1981)

Lemert, C. C. and Gillan, G. 1982. *Michel Foucault: Social Theory as Transgression* (New York)

Lévi-Strauss, C. 1963a. *Anthropologie structurale* (Paris 1958); trans. C. Jacobson and B. Grundfest Schoepf as *Structural Anthropology* (New York 1963)

    1963b. *Le Totemisme aujourd'hui* (Paris 1962); trans. R. Needham as *Totemism* (Boston 1963)

    1966. *La Pensée sauvage* (Paris 1962); trans. as *The Savage Mind* (Chicago 1966)

    1969a. *Les Structures élémentaires de la parenté* (Paris 1949; second edn

1967); trans. R. Needham et al. as *The Elementary Structures of Kinship* (Boston 1969)

1969b. *Mythologiques: Le Cru et le cuit* (Paris 1964); trans. J. and D. Weightman as *The Raw and the Cooked* (New York 1969)

1973a. *Anthropologie structurale deux* (Paris 1973)

1973b. *Mythologiques: Du miel aux cendres* (Paris 1967); trans. J. and D. Weightman as *From Honey to Ashes* (New York 1973)

1977. *Tristes tropiques* (Paris 1955; second edn 1973); trans. J and D. Weightman as *Tristes Tropiques* (New York 1977)

1978. *Mythologiques: L'Origine des manières de table* (Paris 1968); trans. J. and D. Weightman as *The Origin of Table Manners* (New York 1978)

1981. *Mythologiques: L'homme nu* (Paris 1971); trans. J. and D. Weightman as *The Naked Man* (Chicago 1981)

1982. *La Voie des masques* (Geneva 1972; second edn Paris 1979); trans. S. Modelski as *The Way of the Masks* (Seattle 1982)

1983. *Le Regard éloigné* (Paris 1983)

1984. *Paroles données* (Paris 1984)

Lipset, S. 1960. *Political Man* (London)

Locke, J. 1967. *Two Treatises of Government*, ed. P. Laslett (Cambridge)

Lukes, S. 1971. *Emil Durkheim: His Life and Works* (London)

1977. 'Power and Structure', in *Essays in Social Theory* (London)

1982. 'Relativism in its Place', in *Rationality and Relativism*, ed. M. Hollis and S. Lukes (Oxford)

McCarthy, T. 1984. *The Critical Theory of Jürgen Habermas*

MacIntyre, A. 1966. *A Short History of Ethics* (New York)

1971. *Against the Self-Images of the Age* (London)

Macpherson, C. B. 1973. *Democratic Theory: Essays in Retrieval* (Oxford)

Major-Moetzl, P. 1983. *A New Science of History: Michel Foucault's 'Archaeology of Western Culture* (Hassocks)

Mann, H.-D. 1971. *Lucien Febvre: La Pensée vivante d'un historien* (Paris)

Mannheim, K. 1953. 'Conservative Thought', in *Essays on Sociology and Social Psychology* (London)

Marcuse, H. 1964. *One Dimensional Man* (London)

Marx, K. 1974. *Das Kapital*, Vol. I (Hamburg 1867); trans. Moore and Aveling as *Capital*, Vol. I (London 1974)

Miller, D. 1977. *Social Justice* (Oxford)

Montefiore, A. (ed.) 1983. *Philosophy in France Today* (Cambridge)

Mortimore, G. and Maund, J. 1976. 'Rationality in Belief', in *Rationality and the Social Sciences*, ed. S. I. Benn and G. W. Mortimore (London)

Nagel, T. 1979. *Mortal Questions* (Cambridge)

Namier, L. B. 1930. *England in the Age of the American Revolution* (London)

1955. *Personalities and Powers* (London)

Nozick, R. 1974. *Anarchy, State and Utopia* (New York and Oxford)

Outhwaite, W. 1975. *Understanding Social Life. The Method Called Verstehen* (London; second edition Lewes 1986)

   1983. *Concept Formation in Social Science* (London, Boston, Melbourne and Henley)

Palmer, R. 1969. *Hermeneutics: Interpretation Theory in Schleiermacher, Dilthey, Heidegger, Gadamer* (Evanston, Ill.)

Parfit, D. 1984. *Reasons and Persons* (Oxford)

Passmore, J. 1974. *Man's Responsibility for Nature* (London)

Pears, D. 1984. *Motivated Irrationality* (Oxford)

Pettit, P. 1975. *The Concept of Structuralism: A Critical Analysis* (Dublin)

Piaget, J. 1965. *The Moral Development of the Child* (London)

Popper, K. 1945. *The Open Society and its Enemies*, 2 vols. (London)

   1959. *The Logic of Scientific Discovery* (London)

Poster, M. 1975. *Existential Marxism in Postwar France* (Princeton, New Jersey)

Poulantzas, N. 1973. *Pouvoir politique et classes sociales* (Paris 1968); trans. T. O'Hagan as *Political Power and Social Class* (London 1973)

Prins, G. (ed.) 1983. *Defended to Death* (Harmondsworth)

Putnam, H. 1978. *Meaning and the Moral Sciences* (London)

   1981. *Reason, Truth and History* (Cambridge)

Quine, W. 1953. *From a Logical Point of View* (Cambridge)

Racerskis, K. 1983. *Michel Foucault and the Subversion of Intellect* (Ithaca, New York)

Rancière, J. 1974. 'On the Theory of Ideology', *Radical Philosophy* 7, 2–15

Rawls, J. 1958. 'Justice as Fairness', *Philosophical Review* 67, 164–94

   1963a. 'The Sense of Justice', *Philosophical Review* 72, 281–304

   1963b. 'Constitutional Liberty and the Concept of Justice', in *Justice* (*Nomos* VI), ed. C. J. Friedrich and J. W. Chapman (New York)

   1967. 'Distributive Justice', in *Philosophy, Politics and Society*, Third Series, ed. P. Laslett and W. G. Runciman (Oxford).

   1971. *A Theory of Justice* (Cambridge, Mass.)

   1975. 'Fairness to Goodness', *Philosophical Review* 84, 536–54

   1980. 'Kantian Constructionism in Moral Theory', *Journal of Philosophy* 87 (9); 515–72

   1982. 'The Basic Liberties and their Priority', in S. McMurrin (ed.), *The Tanner Lectures on Human Values*, III (Cambridge)

Regan, T. and Singer, P. (eds) 1976. *Animal Rights and Human Obligations* (Englewood Cliffs, New Jersey)

Reiss, H. (ed.) 1972. *Kant's Political Writings* (Cambridge)

Ricoeur, P. 1970. *De l'interprétation. Essai sur Freud* (Paris 1965); trans. D. Savage as *Freud and Philosophy: An Essay on Interpretation* (New Haven 1970)

   1980. *The Contribution of French Historiography to the Theory of History*. Zaharoff Lecture for 1978/9 (Oxford)

1981. *Hermeneutics and the Human Sciences*, ed. and trans. J. B. Thompson (Cambridge)

Rorty, R. 1979. *Philosophy and the Mirror of Nature* (Princeton)

1982. 'Philosophy as a Kind of Writing: An Essay on Derrida', in R. Rorty, *Consequences of Pragmatism* (*Essays: 1972–1980*) (Minneapolis)

Rosen, L. 1971. 'Language, History, and the Logic of Inquiry in Lévi-Strauss and Sartre', *History and Theory* 10, 269–94

Rossi, I. (ed.) 1982a. *Structural Sociology* (New York)

1982b. *The Logic of Culture: Advances in Structural Theory and Method* (South Hadley, Mass.)

Runciman, W. 1972. *A Critique of Max Weber's Philosophy of Social Science* (Cambridge)

1983. *A Treatise on Social Theory*, Vol. I: *The Methodology of Social Theory* (Cambridge)

Ryan, A. 1984. 'Socialism and Freedom', in *New Fabian Essays on Socialism*, ed. Ben Pimlott (London) 101–16

Sahlins, M. 1976. *Culture and Practical Reason* (Chicago and London)

Saussure, F. de. 1983. *Cours de linguistique générale*, ed. C. Bally and A. Sechehaye (Paris 1916; second and rev. edn 1922); trans. R. Harris as *Course in General Linguistics* (London 1983)

Scanlon, T. M. 1982. 'Contractualism and Utilitarianism', in Sen and Williams 1982

Scheffler, S. 1982. *The Rejection of Consequentialism* (Oxford)

Schilpp, F. 1943. *The Philosophy of Bertrand Russell* (New York)

Schutz, A. 1972. *Der Sinnhafte Aufbau der sozialen Welt* (Vienna 1932); trans. George Walsh and Frederick Lehnert as *The Phenomenology of the Social World* (Evanston, Illinois 1967; London 1972)

Scruton, R. 1980. *The Meaning of Conservatism* (London)

Sen, A. 1981. *Poverty and Famines* (Oxford)

Sen, A. and Williams, B. (eds) 1982. *Utilitarianism and Beyond* (Cambridge)

Sheridan, A. 1980. *Michel Foucault: The Will to Truth* (London)

Singer, M. 1984. *Man's Glassy Essence: Explorations in Semiotic Anthropology* (Bloomington)

Skinner, Q. 1969. 'Meaning and Understanding in the History of Ideas', *History and Theory* 8, 3–53

1981. 'The End of Philosophy?' *The New York Review of Books* 28: 4, (19 March), 46–8

1984. 'The Idea of Negative Liberty: Philosophical and Historical Perspectives' in *Philosophy in History*, ed. R. Rorty, J. Schneewind and Q. Skinner (Cambridge)

Skocpol, T. 1979. *States and Social Revolutions* (Cambridge)

Smart, B. 1983. *Foucault, Marxism and Critique* (London)

Smart, J. and Williams, B. 1973. *Utilitarianism: For and Against* (Cambridge)

Stegmüller, W. 1976. *The Structure and Dynamics of Theories* (New York)

Stoianovich, T. 1976. *French Historical Method: The Annales Paradigm*, with a foreword by Fernand Braudel (Ithaca and London)

Stone, L. 1979. 'The Revival of Narrative: Reflections on a New Old History', *Past and Present* 85, 3–24

Strawson, P. F. 1964. 'Truth', in G. Pitcher, *Truth* (Englewood Cliffs)

Sumner, L. (ed.) 1981. *Abortion and Moral Theory* (Princeton, New Jersey)

Tawney, R. H. 1932. *Equality* (London)

Taylor, C. 1967. 'Neutrality in Political Science', in *Philosophy, Politics and Society*, Series III, ed. P. Laslett and W. G. Runciman (Oxford)

　　　1971. 'Interpretation and the Sciences of Man', *Review of Metaphysics* 25, 3–51

　　　1984. 'Philosophy and its History', in *Philosophy in History*, ed. R. Rorty, J. Schneewind and Q. Skinner (Cambridge)

Thompson, E. P. 1978. *The Poverty of Theory and Other Essays* (London)

Thompson, J. 1981. *Critical Hermeneutics. A Study in the Thought of Paul Ricoeur and Jürgen Habermas* (Cambridge)

Thompson, J. and Held, D. 1982. *Habermas: Critical Debates* (London)

Toulmin, S. 1964. *The Uses of Argument* (Cambridge)

Tuck, R. 1979. *Natural Rights Theories: Their Origin and Development* (Cambridge)

Wach, J. 1929. *Das Verstehen*, Vol. II (Tübingen)

Walzer, M. 1977. *Just and Unjust Wars* (New York)

　　　1983. *Spheres of Justice* (New York)

Weber, M. 1968. *Wirtschaft und Gesellschaft* (Tübingen 1921); trans. and ed. G. Roth and C. Wittich as *Economy and Society* (New York)

　　　1975. 'Roscher und Knies und die Logischen Grundlagen der Nationalökonomie' (*Schmollers Jahrbuch* 1903, 1905, 1906); reprinted in M. Weber, *Gesammelte Aufsätze zur Wissenschaftslehre* (Tübingen 1922); trans. Guy Oakes as *Roscher and Knies* (New York 1975)

　　　1976. *Die Protestantische Ethik und der 'Geist' des Kapitalismus* (*Archiv für Sozialwissenschaft und Sozialpolitik* 1904–5); trans. Talcott Parsons as *The Protestant Ethic and the Spirit of Capitalism* (London 1930; 2nd edn London 1976)

Weldon, T. 1953. *The Vocabulary of Politics* (Harmondsworth)

Will, G. 1984. *Statecraft as Soulcraft* (New York)

Winch, P. 1958. *The Idea of a Social Science* (London)

Wittgenstein, L. 1958. *Philosophical Investigations*, 2nd edn, ed. G. E. M. Anscombe (Oxford)

Wolff, J. 1975. *Hermeneutic Philosophy and the Sociology of Art* (London)

Wolff, R. B. 1977. *Understanding Rawls* (Princeton, New Jersey)

Wright Mills, C. 1959. *The Sociological Imagination* (New York)'

Index of names

Index

Engels, F., 18, 143, 156

Febvre, L., 180–2, 185–6, 189, 193,
    195–6
Feyerabend, P., 7–8, 12, 19, 31
Fish, S., 28
Fleck, L., 100
Ford, H., 114
Foucault, M., 9, 11–13, 19, 23, 46, 49,
    58–62, 64, 67–81, 103, 169, 195
Freud, S., 6, 36n, 55, 163, 175
Fried, C., 118
Fullinwider, R. K., 118
Furet, F., 197

Gadamer, H. G., 6n, 7, 19, 23–39, 50–1,
    61–3, 103, 125
Galileo, 145
Gandhi, M. K., 112
Geertz, C., 12n, 13n, 14n
Gellner, E., 34
Geuss, R., 18n, 139
Giddens, A., viii, 17, 19n, 33–5, 37, 156,
    193
Goedel, K., 54–5
Gordon, C., 80–1
Goubert, P., 182, 195
Gurvitch, G., 181
Gutting, G., 100

Habermas, J., 5, 6n, 9, 16–17, 19, 31–4,
    36–8, 61–2, 99, 103, 123–39
Hacking, I., 69
Hampshire, S., 103
Harari, J., 176
Hare, R. M., 4
Hart, H. L. A., 15–16, 19, 117, 119
Hayek, F. A. von, 106
Hegel, G. W. F., 27, 46, 48–9, 61
Heidegger, M., 7, 13, 19, 23, 26, 30, 45,
    47–9, 58, 63
Heisenberg, W. K., 90
Held, D., 138–9
Hempel, C. G., 4n
Hesse, M., 139
Hexter, J. H., 185, 194, 198
Hirsch, E. D., 28
Hirst, P. Q., 157
Hobbes, T., 108
Hollis, M., 16n
Horkheimer, M., 123
Hoy, D. C., vii, 50, 52, 56, 58–9, 62
Hughes, H. S., 194, 196
Hume, D., 16, 108
Husserl, E., 30, 48

Iggers, G. G., 197
Izard, M., 176

Jakobsen, R., 164, 168
James, S., viii, 18n, 19, 157

Kant, I., 15–16, 46–9, 51, 63, 108, 111
Keane, J., 139
Kédourie, E., 197
Kellner, H., 194, 198
Kojève, A., 49
Kristeva, J., 54–5
Kuhn, T., 10–11, 12n, 13n, 19, 23,
    83–100, 131

Lacan, J., 5, 167, 195
Ladurie, E. Le Roy, 180, 186–8, 190,
    195–7
Laing, R. D., 9
Langlois, C. V., 179
Laslett, P., 4n
Le Goff, L., 195
Leach, E., 167
Lenin, V. I., 143, 156
Lessing, G. E., 34
Levi-Strauss, C., vii, 18–19, 45, 161–75,
    190–1, 193–5
Lévy-Bruhl, L., 181
Lewis, J., 157
Lipset, S., 4
Locke, J., 15, 106, 108
Lowie, R., 165
Luckmann, T., 34
Lukes, S., 16n, 37, 157

McCarthy, T., 39
MacIntyre, A., 8, 12n
Macpherson, C. B., 116
Major-Moetzl, P., 81
Malinowski, B., 167
Mallarmé, S., 170
Mann, H. D., 196
Mannheim, K., 100
Marcuse, H., 14
Marx, K., 3, 17–18, 23, 36n, 78, 116,
    124–6, 134–5, 138, 143–52, 154,
    156–7, 163
Mason, M., vii
Mauss, M., 166, 181
Mead, M., 167
Merleau-Ponty, M., 17, 47
Mill, J. S., 103–4, 107
Miller, D., 118
Montefiore, A., 197
Montesquieu, C. L. de S., 179